PEOPLEPOWER

Herbert S. PARNES

PEOPLEPOWER

Elements of Human Resource Policy

SAGE PUBLICATIONS
Beverly Hills   London   New Delhi

Copyright © 1984 by Sage Publications, Inc.

For information address:

SAGE Publications, Inc.
275 South Beverly Drive
Beverly Hills, California 90212

SAGE Publications India Pvt. Ltd.
C-236 Defence Colony
New Delhi 110 024, India

SAGE Publications Ltd
28 Banner Street
London EC1Y 8QE, England

Printed in the United States of America

Library of Congress Cataloging in Publication Data

Parnes, Herbert S., 1919-
    Peoplepower: elements in human resource policy.

    Includes Index.
    1. Manpower policy. 2. Human capital. 3. Labor
supply. I. Title.
HD5713.P37   1984   331.11   84-2085
ISBN 0-8039-2276-0
ISBN 0-8039-2277-9 (pbk.)

FIRST PRINTING

CONTENTS

To Atha

PREFACE

This book is written after more than thirty years of teaching and research in the fields of labor economics and human resource policy. It reflects the way I have come to think about these subjects, and is intended as a text for a one-semester introductory survey of human resource policy for students at either the undergraduate or graduate level who have had little or no exposure to economics. Most instructors will doubtless wish to supplement it with additional assigned readings; with more liberal supplementation the volume might be used in a two-semester course, the first of which would focus on the labor market (Chapters 1-8) and the second on human resource policy issues (Chapters 9-15).

Anyone who writes a book of this kind understands how much of whatever merit the product may have derives from the contributions of others. The works that I have consciously used as references are acknowledged throughout the text, but—even at the risk of unintended omissions—I should like also to express my indebtedness to a number of persons whose contributions have been longer term, more diffuse, and, at the same time, more fundamental. These include my parents, Bess and Joseph, who shaped the way in which I view the world; Elmer Graper and James Charlesworth, who many years ago at the University of Pittsburgh ignited my interest in political science; Russell Dixon, whose textbooks and personal conversations at Pittsburgh developed my understanding of and attachment to institutional economics; Carroll Daugherty, whose *Labor Problems in American Industry* excited my original interest in labor economics; H. Gordon Hayes, Alma Herbst, and Edison Bowers, who conditioned my view of the field during my graduate work at Ohio State University; Samuel C. Kelley, Thomas Chirikos, and Donald Sanders, my colleagues at Ohio State who joined me in creating an interdisciplinary seminar in human resource policy for which several chapters of this volume were originally written; Belton Fleischer and Donald Parsons of

Ohio State's Department of Economics, who caused me to understand that microeconomic theory is not completely without merit, even if not as completely useful as they believe. Some of the aforementioned who are still alive may not like the product; none on the list can escape partial responsibility for it.

I have short-run debts as well. Without implicating him in the book's remaining shortcomings, I must thank Michael Borus for his careful reading of the text, which uncovered errors and led to numerous suggestions for improvement. The same role was played by James Chelius in the sections of the text dealing with workers' compensation and the Occupational Safety and Health Act; and by Ernest Gross in the section on antidiscrimination policy.

My greatest debt I save for last. To my wife, Atha, I offer my gratitude for her continuous support and almost irrational loyalty during our life together. In the nearer term, I thank her for the many hours she spent at the word processor and for knowing, even when I did not, that the book would be completed.

—*Herbert S. Parnes*

1

Introduction

This is a book about people. It views people, however, from a very limited perspective—from the vantage point of their roles as workers. The central concern of the volume is with measures for improving the effectiveness of human beings in their productive roles and for enhancing the degree of satisfaction that they derive from those roles.

THE CONCEPT OF HUMAN RESOURCES

This interest in people as producers is, of course, implied by the choice of the term "human resources." The dictionary definition of the word "resource" emphasizes its instrumental nature: "something that lies ready for use or that can be drawn upon for aid or to take care of a need" (Webster's New World Dictionary: 1974: 1211). Thus, just as natural resources refer to such bounties of nature as timber and coal that are used to produce goods and services for the satisfaction of our needs and wants, so human resources refer to human beings whose productive contributions also satisfy those wants. The big difference, of course, is that in the case of human resources it is the same individuals who are both the agents of production and those for whose welfare and happiness all production takes place.

The fact that human beings are the end for which all productive activity takes place causes some people to be irritated, and others to be infuriated, by a willingness to view humans as mere instruments—that is, as resources. This issue should be confronted at the very beginning of our analysis. To suggest that it is useful and desirable to study human beings from the limited perspective of their roles as producers is not necessarily to suggest that the productive role of an individual is of primary importance. Men and women obviously play a variety of roles that are exceedingly important both from the standpoint of the individual and from the standpoint of society at large. They are parents, spouses, members of a neighborhood and community, citizens of a nation and of the world. Above all, they are thinking, feeling beings whose self-fulfillment is a legitimate concern in its own right for society as well as for the individual. Merely to mention these several roles should be sufficient to indicate the sterility of attempting to ascertain some order of priority among them. The fact of the matter is that all of them are important, and a wholesale failure in any one of them may endanger adequate performance in others. Moreover, there are inextricable interconnections between the productive roles of human beings and each of these other roles.

To illustrate, it is clear that the way in which men and women serve as parents is of some consequence for the degree of success that their children will enjoy in *their* productive roles. In their roles as citizens women and men—at least in a democratic society—ultimately determine the economic and social policies of governments that have a potentially great impact on economic growth and development. Consequently, even if one were to be committed in a simple-minded way to the single goal of economic growth it would be necessary to pay attention to how adequately human beings perform their roles as citizens, for without a broad base of popular understanding it is unlikely that social policy can be well informed.

Finally, it takes only a moment's reflection to realize that the adequacy of individuals in their productive roles substantially conditions the way in which other roles will be performed and the extent to which the goal of individual self-fulfillment can be met. While it is true that we do not live by bread alone, it is equally true that one does not move very far in other important spheres of life without adequate income, which in most cases depends largely on success as a producer. Moreover, the link between productive activity and self-fulfillment lies not simply in the importance of adequate sustenance but also in the fact that productive activity can itself be an important means of self-expression and self-fulfillment.

Thus, the term human resources is a useful, albeit limited, way of viewing people for certain purposes. It enables one to focus on a set of interrelated problems that face individuals and societies; while these problems are by no means coextensive with all of life, they are nonetheless important and worthy of study.

HUMAN RESOURCE POLICY

The subtitle of this volume is *Elements of Human Resource Policy*. Having explored the meaning of the term human resources, we can turn now to the concept of "policy." A policy is a course of action designed to accomplish some goal or objective. Public policy refers to a course of action pursued by society through its instrumentalities of government. Of course, there are policies in the private sphere as well. Business firms have pricing policies, financial policies, and personnel (human resource) policies, to mention only a few. Individuals, in their various roles, also formulate and execute policies. For example, parents generally explicitly or implicitly pursue a set of policies in the rearing of their children.

Whether one considers policy in the public or private domain, it is important to recognize that policy prescription—that is, making decisions with respect to appropriate courses of action—always involves two quite different kinds of intellectual processes. The first of these is the determination of objectives or goals, and the second is the analysis of the consequences of alternative courses of action for the attainment of those goals. The setting of goals, by its very nature, requires the making of value judgments—that is, the specification and ordering of the values that are to be pursued. There are at least two factors that complicate this process. One is the considerable variation in value hierarchies among different individuals—the relative importance they attach to different values. In this realm there is of course no way of demonstrating who is "right."

The other complicating factor, even for a single individual, is that many values or goals are to some extent inconsistent with one another, so that moving in the direction of one may require giving up a little of another. To take a very simple example, the objective of getting to an appointment on time may be incompatible with the objective of conserving energy by walking rather than driving one's car. A parent's goal of encouraging a child's independence may collide to some extent with the goal of protecting his or her health and safety. In the context of the choices that must be made by societies, it is easy to think of instances in which the social goal of maximum individual freedom is at odds with the goal of maximum individual security or where the pursuit of greater equity in income distribution may pose some threat to efficiency. When choices of these kinds have to be made, there is no "scientific" way of arriving at answers.

The second type of intellectual process involved in a policy decision is one to which the scientific method *is* relevant. This is the process of ascertaining the effects a particular course of action will have on the attainment of whatever goals are important to the individual, the organization, or the society. For convenience, this aspect of the policy decision may be referred to as the analytical question, in contrast to the value question that has already been described. Analytical questions involve the application of the scientific method; that is, within the conceptual framework of some theoretical formulation, evidence is collected that can shed light on the relationships among selected variables—for example, the effect of unionism on wages, the impact of specified government programs on unemployment, the relationship between the level of pension benefits and the retirement rate. Needless to say, the fact that questions of this kind are susceptible to scientific investigation does not necessarily mean that answers are easily obtained. Very frequently evidence is ambiguous; different studies, perhaps based on somewhat different samples or based upon somewhat different analytical methods, produce different findings. Thus, disagreements on matters of policy may occur because of different readings of the evidence on what we have called analytical questions. But no matter how unambiguous the evidence, informed men and women of good will may nevertheless disagree on policy issues simply because of differences in their value hierarchies.

The points that have been made above are relatively simple and obvious, but are of fundamental importance and will arise repeatedly in the remainder of this volume. It is useful therefore, to illustrate them by reference to a specific human resource policy issue relating to unemployment compensation. Although this institution will be examined in detail later in the volume, we can observe here that it is an arrangement under which individuals who become unemployed may receive cash payments based on previous earnings that are designed to compensate for some of the income loss resulting from their enforced idleness. One of the most immediate policy questions in developing an unemployment compensation system is how high the benefit level should be relative to the lost wages of the unemployed worker. The higher the benefit level, the more adequate is the degree of protection provided. Moreover, the higher the benefit level, the smaller the impact of any level of unemployment on mass purchasing power, and thus the greater the stabilizing effects on the economy. On the other hand, the higher the benefit level, the greater the risk that unemployment benefits will serve as disincentives to work, with consequent prolongation of unemployment and reduction in the potential output of the economic system. Finally, the higher the benefits the greater the costs of the program.

Now, given all of these consideration, how does one resolve the policy issue of how high unemployment benefits should be relative to the previous earnings of the unemployed? The analytical questions are fairly clear, although answers are by no means easy. What is the relationship between level of benefits and economic stability? In other words, how much additional stability would be generated if the benefit level were, let us say, 75 percent, rather than 50 percent of lost wages? What disincentive effects would such a rise in the benefit level create—to what extent would individuals be satisfied to live on unemployment compensation benefits rather than seek work vigorously?

Let us suppose that it were somehow possible to provide precise answers to these questions—that one knew, for example, that increasing the benefit level by 25 percentage points would reduce the incentive to work by 10 percent and would reduce the probability of recessions by 30 percent. Armed with this kind of precise knowledge, would it be possible to arrive at an unambiguous policy prescription? The answer is clearly no, at least not until one knows what the values of the policymakers are. If the preservation of work incentives looms sufficiently large in their system of values, even a sacrifice of 10 percent in this area would be too great a price to pay for an 80 percent advance toward making the economy depression-proof.

To summarize, it is important to recognize the distinction between value questions and analytical questions. In the realm of values one is guided by one's biases (i.e., one's inclination toward one value as opposed to another). In the realm of analysis, on the other hand, one can and should be "scientific" although this is admittedly not always easy to achieve. In any case, as policies always require a combination of value judgments and analysis, there is no way of arriving at a policy prescription on the basis of the scientific method alone.

THE ELEMENTS OF HUMAN RESOURCE POLICY

Let us now turn to an examination of the components of a comprehensive human resource policy for society. Our objective is to explore the various categories of issues and programs that are subsumed under the heading of human resource policy. As with any classification system, the one proposed here is to some extent arbitrary; it is certainly not the only way of categorizing human resource policies, but it is sufficiently comprehensive to embrace all of the relevant types of policies that have been implemented or proposed in societies representing a wide range of socioeconomic structures.

Human resource development. Under the rubric of human resource development we include all of those policies designed to enhance the effectiveness of human beings in their productive activities. The most obvious and perhaps the most important programs in this category are those that create vocational skills, defined very broadly to include all kinds of knowledge and abilities related to the performance of occupational roles. In this context, reading and writing and arithmetic are every bit as "vocational" as carpentry or weaving or metalworking. Also included under the heading of human resource development are programs designed to create labor market skills—those that enable an individual to function effectively and intelligently in the labor market. Basic to such skills is an understanding of the available occupational alternatives and of the avenues of preparation for each; of the methods of conducting a productive search for work; of how to present oneself to an employer in such a way as to maximize the probability of being hired.

Finally, human resource development embraces the development of attitudes and behavior patterns consistent with the requirements of the world of work. We frequently overlook the considerable amount of regimentation that an industrialized economy imposes on those who participate in it. To take an extreme illustration, workers on an assembly line have to report to work regularly and on time, must work at a specified pace, must take rest periods at prescribed times, and so forth. It is clear that human beings have no innate predisposition to this kind of behavior; however, the socialization process in industrial societies tends to inculcate a set of attitudes and behavior patterns in individuals that are consistent with these requirements. The processes by which this is done are sometimes subtle, but nonetheless real; anyone who has gone through an educational system has experienced such conditioning.

Some of the most intractable problems in human resource development lie precisely in this sphere. In developing economies, where an objective of public policy is frequently to create rapid industrialization, attitudes and ways of life have to be transformed on a wholesale basis. But the problem is by no means unknown in economically advanced countries. Among the inhabitants of some inner city ghettoes of the United States, for example, years of poverty, frustration, and futility have frequently created attitudes and modes of behavior that are incompatible with "mainstream" employment. In situations of these kinds, the mere creation of work skills is not sufficient.

Human resource development is thus a rather broad concept; and as a consequence, the institutions through which it takes place are many and varied. Perhaps the most obvious and most important are the formal educational institutions of a society, but even when one focuses narrowly on the creation of work skills there are many relevant institutions in addition to formal education— apprenticeship arrangements, training in the armed services, proprietary training institutions like barber schools, and perhaps most important of all, training on the job. On-the-job training includes not only formal programs that may be arranged by employers to create specific work skills, but also the informal acquisition of skill that occurs simply as the result of work experience. A worker hired to perform a particular job in an establishment learns a great deal about that job after beginning to practice it, both by picking up pointers from fellow workers and by perceiving from experience ways of performing more efficiently. Moreover, the worker frequently learns about other jobs by talking to workers who are in them or by being given the opportunity to try a machine, and in these ways may build up entirely new work skills. Acquisition of labor market skills and of appropriate work attitudes involves even more subtle processes and occurs in a variety of ways; in addition to the institutions already mentioned, the home and the family, the church, and the media of mass communications all play roles.

Human resource allocation. The process of human resource allocation refers to the distribution of human beings who have acquired work skills of various kinds among the millions of specific jobs in an economy. The allocative process, in other words, involves moving workers into those occupations, industries, geographic areas, and specific firms in which they are needed. It is, of course, a continuous process, occurring in response to changes in the demand for different kinds of labor, changes in the fortunes of individual enterprises, or changes in the desires of individual workers for different types of employment. For all these reasons workers move from one job to another, from one employer to another, from one location to another. Viewed in this perspective, it is clear that human resource allocation is an important process both for assuring that society's needs for labor are met and for allowing the aspirations of workers to be fulfilled.

The process of labor allocation is accomplished largely automatically through the institution of the labor market—that is, through the variety of ways in which employers make their demands for workers known and in which workers obtain jobs. An objective of human resource policy is to make that process operate as smoothly and as effectively as possible. The instruments for doing so include the operation of public employment offices, the regulation of private employment agencies, and a host of policies designed to stimulate desirable kinds of labor mobility and to inhibit those kinds of mobility that are purely wasteful (e.g., aimless shifting among jobs because of lack of adequate information about the labor market).

Human resource conservation. As the phrase implies, human resource conservation embraces policies designed to conserve the valuable skills and know-how that human beings may possess. Two major types of policy are subsumed under this category. Income maintenance programs sustain individuals during periods when for one reason or another it is impossible for them to remain productive—for example, unemployment insurance; workers' compensation, which pays both medical and cash benefits to workers who have suffered an industrial injury or an occupational disease; and disability compensation programs providing benefits for disabilities that are not work connected. Other forms of income maintenance (e.g., retirement benefits and welfare payments) are perhaps less obviously related to productive roles; but even those may legitimately be thought of as falling within the sphere of human resource policy as that term has been defined. Pensions, for instance, may be viewed as a form of deferred compensation for a lifetime of productive activity. Welfare benefits—even if unrelated to work activity of household heads—may allow the children in recipient families to be ultimately more productive than they otherwise would be. A second aspect of human resource conservation relates to maintaining the health and vigor of the population. Here, a variety of public programs having the objective of reducing mortality and illness are relevant, including the operation of public health services and the financing of medical care.

Human resource utilization. Human resource utilization is perhaps the most difficult of the categories to define. In its broadest sense, it can embrace all of human resource policy. Starting with the notion of a completely "raw" population, effective human resource utilization would encompass every means of enhancing the productive capabilities of that population, and would thus include all of the categories of policy already described. However, in the present context, reference is primarily to what goes on within the individual employing establishment. In other words, after human resources are developed and allocated, effective human resource utilization refers to efforts to eliminate waste in the employment of these resources, including the minimization of absenteeism, the reduction of industrial accidents and occupational diseases through industrial safety and hygiene programs, the elimination of discrimination, and, in general, the development of personnel and industrial relations policies for enhancing the productivity and welfare of the individual worker. Thus, the totality of personnel and industrial relations policy falls into this category. *Public* policy in this sphere is implemented through the practices that governments themselves pursue in their roles as employers and through legislation or regulations that govern the personnel practices of private employers.

Promoting full employment. The maintenance of high levels of economic activity and employment—an important aspect of general economic policy—is a sine qua non for the successful achievement of all the objectives of human resource policy that have been described. As has been seen, the ultimate purpose of human resource policy is to enable a nation to mobilize and utilize its population most effectively in the pursuit of its manifold objectives and, at the same time, to ensure the individual members of that population opportunities for self-fulfillment. Unless the society is successful in operating its economy so as to produce an adequate number of jobs for all who want them, the other objectives of human resource policy either make little sense or are unachievable. There is not much point in preparing individuals for jobs that do not exist; there is no need to strive for marginal improvements in efficiency through an improved allocation of human resources when there is gross waste resulting from enforced idleness.

HUMAN RESOURCE POLICY AND OTHER ASPECTS OF SOCIAL POLICY

However important the objective of improving the productive efficiency of the population, this is clearly not the sole aim of social policy. Moreover, many of the instruments of human resource policy are equally relevant to social purposes that have nothing to do with the world of work. Thus, in making decisions about these instruments it would be at least as unwise to operate exclusively within a human resource framework as to ignore human resource considerations entirely.

Perhaps the most obvious illustration is provided by education. It is clear from what has already been said that the educational system has profound implications for how effectively its products perform in the world of work, and this suggests that those responsible for the educational system must have in mind the important objective of vocational preparation. However, it is equally clear that education serves a number of other very important purposes in a society, including preparation for citizenship. This means that decisions about the character of the educational process must recognize this objective as well. Thus, the formulation of educational policy must be guided simultaneously by a number of very different considerations. The relationship is illustrated by the diagram shown in Figure 1.1. There are many aspects of educational policy that have no direct bearing on human resource policy; conversely, many aspects of human resource policy are unrelated to education. However, there is an important area of overlap that is of equal concern to educational specialists and human resource specialists.

What is true in the case of education applies equally to many other facets of human resource policy. Consider, as another example, human resource conservation programs. While good health has an obvious bearing on productive efficiency, it is also

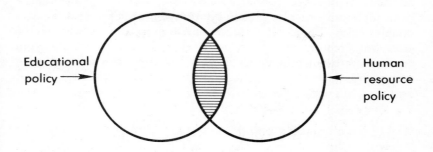

Figure 1.1:   **Relationship Between Human Resource Policy and Educational Policy**

valued in its own right. Consequently, those responsible for health policy must be cognizant of its implications for individuals in their roles as workers, but surely must not base all their decisions on these considerations alone. Similarly, while unemployment compensation programs have been seen to be justified by a desire to protect and conserve valuable productive skills, even if this were not the case such programs could surely be endorsed on the basis of humanitarian considerations. As a final illustration, antidiscrimination measures have been discussed in the context of human resource utilization because discrimination involves an economic waste. However, discrimination has also generally been recognized as morally evil, and programs to combat it do not necessarily require justification in terms of maximizing output.

All of this demonstrates the inextricable interrelationships between human resource policy and other aspects of social policy. Moreover, such interrelationships prevail *within* the domain of human resource policy as well. We have seen that vocational skill creation takes place not only through the formal educational system but through such other means as apprenticeship programs and on-the-job training. Policies relating to one of these areas must therefore be formulated in the light of those that apply to others. Similarly, as the characteristics of income maintenance programs may influence the the extent to which workers are willing to make various kinds of job changes, policies relating to human resource allocation and those relating to income maintenance ought to be formulated with reference to each other.

And so, the several categories of human resource policy cannot be conceived as watertight compartments. What goes on in one sphere frequently has important ramifications in another. It follows that intelligent human resource policy cannot be formulated piecemeal but must be perceived as an interrelated system. The special competence of the human resource specialist it to perceive the human resource implications of all aspects of social policy and to perceive how the several elements of human resource policy fit together.

HUMAN RESOURCE POLICY IN DEVELOPING AND ADVANCED ECONOMIES

The critical role of human resource policy in economic and social development has been highlighted during the past quarter of a century by the aspirations and experiences of developing economies. Although the early economic development plans of such countries—created largely by consultants from developed countries—frequently emphasized the creation of physical capital, it quickly became apparent that there was little point in a nation's building steel mills unless it also took steps to assure the development of required numbers of metallurgists, skilled craftspersons, accountants, personnel workers, and so on, to staff them. And so human resource development plans became important elements in economic development planning beginning in the 1960s. Labor economists, particularly in the United States, turned their attention to the role of human resources in economic development (e.g., Harbison and Myers, 1964).

At the same time, increasing attention was being given in industrialized countries as well to the contribution of human resources to economic growth and economic well-being. American economists, beginning with Theodore Schultz's 1960 presidential address to the American Economic Association (Schultz, 1960), rediscovered the concept of human capital—the productive capabilities acquired by human beings—and its importance to economic growth. The Organization for Economic Cooperation and Development sponsored a conference in Washington in 1961 among its 20 European and North American national members, the theme of which was the role of education in economic and social development (OECD, 1961). In addition to this kind of emphasis on the *development* of human resources, many western European nations and the United States gave increasing attention during the 1960s to a variety of measures for minimizing unemployment and for promoting more effective allocation and utilization of human resources.

The conceptual framework for human resource policy that has been described in this chapter is extremely general and is equally applicable to all societies, irrespective of their stage of economic development and of their particular institutional arrangements. Specific problems will of course vary from one country to another; moreover, policies will also vary because even if problems are identical in two countries, policies will reflect whatever differences may exist in political, social, and economic institutions and in other aspects of national culture. Nevertheless, it seems legitimate to argue that *every* country that wishes to assure the most effective employment of its population for the fullest satisfaction of both individual and national goals must give attention to the kinds of measures that have been classified here under the headings of human resource development, allocation, conservation, and utilization.

HUMAN RESOURCE POLICY IN THE UNITED STATES: A HISTORICAL OVERVIEW

In the United States human resource policy can be, and is, formulated and implemented at the national, state, and local governmental levels. Under our federal system, the national government has only delegated powers, the remainder being reserved to the states. Most national legislation relating to human resources has been based on the powers of Congress under the Constitution to tax, to appropriate funds, to provide for the national defense, and to regulate interstate commerce. During the first century and a half of our national existence many types of congressional action relating to human resources were precluded by the narrow interpretation placed upon some of these powers by the federal courts as well as by the courts' interpretation of the Fifth Amendment's prohibition of the taking of property without "due process of law." State action was also frequently thwarted by a similar interpretation of the due process clause of the Fourteenth Amendment, applicable to state governments.

In the 1930s, however, these judicial roadblocks to a variety of types of social welfare legislation were eliminated by a series of Supreme Court decisions that broadened the interpretation of the congressional power to regulate interstate commerce and reinterpreted the meaning of the due process clauses of the Fifth and Fourteenth Amendments. To take but two examples, the regulation of minimum wages, which had previously been held to be an unconstitutional exercise of power at both the national and state levels, now became a legitimate activity for both Congress and state legislatures; congressional regulation of industrial relations, which had previously been held to violate the Constitution, was henceforth a legitimate exercise of Congress's power to regulate interstate commerce.

A very large majority of the public programs in the United States relating to human resources are a product of the past half century; nevertheless, there are examples much earlier in our national history of public concern for human beings in their productive roles. The following paragraphs present a brief overview, without pretending to be exhaustive, of the development of human resource policy in the United States.

Human resource development. Concern for the development of human resources is evident even prior to the formation of our national union. Under the Articles of Confederation, the Continental Congress provided in the Northwest Ordinance of 1787 for the support of public education in the newly organized Northwest Territory. Public education, of course, has historically been primarily a function of state and local governments in the United States. Nevertheless, the national government has provided financial support and through such support has influenced policy. For example, the Morrill Act of 1862 provided federal lands in support of colleges in the several states to teach the "agricultural and mechanical arts"—the basis for the so-called land grant colleges. In 1917, the Smith-Hughes Act was passed, providing grants-in-aid to the states for the operation of vocational education programs. This federal program was considerably expanded and modified by the Vocational Education Act of 1963 and the amendments enacted in 1968.

The launching of the Soviet Sputnik in 1957 made it clear that the United States was lagging behind Russia in the space race and called attention to the need for strengthening scientific and technical education in this country. This was an important stimulus to an expanded role of the national government in supporting all levels of education. Illustrative pieces of legislation are the National Defense Education Act of 1958, the Elementary and Secondary Education Act of 1965, and the Higher Education Act of the same year. An additional instrument of human resource development that government has helped to fashion is apprenticeship. While apprenticeship programs are largely the creatures of employers and unions, the national government has facilitated their creation under the National Apprenticeship Act of 1937.

The 1960s witnessed a veritable revolution in human resource policy in the United States, with the national government increasing its role along a number of lines. An important element in this series of innovations was the inauguration of "manpower programs," first under the Area Redevelopment Act of 1961 and the Manpower Development and Training Act (MDTA) of 1962, and then under the Economic Opportunity Act of 1964—the major legislative manifestation of the Johnson administration's "war on poverty."

The MDTA emerged originally as a means of providing retraining opportunities to individuals whose skills had been made superfluous by technological change. However, early experience under the program demonstrated that this was less of a problem than had originally been supposed and that the real needs for training were among certain categories of disadvantaged individuals who had never acquired skills that would assure them a satisfactory niche in the labor market. Therefore, as it developed and was supplemented by the Economic Opportunity Act and modified by the Comprehensive Employment and Training Act of 1973 (CETA) and the Job Training Partnership Act of 1982 (JTPA), the program focused largely on these disadvantaged groups, providing a variety of services—including training and work experience— designed to bring them into the mainstream of economic activity.

Human resource allocation. In the United States the principal activities of government in human resource allocation have been the regulation of private employment agencies and the operation of the public employment service. The former function has been performed exclusively by the states; the latter has been a joint effort of the national and state governments. In 1933, the Wagner-Peyser Act established the federal system of public employment offices operated by the states under guidelines established by the national government, which finances the system. In addition to serving as a free employment exchange for workers and employers, the public employment service offers counseling and testing services to workers and certain types of technical assistance in the personnel field to employers. Except during major wars, there has been no other public intervention in the process of human resource allocation in the United States, although there have been several small-scale experimental programs designed to stimulate the geographic mobility of unemployed workers.

Human resource conservation. Income maintenance in the United States is accomplished through a variety of social insurance and social assistance programs. The former provide benefits as a matter of right to eligible individuals who suffer the particular form of income loss against which the program is designed to provide protection. The latter offer benefits only to individuals or families who can demonstrate need. The earliest social insurance to develop in the United States was workers' compensation, which provides cash benefits as well as medical services to workers who suffer disabling injuries in the course of their employment or who contract a disease that is uniquely associated with their type of work. A workers' compensation law exists in each of the 50 states, having developed over the period from 1911 to 1948. Beginning in the late 1940s a handful of states also adopted temporary disability compensation laws that provide benefits up to a maximum of six months for disabling illness or injuries that are not work connected.

Unemployment compensation is also a product of state laws, but in this case the legislation was stimulated by provisions of the Social Security Act of 1935, which also established certain standards that the state laws had to meet. The Social Security Act also established a national system of old age pensions, as well as cash benefits to the dependents of retired workers and to the dependent survivors of covered workers who die either before or after retirement. Since the 1950s benefits are also payable to the permanently and totally disabled. In 1974 with the passage of the Employee Retirement Income Security Act (ERISA) the national government entered the income maintenance arena in another way—by protecting the pension rights of workers under private employer plans.

The national government's role in social assistance programs was also inaugurated by the Social Security Act and its amendments. The largest program, popularly known as "welfare," is Aid to Families with Dependent Children (AFDC), which pays benefits to needy children in families without a male parent (or, in about one-half of the states, where the father is unemployed). These are actually state programs, with a major portion of the financing coming from the national government. A national Supplemental Security Income (SSI) program provides benefits to persons in financial need who are 65 years of age or older, blind, or permanently and totally disabled. Under national programs, persons whose income falls below prescribed levels may qualify for rent subsidies and for food stamps, which are used in lieu of cash to purchase groceries.

In the realm of health programs, the principal governmental actors have been state and local governments through their departments of health. The major national programs that underwrite health care for individuals are the Medicaid program, which makes grants to states for the payment of medical bills for the "medically indigent"; the Medicare program, which offers medical care insurance to individuals 65 and older and to the recipients of social security disability benefits; and the Neighborhood Health Center Program, originally developed under the Economic Opportunity Act, under which funds are provided by the national government for the operation of health care agencies in poverty neighborhoods. All of these programs were initiated in the 1960s. Important legislative developments of the 1970s include the National Health Planning and Resource Development Act, which makes provision for health planning at the regional and state levels and the Health Maintenance Organization (HMO) Act that provided financial aid for the development of HMOs—group practices providing comprehensive prepaid medical services with emphasis on preventive care.

Human resource utilization. The dreadful working conditions that characterized the early days of the industrial revolution in the United States evoked demands for the protection of workers by government through the setting of standards in the realm of wages, hours, physical working conditions, and child labor. As has been seen, the intrusion of state or national governments into these aspects of the employment relationship was generally viewed unfavorably by the courts as violating constitutionally guaranteed freedom of contract. Although generalization is difficult, it may be said that courts were more willing to accept state laws that bore a clear relationship with protecting the health and physical well-being of workers. Thus, generally speaking, regulation of hours—especially in hazardous industries—was more likely to withstand judicial scrutiny than regulation of wages. Because of their more vulnerable position, women and children were regarded to be more appropriate subjects for such laws than were adults males; and by the 1930s all about a handful of states had adopted legislation regulating the working hours of women. However, laws that impose special restrictions on the employment of women have been held by the courts to violate the civil rights legislation of the 1960s.

As has been seen, by the end of the 1930s the constitutional barriers to legislation governing employment relations had crumbled. Over half of the states now have laws establishing minimum wages for workers in at least some industries, and all states have laws relating to a variety of other aspects of employment. The Fair Labor Standards Act was passed in 1938, establishing minimum wages, a standard workweek of 40 hours with the requirement of premium pay for hours in excess of that number, and outlawing child labor. Even earlier the Davis-Bacon Act of 1931 and the Walsh-Healey Act of 1936 had required the payment of prevailing wages on work performed under government contracts, the former applying to construction contracts and the latter to all others.

The other major development in the sphere of employment relations during the 1930s was the enactment of the National Labor Relations Act of 1935. This monumental piece of legislation effectively guaranteed for the first time the right of workers in industries affecting interstate commerce to organize into unions and to bargain collectively with employers without "interference, restraint, or coercion." As amended by the Taft-Hartley Act of 1947 and the Landrum-Griffin Act of 1959, it has continued to provide the basic framework for industrial relations in the United States and has served as a model for many state laws applying to intrastate commerce and to industrial relations in the public sector.

Two other major interventions of the national government in the sphere of human resource utilization were later developments. One of these was an entrance into the field of industrial safety and hygiene, long the exclusive province of state governments. In 1970 the Occupational Safety and Health Act was passed, providing for the establishment of minimum federal standards and for enforcement of these standards by federal and/or state agencies.

The second development was in the realm of labor market discrimination. Presidential executive orders attempted to deal with racial discrimination during World War II and in the early postwar period. After the war, fair employment practice laws were enacted in more than half of the states and in a number of municipalities. However, the major breakthrough in this area was the passage of the Civil Rights Act of 1964, Title VII of which outlawed discrimination in employment based on race, sex, religion, or national origin. Discrimination based on age (between

40 and 65—40 and 70 beginning in 1979) was outlawed by the Age Discrimination in Employment Act of 1967. The national government also combats employment discrimination through its power to impose conditions on organizations enjoying government contracts. Under executive orders, the Office of Federal Contract Compliance in the Department of Labor polices contractors to assure that there is no discrimination based on race, sex, ethnicity, or physical handicap.

Promoting full employment. The national government assumed the responsibility for maintaining high levels of "employment, production, and purchasing power" in the Employment Act of 1946. This statute established the Council of Economic Advisers to the President and the Joint Economic Committee of Congress and imposed on the President the obligation to present to Congress an annual Economic Report. In the light of pre-Keynesian economic thinking and public policy, this was a revolutionary piece of legislation: It not only acknowledged that full employment was not automatically assured by the free operation of the economy, but recognized its attainment as a responsibility of the national government.

What the Employment Act of 1946 did for problems of cyclical unemployment, the Manpower Development and Training Act of 1962 (replaced by CETA and JTPA) did for problems of structural unemployment. In addition to establishing training and work-experience programs—and until 1982, programs of public service employment—this legislation acknowledged the president's responsibility to exercise surveillance over the operation of the labor market and to recommend to Congress programs designed to assure balance between the demand for and the supply of labor. In 1978 Congress enacted the Full Employment and Balanced Growth (Humphrey-Hawkins) Act, which announced the objective of making a "practical reality" of the right to jobs for all adult American job seekers able and willing to work. Target unemployment and inflation rates were also established, although these turned out to be unrealistically low. The importance of these statutes should not be overemphasized, for the acknowledgment of responsibility does not guarantee its effective discharge, and full employment has proved to be an elusive target in recent years. Nonetheless, when one compares the historical role and activity of the national government in employment policy with those that have prevailed since World War II it is clear that there has been a dramatic change.

Summary. The catalogue of human resource programs that has been presented is by no means complete. No mention has been made, for example, of the special legislation in the railroad industry that provides pensions and unemployment insurance for railroad workers and that governs industrial relations in that industry as well as in the airlines. Nor has anything been said about a host of human resource programs designed for veterans, including the important educational benefits of the so-called G.I. Bill of Rights.

Nevertheless, the major programs have been at least mentioned; many of these will be explored in detail in subsequent chapters. As the historical review indicates, while human resource considerations have never been completely absent in the deliberations of national and state legislatures, the major components of human resource policy in the United States are largely the product of the 1930s and the 1960s. The complete collapse of the economic system in 1933 spawned the New Deal, which generated numerous social and economic reforms including many in the realm of human resource policy. The 1960s witnessed another spate of human resource legislation. Concern for problems of structural unemployment and increasing social sensitivity to the blights of poverty and labor market discrimination generated such important innovations as MDTA, the Economic Opportunity Act, and antidiscrimination legislation.

By the end of the 1970s the United States had taken substantial strides in the development of a comprehensive human resource program. With the election of Ronald Reagan to the presidency in 1980, it was clear that further innovation in this sphere was not to be expected. Indeed, during his administration there were numerous evidences of a turning back in many aspects of human resource policy. Whether these signaled a real reversal of trend or merely a temporary pause, at this writing remains to be seen.

QUESTIONS FOR DISCUSSION

1. Do you believe that a woman who devotes her full time to the care of home and family should be regarded as a "human resource?" What about the 4-year-old child? The 78-year-old retiree?

2. Without regard to whether you agree with it, label each of the following as either a value statement, an analytical statement, or a policy prescription.

(a) Unemployment is a more serious social problem than inflation.
(b) Inadequate training is the most fundamental cause of youth unemployment.
(c) Unemployment compensation benefits in the United States are too high.
(d) Minimum wage laws hurt those they are designed to help.
(e) Preservation of individual dignity and self-respect is worth the loss of some work incentives.
(f) Seniority systems tend to reduce productive efficiency.

3. Can you think of human resource policy issues that are not accommodated by the conceptual framework suggested in this chapter? If so, what modifications in the framework would you suggest?

4. How do you account for the spate of human resource legislation during the 1930s and the 1960s? Do the 1980s represent a permanent reversal of trend or a temporary pause?

2

Human Capital

It is but a short intellectual hop from the concept of human resources to the economist's concept of human capital, for that term refers to the productive capabilities of human beings. More specifically and precisely, human capital embraces the abilities and know-how of men and women that have been acquired at some cost and that can command a price in the labor market because they are useful in the productive process. Economists have a way of thinking about human capital that they believe is useful for purposes of deciding how much and what kinds of such productive capabilities individuals and societies ought to develop. It is the purpose of this chapter to explore and to evaluate that system of thought.

There are very substantial similarities between human capital and physical capital. Generally speaking, the term capital in economics refers to produced goods that are to be used in the process of further production. A factory building and the equipment in it, for example, are capital because they have been produced not in order directly to satisfy human wants but rather because they facilitate the production of other goods (e.g., shoes). Similarly, the leather that is brought into the shoe factory as the raw material from which the final product will be fashioned is also thought of as capital, and for the same reason.

The process of creating capital is known as investment. In popular usage this term frequently refers to using funds to earn a return—for example, "investing" one's savings in General Motors stock or in the purchase of a retail grocery store. Technically, however, investment refers to the actual creation of capital goods—for example, the construction of a building to serve as a grocery store and the acquisition of equipment and inventories of groceries to be used in it.

Now the creation of capital in this sense is obviously costly; that is, capital can be acquired only by using resources that could have been put to other uses—uses more immediately related to satisfying peoples' wants for goods and services. The reason that individuals and societies invest in capital, then, is because such investment is productive in the sense that the quantity of the ultimate product—shoes, let us say—is sufficiently greater than it would have been had they been produced "by hand" to warrant the costs of acquiring the capital. When one looks at it in this way, it is clear that one means of deciding whether a particular investment in capital is worthwhile is to inquire whether the benefits that flow from it—that is, the increased product attributable to the investment—is worth at least as much as the cost of making the investment.

There is one additional aspect of investment theory that must be mentioned before we can turn our attention to how all of this relates to the human resource issues with which we are primarily concerned. That is the effect of the principle of diminishing returns on investment decisions. The economic principle of diminishing returns—or diminishing marginal productivity, as it is frequently called—holds that as additional units of a productive factor (e.g., a certain type of capital) are added to fixed quantities of the other factors of production, a point will be reached beyond which the marginal product of that productive factor will decline. In other words, beyond that point each additional unit of the item of capital in question will add less to the final product (e.g., shoes).

There are many simple-minded illustrations that may be used to demonstrate the universality of the principle. Consider, for instance, a group of 15 men, each equipped with a shovel, whose mission is to transport a quantity of topsoil from one location to another. Let the variable factor of production be wheelbarrows, and consider the effect of increasing the number of wheelbarrows on the number of cubic feet of soil transported per hour between the two locations. The addition of one wheelbarrow may be expected to have a considerable "marginal product"—that is, will increase substantially the amount of soil carried per hour. The addition of a second wheelbarrow may have an even greater effect, in which case the marginal product would have increased. The principle of diminishing marginal productivity simply asserts that such a relationship between output and the increased investment in wheelbarrows cannot continue indefinitely. At some point—perhaps in this illustration when the sixteenth wheelbarrow is added—its contribution to increasing the output will be smaller than that of its predecessor.

Now this phenomenon of diminishing marginal productivity provides a very useful set of guidelines to a businessperson in deciding upon how much to invest in each type of capital—or, indeed, in how best to combine all the factors of production used in a particular enterprise. The investment criteria are two-fold. First, as between two different types of investment, the objective is to equalize the ratios of marginal revenue to marginal cost. As this ratio represents the effect of an additional dollar of investment on total profits, application of the criterion simply assures that the business gets the "biggest bang for the buck." To modify somewhat the simple example used earlier, if the ratio in question is 1.5 for wheelbarrows and 2.1 for shovels when eight wheelbarrows and ten shovels are being used, this signifies that the firm's profits would be greater if it had invested somewhat more in shovels and somewhat less in wheelbarrows.

The second investment criterion holds that investment in each type of capital should continue up to the point where the ratio of marginal revenue to marginal cost is exactly 1.0. The rationale underlying this principle should be quite clear: As long as the ratio is higher than 1.0, each dollar of investment is adding more than a dollar to the firm's revenues, and the excess is profit. Thus, the firm is in the best position when an additional dollar of investment will add exactly that amount to its revenues.

HUMAN CAPITAL VERSUS PHYSICAL CAPITAL

Now what has all this to do with human capital and, more particularly, with issues in human resource policy? As will be seen, many economists argue that the rationale relating to business investments in physical capital that has been described above is equally relevant to individual and social decisions relating to many kinds of human resource policies. Without attempting to prejudge the issue at this point, we will first examine the similarities and differences between human and physical capital and then describe the way in which economists have used human capital theory as a basis for human resource policy prescription.

Similarities. However useful the concept may or may not be, it is fairly clear that one can draw a number of parallels between human capital and physical capital. As Theodore Schultz (1960: 1) has observed, "Although it is obvious that people acquire useful skills and knowledge, it is not obvious that these skills and knowledge are a form of capital, that this capital is in substantial part a product of deliberate investment."

To begin with, it seems reasonable to acknowledge that the acquisition of skills is a costly process in the sense that it uses resources—including the time of the individual acquiring the skills—that could have been devoted to other purposes. The most obvious example is the accumulation of skills through an educational or training program. The real costs include the building, equipment, and educational and training materials devoted to the process, as well as the services of the teachers and other personnel associated with the institution. A somewhat less obvious component of the cost is the foregone earnings of the trainee while engaged in the educational or training activity.

While formal education and training are commonplace examples, a moment's reflection will suggest other forms of skill acquisition that fit the same conceptual framework. When a professional dancer or musician spends hours a day practicing or when a professional athlete devotes equal amounts of time to training, their objective is generally to preserve or enhance the skills that they utilize in the labor market. And the process is a costly one, not only in terms of the equipment and facilities they use, but largely in terms of the valuable time they devote to the process. Similarly, when a parent spends time reading to a child, or accompanying her or him on a walk through the woods, this may be thought of as a subtle—albeit very important—form of human capital investment. The process is at least potentially costly by virtue of the foregone opportunities of the parent; the potential contribution to the ultimate work skills of the child, however indirect, may be very great indeed.

A second similarity between investments in human and physical capital is that the former, like the latter, are generally motivated at least in part by a desire to improve productivity. Thus, as in the case of physical capital, costs of acquisition can be more than compensated by the greater return that the capital makes possible.

Finally, it needs to be recognized that both types of investment may be either private or public, and that each may be evaluated either from an individual or a societal perspective. In the case of physical capital, just as an individual entrepreneur may invest in a factory building, so may a community invest in a bridge, a recreation hall, or a hospital. In the case of human capital, there can be collective investments by society in the education and training of its citizens just as there may be private investments in such means of skill acquisition. Indeed, in the case of human capital the very same investments may be viewed either from a private or a public perspective. As will be seen, however, the measurements of costs and benefits will generally differ as between these two cases.

Differences. The similarities between physical and human capital should not obscure the very great differences that exist between them in several respects. Perhaps the most important of these is that some portion of skill creation is incidental to consumption; its cost, therefore, cannot be considered to be exclusively an investment. From the vantage point of an individual, for example, most educational activity is not engaged in solely as a means of increasing productivity. It is enjoyable in its own right either because it is entertaining or satisfying as it occurs or because it may serve to enhance one's quality of life in future years. Even more so, one may hope that the time that a parent spends with a child brings its own satisfactions, irrespective of its ultimate contribution to the child's productivity in the labor market.

In these respects, therefore, there is a very large difference between a business executive's investing in a factory and a student's investing in a college education. In the former case, the sole motive is generally to increase profits, and there is no ambiguity either in defining or in measuring costs and benefits. In the example of the student or of the parent, on the other hand, if the benefit is to be defined as increased earnings, there is then the problem of ascertaining what part of the cost was true investment (i.e., undertaken solely to increase earnings) and what part represented consumption; and this, of course, is not easily resolved. At first thought it might seem that one could escape the problem by ignoring the distinction in costs and including among the benefits the value of consumption as well as the increased earnings. But here the problem of estimating and attaching money values to the "consumption" benefits is equally intractable.

A second major difference between human and physical capital is that the former, in the absence of slavery, cannot be owned by anyone other than the individual in whom the capital resides. This has several important implications. One of them is that in deciding how one's human capital is to be employed, a variety of individual tastes will be influential. As the person is inseparable from his or her skills, these skills will not necessarily be rented to the highest bidder (as would normally be true of a building or a machine); the congeniality of the type of work, of the persons with whom one works, and of the location of the job will all loom large in the decision. Another consequence of the inseparability of human capital from its owner is that the financing of human capital investment is different from and generally more difficult than the financing of investments in physical capital. In the case of a factory, a businessperson can borrow funds for its construction, using the factory building itself as collateral for the loan. Default on the loan allows the holder of the mortgage to gain ownership of the building. A comparable arrangement in the case of human capital is, of course, impossible.

Third, human capital differs from physical capital in that the productive capacity of the former depends upon the volition of the individual in whom it resides. An electrically driven machine with given specifications can generally be relied upon to work as it was intended to once it is plugged in; there is no similar assurance of performance on the part of a human being who has been through a prescribed training program. Speaking more generally, one may say that there tends to be greater variability in the productive capacity of a given amount and kind of human capital investment than in the case of investment in physical capital. In part this reflects variation in innate ability and prior experience; in part, however, it also reflects variation in initiative, motivation, and a multitude of personality traits. Whatever the causes, the conclusion is one that has been mentioned in another context in Chapter 1 — namely, that attempts to improve the productive effectiveness of human beings cannot afford to focus exclusively on programs of skill acquisition.

H UMAN CAPITAL INVESTMENT DECISIONS

As has been mentioned, economic theorists utilize human capital theory to suggest how investment decisions ought rationally to be made both by individuals and societies. In this section we present a simple, nontechnical illustration of this approach that is applicable to an individual, and then show how it would have to be modified to provide a basis for evaluating a social investment.

Individual investment in education: an illustration. Consider for a moment a young man who has just completed high school at age 18 and who is considering two alternative occupations that are, intrinsically, equally satisfying to him. One of these— occupation A—requires a four-year college education that costs $4,000 per year; with the degree the individual can look forward to receiving $13,000 per year in real terms (adjusted for changes in the price level) for the 43 years until his retirement at age 65. The other—occupation B—can be entered immediately and will pay a real annual income of $8,500 for the 47 years until retirement. Assuming that the young man will elect to attend college only if it would be economically advantageous, which of the two occupations should he choose?

The example is obviously grossly oversimplified, especially as it is unrealistic to assume that the individual will remain in the same occupation for a lifetime and that, even if he did, real earnings would be constant. It is perhaps even more unrealistic to believe that the choice between attending college and going to work immediately upon graduating from high school would be made exclusively on economic grounds by means of a cold monetary calculus. Nevertheless, the example provides an opportunity to throw the economic analysis into bold relief and to explore the rationale underlying it.

The essence of the problem is to ascertain whether the cost of attending college will be at least compensated by the higher earnings made possible by that investment. What makes the problem less than completely straightforward is the fact that the costs incurred and the benefits received occur during different time periods, which requires the introduction of the interest rate. The point is that a dollar at the present is worth more than a dollar at some future point, and how much more is a function of the discount rate, or the rate of interest.

A simple illustration will make this clear. If the interest rate is 10 percent per year, a dollar placed in the bank today will "grow" to $1.10 a year from now. By the same token, a dollar payable a year from now is today worth only $1.00/1.10, or 90.9 cents. More generally, the present value of any sum payable at some future date is given by the formula

$$PV = S/(1+r)^t$$

where S is the sum in question, r is the annual interest (discount) rate, and t is the number of years in the future at which the sum is payable.

With this in mind, let us now return to the investment decision facing our hypothetical young high school graduate. His problem is to compare the net present value of the lifetime earnings streams of occupations A and B. As has been seen, for this purpose it is necessary to use an appropriate interest rate, which, let us assume, is 8 percent. To make the arithmetic simpler, we will assume that the interest is compounded annually and that all income and costs are paid at the end of the year to which they apply (see Table 2.1).

From an annuity table we can ascertain that the present value of a payment of $1.00 per year over a 47-year period is $12.1643. (This means, incidentally, that if one deposited that amount in a bank paying 8 percent interest compounded annually, one could withdraw a dollar a year for 47 years and would end up with a balance of zero upon making the forty-seventh withdrawal.) Thus, the present value of the income stream from occupation B is $8,500 × $12.1643 = $103,397.

Occupation A can be entered only four years from now. At that time, the discounted value of the earnings stream over the 43-year period till retirement is $156,562. This figure, however, needs to be discounted to the present in order to make it comparable to the corresponding figure for occupation B. Thus, the present value of the earnings stream from occupation A is equal to $156,562/ $(1+.08)^4$ = $115,077. From this amount, however, one needs to deduct the present value of the cost of the college education, which is $4,000 per year. This calculation can be made as follows:

$$PV = \$4,000/1.08 + \$4,000/(1.08)^2 + \$4,000/(1.09)^3 +$$
$$\$4,000/(1.08)^4 =$$
$$\$3,704 + \$3,429 + \$3,175 + \$2,940 = \$13,248$$

Alternatively, one can multiply 4,000 by $3.3121, the present value of a $1.00 annuity paid for four years.

Thus, the net present value of the earnings stream in occupation A is $115,077—$13,248, or $101,829. This, it will be noted, is $1,568 smaller than the present value of the earnings stream in occupation B, which signifies that the investment in the college education is not worth while and that the student should select occupation B.

There is an alternative way of arriving at the same conclusion. Let us calculate the present value of the benefits of making the investment in the college education and compare that with the costs of the investment. The benefits, of course, are the discounted value of the difference between the two earning streams over the 43-year period between graduation from college and time of

TABLE 2.1 Illustration of Calculation of Value of Investment in College

Method I

(1) Value of income from A at time of graduation from college:	$13,000 \times \$12.0432 =$	$156,562
(2) Present value of income from A:	$\$156,562/(1.08)^4 =$	115,077
(3) Present value of cost of college:	$4,000 \times \$3.3121 =$	13,248
(4) *Net* present value of income from A:	$(2 - 3) =$	101,829
(5) Present value of income from B:	$8,500 \times \$12.1643 =$	103,397
(6) Present value of investment in college:	$(4 - 5) =$	−1,568

Method II

(1) Difference in annual income between A and B:	$=$	4,500
(2) Discounted value of difference in income streams at time of graduation from college:	$4,500 \times \$12.0432 =$	54,194
(3) Present value of benefit of investment:	$\$54,194/(1.08)^4 =$	39,834
(4) Present value of cost of investment:	$12,500 \times \$3.3121 =$	41,401
(5) Present value of investment:	$(3 - 4) =$	−1,567
(6) Benefit-cost ratio:	$(3\,/\,4) =$	.96

NOTE: Occupation A: Earnings of $13,000 per year for 43 years.
Occupation B: Earnings of $8,500 per year for 47 years.
College: Cost of tuition and books = $4,000 per year.
Interest rate: 8 percent.
Present value of annuity of $1.00 payable for 43 years = $12.0432.
Present value of annuity of $1.00 payable for 47 years = $12.1643.
Present value of annuity of $1.00 payable for 4 years = $3.3121.

retirement. The costs, on the other hand, are the discounted value of the annual direct outlays for college ($4,000 per year) and the foregone earnings that the youth could have garnered over the 4-year period with his high school diploma.

The difference in income streams at time of graduation from college is $4,500 per year for 43 years, the discounted value of which at that time is $4,500 \times \$12.0432 = \$54,194$. Discounting that to the time of high school graduation yields a present value of $\$54,194 \div (1.08)^4 = \$39,834$. The present value of the cost of the investment is $\$12,500/1.08 + \$12,500/(1.08)^2 + \$12,500/(1.09)^3 + \$12,500/(1.08)^4 = \$41,401$. Thus, the benefits are lower than the costs by $41,401—$39,834, or $1,567, the same conclusion that was arrived at earlier.

Social investments in education. The rationale that has been illustrated in the case of our hypothetical high school graduate also underlies the efforts that economists have made to evaluate social investments in education and other forms of human capital. Specifically, the objective has generally been to compare the costs of the investment with the benefits that accrue to society through increases in real income—that is, the production of greater amounts of goods and services.

In making such calculations the costs are usually not identical with the summation of individual costs, as society generally bears costs that are not reflected in what individual students pay. This is especially clear in the case of elementary and secondary education, but occurs in the case of higher education as well considering that much of the cost of both private and public higher education is subsidized. Foregone earnings are included in social costs just as they are in private calculations, as they represent the production that society has lost by having students in school rather than at work.

How does one estimate the increased production that is attributable to a social investment in education? Economists have generally done this by comparing earnings differences between individuals having different levels of education and assuming (on the basis of the marginal productivity theory of wages) that these differences in earnings reflect differentials in contribution to the social product. More specifically, census data on earnings by educational level and age are generally used to generate discounted values of lifetime earnings streams of categories of individuals with varying amounts of education. The difference, say, between this value for persons with 11 years of education and those with 12 years of education is taken to reflect the benefits attributable to completing high school as compared with dropping out after the eleventh grade. Expressing this value as a ratio to the cost of providing the twelfth year of education yields the benefit-cost ratio of the social investment in the twelfth year of schooling.

FORMS OF HUMAN CAPITAL INVESTMENT

Until now our examples of human capital investment have focused exclusively on education. However, there are other categories of investment, and those should be at least mentioned. Most closely related conceptually to education are various kinds of training programs. Like education, these may be evaluated either from a private or from a social point of view, and the methods are essentially the same as for education. That is, benefits measured in terms of earnings differentials are related to costs to ascertain whether the investment is "profitable."

Health is another form of investment in human capital. Expenditures on health care can be viewed as a means of improving the productive capability of an individual, and benefit-cost calculations can be made from either a private or a public point of view. As in the case of education there is the very real problem of differentiating between that part of an expenditure on health that is investment and the part that is consumption. Whether one views the matter from an individual or from a social perspective it is clear that expenditures on health have purposes other than simply to increase productivity.

Perhaps less obvious than the examples that have been mentioned to this point, migration may also be viewed as an investment in human capital. Moving from an area in which earnings are low (or nonexistent) into one in which they are higher clearly involves a gain from the vantage point of the individual and, if one accepts earnings as a measure of contribution to social product, from the vantage point of society as well. Thus, an individual can compare the costs of moving with benefits measured in terms of increased earnings in order to decide whether a move is worthwhile. Similarly, society can compare the costs of programs designed to promote mobility (e.g., moving subsidies) with the social benefits measured in terms of increased product. Finally, and in the same context, job search even within a given local area may be viewed as a form of human capital investment. From the standpoint of the individual it involves costs (e.g., time devoted to search, employment agency fees, newspaper ads, etc.), but it also promises benefits in the form of higher earnings. Likewise, from a social point of view one may compare the costs of providing more adequate labor market information with the benefits that accrue to a more favorable allocation of labor.

Thus, all forms of human capital investment are conceptually amenable to the same kind of benefit-cost calculus. Either the individual or the society may inquire whether the investment "pays off." In either case, all relevant costs must be compared with the benefits of increased productivity that accrue to the investment, and these benefits are generally estimated by comparing the earnings of individuals who have acquired the type of capital in question with the earnings of those who have not.

COMPARING ALTERNATIVE FORMS OF INVESTMENT

Up to this point we have illustrated the way in which an individual or a society can ascertain whether a given investment is worthwhile. If the benefit-cost ratio exceeds unity—that is, if the present value of benefits exceeds the present value of costs, the answer to this question is "yes." However, frequently the more important question is which type of investment in human capital has the higher payoff.

An individual may wish to decide whether a college degree or a certificate from a technical institute represents a "better deal"; whether it is a better investment to pursue a law degree or a degree in medicine; whether it is preferable to complete high school and become a bank teller or to drop out after eleven years and go to barbers' school. Similarly, policymakers may wish to know whether one type of training program is more valuable than another; whether it would be better to spend a billion dollars on vocational rehabilitation or on subsidizing geographic mobility; whether expansion of vocational secondary education or of adult literacy programs represents a sounder social investment.

All of these questions may be approached in precisely the same way. Considering that it is at least conceptually possible to evaluate the benefits and costs of all forms of investment in human capital, all that is required is a method of comparing the relative merits of different alternatives. There are actually two methods that have been used to accomplish this. One is simply to compare the benefit-cost ratios of different forms of investment and to choose the one with the highest ratio. The other is to calculate *internal rates of return*, and to choose the investment with the greatest yield. The internal rate of return is defined as that rate of discount that equates the present value of costs with the present value of benefits of a particular investment.

Whichever method is used, the rules for sound investment decisions are analogous to those that were described earlier as governing the investment decisions of businesspersons. The objective of social policy, in other words, should be to equalize the ratio of marginal benefits to marginal costs for all forms of investment and to continue each type of investment until this ratio equals unity. Using the internal rate of return approach, such rates should be equalized across all forms of investment and investments of each type should continue until the internal rate of return equals the social interest rate (Thurow, 1970: 109-110).

AN EVALUATION OF HUMAN CAPITAL THEORY

Human capital theory—the bare outlines of which have been presented in this chapter—may be looked at from several related points of view. On the one hand it is a conceptual framework—a way of viewing some of the important aspects of life. From another perspective, it offers an explanation of a number of phenomena relating to human resources. Finally, as has been seen, it purports to provide a more or less "scientific" means of making human capital investment decisions.

As a way of viewing human resource problems. It is probably helpful to recognize that there are a variety of ways of contributing to the productive efficiency of human beings, that most of these involve costs, and that there are trade-offs among different forms of investment. Moreover, it is certainly useful to acknowledge that many types of social programs that can be justified on humanitarian grounds have economic payoffs. That unemployment compensation in the social sphere is analogous to the maintenance of unutilized machinery may be a cold-blooded way of looking at a social program, but is nonetheless valid. That antidiscrimination measures are not only justified by ethical considerations but have an economic payoff is also worthy of recognition. At the very least this line of reasoning leads to the conclusion that the costs of programs of these kinds ought not to be considered as a net burden to society.

As a unified explanation of human resource phenomena. Some economists have pointed out that human capital theory provides a relatively parsimonious explanation of a variety of seemingly unrelated phenomena. Theodore Schultz (1960), for example, has listed the following observations. (1) The lower unemployment rates of skilled than of unskilled workers reflect the fact that the former have been the beneficiaries of greater investments in specific human capital made by the companies for whom they work; the lesser likelihood of their being laid off represents the firms' attempts to protect these investments. (2) The steeper age-income profiles of the skilled than of the unskilled—that is, the greater rise in income with increasing age—reflects the payoffs to the greater human capital investments that skilled workers have made in themselves. (3) The greater tendency of young than of older workers to change jobs or to migrate reflects the fact that, other things being equal, the benefits of mobility are greater for younger workers because the payoff period for them is longer. (4) The fact that total output has grown much faster over the years than the growth of labor and capital inputs reflects the qualitative improvements in both labor and capital, the former representing investments in human capital. (5) The rapid reconstruction of

Europe following World War II despite the wholesale devastation of physical capital is largely explainable in terms of the fact that *human capital*—the know-how and skills locked in the minds and hands of workers—was largely unaffected.

As an investment criterion. As a means of arriving at rational investment decisions, the use of human capital theory has a number of limitations. Perhaps the most significant is the impossibility of including in a benefit-cost calculus all the benefits of a human capital investment. As has been seen, on the basis of a set of simplifying assumptions it is at least conceptually possible to estimate the effects of a human capital investment on earnings or—from a social perspective—on social product. But even if one were satisfied with this measure, it would clearly not measure all of the *economic* contributions of the investment (e.g., education). To the extent that education contributes to a decline in crime and delinquency, or to the extent that it enhances the quality of economic decisions made by the electorate, there would be unmeasured economic benefits. Moreover, a host of *noneconomic* benefits may result from an investment in education. It is doubtful that all of these can be identified, but even if they could, their measurement would be difficult if not impossible. And, finally, even with complete and precise measures there is no way of combining them into a common metric that would permit their comparison with costs.

Most economists who use benefit-cost calculations would acknowledge the foregoing criticisms. They admit that the conventional approach measures benefits in only a very limited perspective, but are inclined to argue that such measures are better than none in a world where policy makers are faced with hard choices. There is doubtless some merit to this point of view; yet it must be pointed out that the use of earnings differentials as a measure of the effect of a human capital investment on productivity is itself fraught with certain dangers.

For one thing, rates of return are always geared to the past. That is, census data on differences in earnings by levels or kinds of education reflect evaluations that the labor market has made *in the past*. They are not necessarily a valid guide to the future, particularly when economic structure is changing rapidly. It is this consideration that argues particularly against the use of rates-of-return analysis as guides to investment decisions in developing economies.

Second, in developing and advanced economies alike, there is no assurance that income differentials among individuals with different amounts of education are in fact attributable to the educational differentials. It is well known that the amount of education an individual achieves is correlated with a number of factors that themselves are likely to influence earnings (e.g., ability, initiative, social contacts, etc.). Thus, earnings differentials are almost certain to overstate the net effects on earnings of differences in education or similar investments. Sophisticated benefit-cost analyses attempt to control for these other factors, but rarely can this be done with anything approaching completeness.

Finally, the entire rationale underlying the measurement of social benefits accruing to investments in human resources rests on the acceptance of the marginal productivity theory of wages— that is, on the proposition that wage differences reflect true differences in productivity. In measuring private returns to human capital investment this is a matter of no concern, for individuals care little whether their earnings reflect their contributions to society. In measures of social returns, on the other hand, unless this is true the entire approach loses its meaning.

Conclusion. The reader is invited to form an individual opinion on the utility of the human capital concept and human capital theory. In my view there is much to commend the concept. It provides a way of looking at certain aspects of human resource policy that appears to be both valid and useful. Moreover, the basic concept underlying benefit-cost analysis—that social investment decisions must necessarily involve juxtapositioning total costs and total benefits—is also surely sound. Nevertheless, the possibility of actually operationalizing this approach to permit reasonably confident policy decisions appears to be limited.

QUESTIONS FOR DISCUSSION

1. What do you perceive to be the relationship between the concepts "human resources" and "human capital"?

2. How useful do you think human capital theory is in (a) explaining the process of occupational choice? (b) providing a basis for social investment decisions? (c) understanding labor market phenomena? (d) thinking about human resource policy issues?

3. What kinds of information would be required to measure the "pure" effect of education on individual earnings? How confident are you that such a measurement can in fact be made?

4. Why would you expect to find differences between private and social rates of return to education?

3

Defining and Measuring
Human Resources

A society that wishes to develop and implement a comprehensive human resource policy obviously needs information on the numbers and characteristics of its current and potential human resources. However, what kinds of definitions and categories to establish for collecting such information and how to go about gathering it are by no means self-evident. In this chapter we examine the several purposes that human resource data should be designed to serve, consider the types of information that are necessary to serve these purposes, and discuss the several ways in which the data may be collected. The statistical data on human resources that are available in the United States will then be described and evaluated.

There is good reason for beginning the discussion with an analysis of the potential purposes of human resource data. In one of the earliest systematic treatises on this subject, A. Jaffe and Charles Stewart (1951) pointed out that "working force" data reflect the total cultural milieu of a society. Data are collected to provide answers to important questions, and what those questions are is determined by the total social, economic, and political structure of the society—which, incidentally, is subject to change over time. Two examples will serve to illustrate this thesis. First, the current system of defining and classifying the labor force is a product of the 1930s when the disastrous collapse of the economy demanded a reliable measure of unemployment that previously had not existed. Second, the fact that many of our statistics on human resources are classified according to skin color (race) reflects a recognition of the problem of racial discrimination that has for so long plagued American society. We do not, after all, present data on unemployment by hair color or by height!

A brief discussion of terminology is useful at the outset. The term "human resources" has not ordinarily been used in the context of data collection and presentation, but the terms that have been used are closely related to that concept as we have defined it. Jaffe and Stewart used the generic term "working force" to refer to that segment of the population engaged (or attempting to be engaged) in the production of goods and services for the market—that is, the "economically active" portion of the population. The latter term, in fact, is currently used in the official statistics of some countries (e.g., *population active* in France).

If one wishes an actual count of the "economically active" it is necessary to develop a set of definitions or rules to determine who is to be included and who is not. Should there, for example, be age limits? What criteria should be used for inclusion of those who want to work but currently do not have jobs (the "unemployed")? Thus, every nation's official statistics are based upon a specific set of definitions that have been developed for delineating and categorizing the "economically active." In the United States we used the term "gainful workers" until the 1940 decennial census. The rather fundamental changes in definitions that were then effected resulted in the adoption and use since that time of the term "labor force." Thus, the term "labor force" has a precise operational meaning (explored in detail below) in a way that "human resources," "working force," and "economically active population" do not.

There are other frequently used generic terms that deserve mention. The economist uses the term "labor"—one of the "factors of production" along with capital and natural resources—to refer to all human effort expended in the productive process. The term "manpower" has also frequently been used, although greater sensitivity to the issue of sexual equality has made it much less popular in recent years. What once was the Manpower Administration in the Department of Labor, for example, has become the Employment and Training Administration.

PURPOSES OF HUMAN RESOURCE DATA

What are the basic purposes that are served by human resource data? Five major categories may be suggested: (1) measuring the health and performance of the economy; (2) identifying problems in human resource utilization; (3) describing and analyzing the economic and social structure; (4) aiding private and public planning; and (5) serving as a basis for the allocation of funds among political units. Each of these will now be elaborated and illustrated.

Measuring the health and performance of the economy. The eagerness with which the public frequently awaits the announcement of the unemployment rate by the Bureau of Labor Statistics on the first Friday of each month provides a good illustration of this function of human resource data. While the unemployment measure is perhaps the single most dramatic element in this context, there are others as well. Figures on employment may also be used as indicators of the health and vigor of the economy and of specific industries. Changes in average weekly hours of work frequently foretell corresponding changes in employment and unemployment. Data on hours of work, in conjunction with figures on output, provide the basis for measuring labor productivity—output per person-hour—which is the most basic proximate determinant of the standard of living of a society. These examples, as well as many others that might be mentioned, relate not only to the global economic system but to geographic and industrial segments thereof. For instance, human resource data reflected the economic woes of the steel, automobile, and construction industries in the early 1980s, as well as the dismal employment outlook in cities like Flint and Detroit.

Identifying problems in human resource utilization. Unemployment is not only an indicator of economic health, but the measure *par excellence* of malutilization of human resources—which demonstrates, incidentally, that the categories that are being used here are not mutually exclusive. However, there are additional facets of utilization. One has only to examine data on the occupational distributions of blacks and whites and of differences in their earnings within occupational and educational categories to suspect the existence of racial discrimination in the labor market, which signifies less than optimal utilization of human resources. The same can be said about occupational and earnings differences between men and women. As a final example, data on turnover (e.g., number of quits per 100 persons on the payroll) would provide clues to utilization problems in individual firms and/or industries.

Describing and analyzing economic and social structure. Human resource data may be used to characterize the economic and social structure of the nation as a whole and of its geographic units. Comparison of the industrial and occupational composition of employment in Chicago with that of Washington leads one to expect greater economic stability in the latter than the former because of the high proportion of cyclically sensitive heavy industry in Chicago and the large component of white collar government employment in the nation's capital. Over time, the increasing proportion of white collar work and of employment in industries that produce services relative to those that produce goods has been a factor operating for greater economic stability nationally.

With respect to social structure, an examination of race and sex differences in labor force participation and in occupational assignments tells us much about the status and roles of blacks and of women in American society. Trends over time in these variables, particularly during the past two decades, are testimony to improvements in the relative positions of both these groups—especially of blacks (see Chapter 9).

Aid to public and private planning. When a firm wishes to establish a new plant and is attempting to decide where to locate it, human resource data are usually an important input into the decision. How adequate is the labor supply in alternative communities? What are the average earnings of workers in the occupational categories that the firm will employ? Even aside from plant location, a firm wishing to develop a long-term human resource plan needs information not only about its own work force but about the potential work force in the relevant labor market area.

What is true of individual firms is equally true of communities, states, and the nation at large. Under the Comprehensive Employment and Training Act "prime sponsors" (states and local areas) were required to develop plans for employment and training programs as a prerequisite to obtaining federal funds for these purposes. Such plans were generally grounded in data on employment, unemployment, and income in the area, classified by age, race, and sex, in order to establish the "universe of need." Decisions about what kinds of training to provide depend upon forecasts of occupational structure, and these are generally based on current data and recent trends. Perhaps the most dramatic example of public human resource planning in the United States is in connection with national defense. During World War II, numerous studies attempted to estimate the potential labor supply of the nation. More recently, studies were directed at assessing the feasibility of an all-volunteer army. For both of these kinds of investigations historical and current data on employment and earnings played an important role.

Allocation of funds among political units. Many of the social programs inaugurated in the United States in the 1960s and 1970s provide for the allocation of funds among states and communities on the basis of human resource data—especially unemployment rates. Unfortunately, local area unemployment estimates have been notoriously weak in the United States, and this particular purpose has strengthened the case—which can also be made on other grounds—for their development.

REQUIRED TYPES OF DATA

In the light of the purposes described above, what kinds of information about the working force ought ideally to be available? Of course, if one gives free reign to the imagination, there is almost no limit to the types of data that would be of potential value—perhaps a complete physical-psychological profile of every individual of working age! However, keeping at least one eye on considerations of feasbility and cost it is possible to delineate several categories of human resource information that are essential to the purposes outlined above.

Geographic detail. Virtually all of the important questions about human resources may be asked in the context of a particular community or state as well as for the country as a whole. This means that national aggregates are insufficient; all of the types of information that we agree upon should be available on a regional, state, and local labor market level.

Activity status. One of the most important things that needs to be known about each individual in the population is how actively that person is currently filling the role of a human resource. Conceptually, we might think of people of working age at any moment of time as falling along a continuum. At one end is the person who under virtually no circumstances could or would accept employment—for example, a severely disabled individual, a 62-year-old male retiree who "has had it" with work, or a young mother holding a firm conviction that her exclusive role is as home-maker. At the other end is the woman or man who has for 15 years worked full-time with only a two-week annual vacation and who has every intention of following the same pattern for the next 25 years. Between these extremes are individuals with varying degrees of capacity for and interest in work—some actively seeking jobs; some willing or even eager to work despite the absence of an active search; some who would take only jobs tailored to their particular needs; some who really have no desire to work but who could be induced to do so under certain circumstances.

While such a gradation of potential human resources would be highly useful, it would be very difficult—if not impossible—to achieve. As a very minimum, however, it is important to be able to differentiate among individuals who are currently employed, those who are not but who wish to be, and those who have no desire to work. As we will see, it is easier to agree upon these categories than to decide what precise criteria are to be used for establishing the boundaries between them.

Occupation, industry, type of worker. It is important to be able to place a tag on every actual or potential human resource describing the particular role in the productive process the individual is or might be performing. An occupational designation refers to the tasks that the person is engaged in, irrespective of where employed—such as a carpenter who may work in construction or as a maintenance man in a university. An industrial designation refers to the product (tangible or intangible) of the employer for whom the person works, irrespective of the specific productive role performed. Thus, the billing clerk at General Motors is classified industrially as motor vehicle manufacturing (more broadly, manufacturing) while the person performing the corre-sponding role at Macy's would fall in the industrial category of department stores (more broadly, retail trade). "Type of worker" is a term used in the official labor force statistics of the United States to differentiate among self-employed individuals, private and public wage and salary workers, and "unpaid family workers"—individuals working without pay in family enterprises.

What about persons who have skills and experience that would permit them to fill more than one occupational and/or industrial role? Ideally information of this type would of course be useful. Especially desirable would be information about an individual's highest skill; comparison of that with current occupational assignment would provide a measure of underutilization. However, it is not easy to obtain reliable information about the skills of individuals other than those they may be presumed to have by virtue of actually serving in a given capacity. As a practical matter, therefore, data on occupation, industry, and type of worker are normally obtained for the current job for those who are employed, and for the most recent job (if any) for those who are not.

Demographic characteristics. For many of the purposes outlined in the preceding section it is important to know something about the personal characteristics of each individual whose activity status is described—sex, race, age, marital status, educational attainment, physical and mental health, and family size and structure. The reasons for wanting to be able to cross-classify human resources by these characteristics and such labor market variables as activity status, occupation, and earnings are fairly obvious but give rise to interesting philosophical questions. If it is true, as has been argued earlier, that racial classifications are important in the United States only because of the problem of racial discrimination, can we logically (even if optimistically) look forward to a day when there will no longer be a point in presenting working force data by race? And if the answer to this is affirmative, could the same be said about sex? The reader might well ponder whether a society in which the status of the two sexes was equalized would nevertheless have reason to make distinctions between males and females in working force data.

In any case, it should be recognized that most of the demographic characteristics listed above are readily obtainable, as they relate to matters with respect to which there is little ambiguity. However, this generalization does not apply to health because there is considerable subjectivity in self-reports and medical examinations would not be feasible. It is not surprising, therefore, that despite their importance measures of health do not appear in regularly available human resource data, although special surveys occasionally provide them. Measures of educational attainment also pose difficulties, albeit less serious ones. Number of years of "regular" schooling is a readily objectifiable measure and is obtained on a regular basis. Other dimensions of educational attainment—type of curriculum, field of specialization, and training outside the formal educational system—are less susceptible to easy measurement and/or classification and are made available only by special surveys.

Hours of work. Intensity of participation in the work force is an important variable from a number of perspectives. Because it provides a more refined measure of human resource input into the productive process than a mere count of bodies, it is useful for measuring changes in levels of human resource utilization over time and differences in such levels among demographic groups. When combined with measures of output it yields measures of labor productivity. As a minimum, one would like information on the number of hours per week each employed person currently works and the number of hours those who are seeking job would like to work. It would also be useful to know how many hours employed person would *like* to work and how many the unemployed would be *willing* to serve.

Wage rates, annual earnings, and total income. For purposes of assessing individual and family welfare and of evaluating labor market conditions it is important to have information on wage rates, annual earnings, and total family income, by source. The wage rate, conceptually, is the basic payment per hour of work, exclusive of overtime, bonuses, and the like; however, methods of compensation are so complex that it is very difficult to obtain information of this kind for many categories of workers (e.g., those paid on an annual basis and those working on piece rates or other types of incentive systems). Total earnings from wages and salaries for an entire year is a less difficult measure, even though it may be subject to substantial reporting error. The most meaningful indicator of family welfare is total family income in relation to the size and composition of the family unit. *Sources* of income are also important for a number of purposes, including the evaluation of such social income maintenance programs as Social Security and unemployment compensation.

Mobility measures. The kinds of information that have been described thus far permit a snapshot description of human resources at a given point in time and a comparison of such snapshots over time. For many purposes, however, it is important to have what might by analogy be referred to as a motion picture— a record that shows the change in status of the same individuals over time. The movement into and out of the working force, between employment and unemployment, among occupations, industries, individual employers, and labor market areas are all forms of human resource (labor) mobility. Mobility data are important not only for understanding individual careers but for evaluating the degree of flexibility of the human factor in production.

Despite their importance, mobility measures are somewhat difficult to obtain on a regular basis. There are two possible approaches: (1) repeated surveys of the same individuals over time so that any aspect of their working force experience at one point can be compared with the same measure at another. Alternatively, (2) in a single survey individuals may be asked retrospective questions relating to a specified point of time in the past that may be compared with their current situation (e.g., occupational assignment in the first week of January last year and in the same week in the current year).

Attitudinal measures. In addition to knowing about what individuals are doing or have done in the labor market, there are reasons for wanting to know about their reactions to their experience. How committed is the person to her or his work role? How satisfying is the current job? What aspects of the job are particularly appealing or onerous? Information of these kinds is useful for at least two important reasons. First, they provide a basis for predicting actual behavior.[1] Second, they indicate the extent to which productive activity is serving one of its functions—namely, contributing to the aspirations and the self-fulfillment of the individual. Despite their importance, however, attitudinal measures are both more difficult to obtain and to interpret than more objective descriptions of status and activity. It is not surprising, therefore, that their use is confined to special surveys rather than being an element of regularly collected official statistics.

SOURCES OF HUMAN RESOURCE DATA

There are four major sources of regularly published human resource data: population censuses, household surveys, establishment surveys, and operational data from social insurance systems (especially unemployment insurance). Each of these sources has its particular strengths and limitations; together they constitute the potential for a comprehensive system of information about a society's human resources.

The census. The decennial census in the United States is a complete count of the population that permits working force status and activity to be cross-classified with a host of demographic characteristics in virtually any desired level of geographic detail. Its chief disadvantages are inherent in its very nature—it provides data only once every ten years and is, moreover, such a massive undertaking that even these cannot be made available until they are already out of date—two or three years after the enumeration. Also, because the information is collected either by mail or by a virtual army of enumerators who cannot undergo intensive training, it is generally not as accurate as that collected from a representative sample by carefully trained interviewers. Nevertheless the decennial census has been a rich source of data for human resource research—especially in the form of computer tapes that provide an amazing array of economic and social characteristics for a one-in-a-thousand sample of the population.

Household surveys. The household survey collects information from a representative sample of households on a periodic basis, and thus has the potential advantages of a census (except for the geographic detail) without the weaknesses mentioned above. Specifically, it is the only means of obtaining a satisfactory current measure of total unemployment; employer surveys can provide information about layoffs, but provide no basis for knowing whether laid-off workers have found other work, or the extent of unemployment among new entrants to the labor market. The Current Population Survey (CPS), which is the household survey that provides official working force data for the United States, will be described in some detail below.

Establishment surveys. Establishment surveys are based on samples of employing units. They are particularly useful for providing current data on employment by industrial category, hours of work, weekly and hourly earnings, and labor turnover.[2] In the United States, establishment-based data are collected by the Bureau of Labor Statistics with the collaboration of the state employment security agencies (which administer unemployment compensation). Some of the statistics collected in this way parallel those yielded by the CPS, yet with significant differences.

Estimates of total employment and of hours of work are illus-trative of differences between the two data sources. Employment data from the CPS relate to the total working force, whether self-employed or wage or salary workers; in the establishment-based survey, certain categories of workers are not covered by the sample—for example, the self-employed, domestic servants, and agricultural workers.[3] Second, the CPS counts persons whereas the establishment survey counts jobs. Thus a dual job-holder is counted only once in the CPS (and is classified according to the job in which the most hours per week are worked) whereas in the establishment survey individuals are counted as many times as they appear on a firm's payroll in the reference week. As the result of these and other differences, CPS employment in 1982 averaged 99.5 million (with 96.1 million in nonagricultural industries), as compared with 89.6 million in the establishment survey. Despite these differences in level, trends in the nonagricultural component of the two series tend to be similar, and careful labor market analysts make use of both.

In the case of weekly hours the CPS collects information on the number of hours of work the individual performed in the reference week, while employers covered by the establishment survey report the number of hours they have *paid for*. Thus paid sick leave and vacation time are included in the latter series, but not in the former. Because of the increasing prevalence of fringe benefits of these types, the establishment-based measure of total hours of human resource input has risen faster than the CPS measure.

Social insurance data. The normal operation of the unem-ployment insurance system yields as a by-product counts of the "insured unemployed" (i.e., persons who file valid claims for unemployment benefits). The fact that these are complete counts rather than estimates based on samples and that they are available on a state and local labor market basis is an ostensible advantage. However, it is probably more than offset by the fact that incom-plete coverage, eligibility requirements and the limited duration of unemployment benefits cause the data to be only a partial count of unemployment. Moreover, insured unemployment becomes a progressively smaller proportion of the total as the economy sinks into a deep recession and exhaustions of unemployment benefits increase. Furthermore, even the interstate comparisons that the data make possible are flawed by the effect that the substantive provisions of the state unemployment insurance laws have on the measures of insured unemployment. Given two states with iden-tical economic characteristics, the one with the more liberal unemployment insurance eligibility and disqualification provisions would manifest a higher insured unemployment rate.

WORKING FORCE DEFINITION IN THE UNITED STATES

As has been noted, an inventory of the working force, or the econcomically active population, requires that operational meaning be given to the several concepts embodied in the data. In this section we examine the operational definitions currently in use in the United States.

Prior to 1940, the basic measure of human resources in the United States was the number of "gainful workers," a term that was defined to include persons 10 years of age and over who reported a "usual occupation." Certain ambiguities stemmed from this definition (e.g., the status of an individual in semiretirement), but the most important limitation was its failure to distinguish between those who were currently plying their trade and those who were not as the result of an inability to find work. The collapse of the economy in the 1930s demanded a satisfactory measure of unemployment; after some experimentation during the decade, the concept of the "labor force" was substituted for that of "gainful workers" in the 1940 decennial census and has been used ever since in both the census and the CPS.[4]

The new system differed from the old in that an individual's status generally depends on his or her *activity* during the calendar week to which the survey refers (the reference week). Under the definitions that have been in force since 1967, the *labor force* comprises all noninstitutionalized persons 16 years of age and over who in the reference week were either *employed* or *unemployed*. The former are individulas (1) who worked at least one hour either for wages or salary or in self-employment during the week in question, or for a minimum of 15 hours without pay in a family enterprise (unpaid family workers); or (2) who held jobs from which they were temporarily absent as the result of vacation, illness, bad weather, or a labor dispute. The unemployed include those who did not work during the reference week but were available for work except for temporary illness and (1) who were on layoff from a job, or (2) who were seeking work at any time during the four-week period preceding the survey.[5]

Several aspects of these definitions deserve elaboration or emphasis. First, the labor force has no independent definition, but is simply the sum of the employed and the unemployed. Second, while there is a lower age limit (16 years of age) for inclusion in the labor force, there is no upper age limit. Third, in deciding whether an individual is employed or unemployed, having a job at any time during the week takes priority over layoff or job-seeking. This means that if a woman is discharged at the end of her workday on a Monday and seeks work for the rest of the week she is classified as "employed" during that week. It also means that a machinist who is on layoff and works four hours on a Saturday afternoon in a service station is treated as employed. Finally, except for persons on layoff, no one is classified as unemployed unless the interviewer is told that during the four-week period preceding the survey the individual engaged in some specified work-seeking activity (e.g., reading want ads, making the round of employers, checking with the union, etc.). Thus, persons who want to work but either discontinue or do not initiate a job search because they perceive that no work is available ("discouraged workers") are not counted among the unemployed. The CPS does attempt to identify such individuals, however, and separate tabulations show their numbers and characteristics.

The structure of these labor force concepts is shown in Table 3.1, which presents annual average data for 1982. It will be noted that the labor force is measured in two ways—the total and the civilian labor force, depending on whether those in the armed services are included. There are two additional concepts illustrated in the table that deserve elaboration. The *labor force participation rate* expresses the total or the civilian labor force as a percentage of the relevant population (total or civilian noninstitutional population). The *unemployment rate* expresses the number of unemployed as a percentage of the civilian labor force (beginning in 1983, the denominator also includes members of the armed forces stationed in the United States). In addition to the global measures illustrated in the table, labor force participation rates and unemployment rates may be calculated for demographic subsets of the total population. Thus, the civilian labor force participation rate of black women 35 to 44 years of age is the number of employed and unemployed black women in that age group expressed as a percentage of the number of 35-to-44-year-old black women in the noninstitutional population. The unemployment rate of

TABLE 3.1 Employment Status of the Noninstitutional Population, 1982 (numbers in thousands)

Noninstitutional population 16 years and older	174,451
Total labor force, including armed forces	112,383
Armed forces	2,179
Civilian labor force	110,204
Employed	99,526
Unemployed	10,678
Not in the labor force	62,068
Total labor force participation rate $(112,383/174,451) \times 100$	64.4
Civilian labor force participation rate $(110,204/172,272) \times 100$	64.0
Unemployment rate $(10,678/110,204) \times 100$	9.7

SOURCE: U.S. President (1983: 196).

teenagers is the number of unemployed 16-to-19-year-olds expressed as a percentage of that age group in the civilian labor force.

THE CURRENT POPULATION SURVEY

How have the data in Table 3.1 been obtained? As has been indicated, the principal source of current labor force data in the United States is the CPS—a monthly enumeration of a sample of about 60,000 households scientifically selected to constitute a microcosm of the total U.S. population. The survey is the joint responsibility of the Bureau of the Census in the Department of Commerce and the Bureau of Labor Statistics in the Department of Labor, the former being responsible for sample design and field procedures and the latter for the content of the surveys and the analyses and presentation of the results.

There is rotation of the households in the sample. Each household is interviewed for a period of four months, drops out for eight months, and then re-enters the sample for a final four months. Interviews are conducted during the calendar week containing the nineteenth of each month, and relate to the activity of members of the household during the week containing the twelfth. The interviewer normally obtains information from one member of the household relating to all of its members 16 years of age or older. The answers provided by the respondent to a series of questions permit census coders to pigeon-hole each individual into one of the labor force categories that have been described. For example, the portion of the interview with Mrs. Thompson relating to her 18-year-old son Donald, might go as follows:

(1) Interviewer: What was Donald doing most of last week, working or something else?

Mrs. T.: He was going to school.

(2) Interviewer: Did Donald do any work last week, not counting work around the house?

Mrs. T.: No, he was just going to school.

(3) Interviewer: Did he have a job from which he was temporarily absent or on layoff?

Mrs. T.: No.

(4) Interviewer: Has Donald been looking for work during the past 4 weeks?

Mrs. T.: Yes, he's been looking for a part-time job for after school and weekends.

(5) Interviewer: What has he been doing in the last four weeks to find work?

Mrs. T.: He's been applying at local supermarkets.

(6) Interviewer: Is there any reason why Donald could not take a job last week?

Mrs. T.: No.

On the basis of these recorded responses, Donald would ultimately be classified as unemployed. Had the response to question 4 been negative, had Mrs. T. not been able to refer to any method that Donald was using to find work, or had the response to question 6 indicated that Donald was not available for work (except by virtue of temporary illness) he would have been classified as out of the labor force. If in response to question 3 Mrs. T. had indicated that Donald was employed part-time by the Kroger Company but had been given the week off in order to prepare for final exams, the remaining questions would not have been asked, and Donald's classification would have been employed—with a job but not at work.

Following the questions that yield labor force and employment status, there is a series of questions that identify the occupation, industry, and type of workers of the job held by employed persons or of the most recent job (if any) of those currently unemployed or out of the labor force. There are also questions for the employed on hours of work; for the unemployed on why the individual started to look for work (e.g., lost job, quit, entered labor force) and whether part- or full-time work is being sought; and for those out of the labor force on work-seeking intentions, whether the individual wants a regular job, and (if so) why he or she is not seeking work. Finally for all individuals there is a series of questions on demographic characteristics, including sex, age, race, marital status, and highest year of school completed.

The basic monthly questionnaire described above is supplemented with regular annual surveys on selected subjects as well as with nonrecurring surveys of various kinds. Illustrative of the former is the March supplement, which obtains data for the preceding calendar year on labor market activity (number of weeks employed, unemployed, and out of the labor force) and on income from all sources; and the October supplement, which collects information on school enrollment status and thus provides the basis for comparing labor force participation and unemployment rates of students and nonstudents. Among the special surveys that have been conducted are studies of interfirm and occupational mobility, pension coverage, and job search methods used by the unemployed.

Population estimates. Data derived from the CPS relate to a sample; these results are "blown up" to reflect the corresponding magnitudes for the entire population. Because of the way in which the sample is designed, it is possible to measure the "sampling error"—that is, the range on either side of the "true" population value within which the estimate yielded by the sample is likely to fall (with a specified level of probability). To illustrate, the standard error of the unemployment rate in 1980 was .11 percentage points, which means that at the 90 percent confidence level (1.6 standard errors) the unemployment rate calculated from the sample (7.1 percent) was within the range of plus or minus 0.2 percentage points (1.6 × .11) of the "true" value.

Seasonal adjustment. It should go without saying that there is a great deal of technical detail in the preparation of the CPS estimates at which the foregoing simple account barely hints. Fortunately most of this can safely remain unknown to even the serious and sophisticated user of human resource data. There is one statistical technique, however, about which one must be aware if intelligent use of the data is to be made, and that is the seasonal adjustment of monthly or quarterly working force data. The seasonal adjustment process is not confined to labor force data but to any time series of economic data that relate to periods shorter than a year. The problem lies in the fact that such data frequently display a more or less regular pattern of variation over a 12-month period (seasonal variation) that results either from changes in the weather (e.g., decline in agricultural production in the winter) or from elements of custom (e.g., rise in department store sales prior to Christmas). Under these circumstances, a given month-to-month change does not necessarily reflect a change in basic economic conditions but merely the variation that is expected every year. The seasonal adjustment process is designed to rid the raw figures of this seasonal influence so that the "real" economic change is more clearly revealed.

To illustrate, whether labor market conditions are good or bad, the unemployment rate has generally increased by more than a percentage point between May and June in recent years largely as the result of the influx of millions of students into the labor market as the school year ends. Given that fact, a rise in the unemployment rate of, say, half a percentage point between May and June in a particular year should actually be regarded as an *improvement* in underlying economic conditions. Indeed, under the hypothetical circumstances described, the unadjusted unemployment rate would rise between May and June while the seasonally adjusted rate would actually decline.

The seasonal adjustment procedures used by the Bureau of Labor Statistics are quite complex, but what they accomplish can be illustrated by the following hypothetical figures for 1978 (Table 3.2). Column one shows the actual unadjusted unemployment rates for each month of the year. Column two shows an hypothetical seasonal index that expresses the (average) unemployment rate for each month as a percentage of the average rate for the year.[6] For example, the seasonal index number for the month of June may be interpreted as indicating that in recent years the unemployment rate for that month has been about 7 percent above the average rate for the year. By the same token, the rate for October has generally been about 7 percent *below* the year's average. (Note that the arithmetic mean of the seasonal index is 1.0.) The seasonally adjusted rate in this example is obtained by dividing the unadjusted rate by the index value. Thus, for June the adjusted rate is 5.8 percent (6.2/1.07). Although the raw unemployment rate rose by 0.7 percentage point between May and June, the adjusted rate dropped by 0.2 percentage point.

It is the adjusted unemployment rate that is generally reported in the news media. In cases (like the example above) where the adjusted rate moves in the opposite direction from the unadjusted

TABLE 3.2 Hypothetical Illustration of Seasonal Adjustment

Month	Unadjusted Unemployment Rate	Seasonal Index	Seasonally Adjusted Unemployment Rate
January	7.0	1.11	6.3
February	6.9	1.13	6.1
March	6.6	1.06	6.2
April	5.8	0.95	6.1
May	5.5	0.92	6.0
June	6.2	1.07	5.8
July	6.3	1.03	6.1
August	5.8	0.98	5.9
September	5.7	0.97	5.9
October	5.4	0.93	5.8
November	5.5	0.95	5.8
December	5.6	0.93	6.0

SOURCE: See note 6 in Chapter 3.

rate, the reports even by sophisticated newscasters are occasionally confused and perplexing. Indeed, when it suits their purposes, political leaders have implied that there is something "fishy" about the seasonal adjustment. However, while there are differences of opinion among experts about how the seasonal adjustment should appropriately be made, there is no disagreement about its propriety.

PUBLISHED WORKING FORCE DATA

The working force data that emerge from the CPS, establishment surveys, and unemployment insurance operations appear regularly in two publications of the Bureau of Labor Statistics: *The Monthly Labor Review* and *Employment and Earnings*. Each issue of *The Monthly Labor Review* contains articles on various topics of interest to human resource specialists as well as brief summaries of recent developments in the labor market and industrial relations, several book reviews, and a list of recent publications in the human resource field. Its "Current Labor Statistics" section presents employment and unemployment data from the CPS; employment, hours, and earnings data for nonagricultural industries from the establishment surveys; selected data from unemployment insurance and employment service operations; and data on prices, productivity, work stoppages, employment costs, and changes in wages and fringe benefits negotiated under collective bargaining.

Employment and Earnings, also published monthly by the Bureau of Labor Statistics, contains statistical data from the same sources but in considerably greater detail.

EVALUATION

How adequately does the system of working force data in the United States serve the purposes that were outlined at the beginning of this chapter? Do the concepts and definitions currently in use provide meaningful measures of the utilization of the nation's human resources? Are there gaps in the available information that are significant from the perspective of formulating and evaluating human resource policy? A consideration of these issues provides a fitting conclusion to our discussion of human resource definitions and measurement.

Questions of these kinds are not merely of academic interest, but have occasioned intense political debate. Controversy about the meaningfulness of the official measure of unemployment has been especially pronounced during periods when the economy is in the doldrums. On one side are those who argue that the unemployment rate seriously understates the magnitude of the human resource utilization problem because it excludes individuals who are involuntarily working part-time, those who in desperation have taken jobs below their level of skill, and discouraged workers who believe that job search would be fruitless. On the other side, some argue that measured unemployment exaggerates the seriousness of the problem by giving the same weight to the 16-year-old seeking a part-time baby-sitting job as to the family breadwinner who has been laid off, and by including individuals whose search for work has been less than assiduous.

Twice during the past quarter of a century this and other issues have been studied by committees of experts whose mission has been to evaluate working force data in the United States and to make recommendations for whatever improvements were perceived to be desirable. The more recent of these was the National Commission on Employment and Unemployment Statistics (NCEUS), chaired by Professor Sar Levitan. Perhaps the most important point to be made about its report (NCEUS, 1979) is that the commission, like its predecessor almost two decades earlier (President's Committee to Appraise Employment and Unemployment, 1962), gave a clean bill of health to the basic soundness and integrity of the existing statistical programs while nevertheless making a number of significant proposals for change:

In combination, these data sources comprise an immense storehouse of information on employment and unemployment. By and large, the most important national statistics are timely, objective, and reasonably accurate, and they have unquestionably played a crucial role in guiding policy formulation. The commission's review of existing data, however, has led it to several areas in which the information system might be improved [NCEUS, 1979: 2].

Specifically, the NCEUS endorsed the continued exclusion of "discouraged workers" from the unemployed, largely because of the absence of a reliable method of identifying those who are "truly" unemployed; but recommended that the separate count of the discouraged be continued under a modified set of definitions. It also recommended that 16 be retained as the minimum age for inclusion in the labor force but suggested that information on school enrollment be collected monthly to permit statistical distinctions between students and nonstudents. The only major recommendation relating to definitions was that the armed forces stationed in the United States be included in the national count of the employed, which would affect the calculation of the national unemployment rate.

The commission urged that additional types of data be made available, notably (1) data cross-classifying individuals by employment status and income and earnings in order to ascertain the degree to which labor market difficulties create economic hardship; (2) "gross flow" data showing the numbers of individuals who move among the labor force and employment status categories (employed, unemployed, out of the labor force) from one month to the next; (3) information on volunteer work to be obtained in a triennial survey; (4) additional information on the unemployed, including the amount and sources of their income and the types of occupations and levels of wages they are seeking; (5) data on job changes of employed workers; and (6) better data for particular groups that are disadvantaged in the labor market—minority racial and ethnic groups, women, disabled persons, and rural workers.

In order to improve the woefully inadequate estimates of employment and unemployment for state and local areas and to provide more reliable data on minority groups, the commission recommended the expansion of the CPS sample by 42,000 households and a doubling of the sample size for minority households. In addition, it recommended the creation of a special supplementary household sample for a trial period of two years in order to experiment with the collection of information on such special topics as underemployment, labor force attachment, and job search activities of the unemployed. Finally, a number of technical improvements were suggested in the collection, processing, and presentation of data from each of the major sources. The estimated annual cost of implementing the recommendations of the NCEUS was in the neighborhood of $35 million, well over half of which would be accounted for by the recommended expansion in the size of the CPS sample.

In keeping with the economy measures of the Reagan administration, Secretary of Labor Donovan rejected all of the commission's recommendations that would have involved additional outlays (Donovan, 1981) but accepted the recommendations concerning definitions. Effective January 1983, the national labor force includes members of the armed services stationed in the United States, and the unemployment rate is based upon this total rather than the civilian labor force. This caused the measured unemployment rate to be about 0.2 percentage point lower than it would have been on the basis of the previous definition.

Not only were the significant NCEUS recommendations for improvement rejected, but there was an actual retrenchment in the human resource statistical program—and indeed in the statistical programs of the national government generally—as the result of budget cuts (Fuerbringer, 1982). Several statistical series of the BLS were abandoned, and publication of the results of the 1980 census was delayed. Many observers in both the academic and business communities who understand the importance of statistical data for sound policy decisions—public and private—have expressed the view that such budget cuts are penny-wise but pound-foolish.

NOTES

1. For example, measures of degree of commitment to the work ethic and satisfaction with current job among middle-aged men have been found to be related, other things equal, to the likelihood of subsequent early retirement. See Parnes and Nestel (1975).

2. Data on turnover (accessions and separations per 100 persons on the payroll) were provided for manufacturing industries in the United States until recently,

when their collection was terminated because of budget cuts initiated by the Reagan administration.

3. Agricultural employment and hours—including self-employed farmers and unpaid family workers as well as hired agricultural labor—are measured by a quarterly survey conducted by the Economics, Statistics, and Cooperatives Service of the U.S. Department of Agriculture.

4. The CPS was developed as a WPA project in the Department of Commerce, and was inaugurated in 1940 under the title of the Monthly Report on the Labor Force.

5. Persons who did not look for work because they were waiting to start new jobs within the next 30 days are also included among the unemployed.

6. These figures were calculated for the present purpose by dividing the published unadjusted rates by the seasonally adjusted rates. In other words, the figures in column two are the seasonal index implicit in the data published by the BLS. Actually, the BLS does not adjust global unemployment rates, but adjusts absolute data on unemployment for four age-sex groups and on employment for the same groups in and outside of agriculture.

QUESTIONS FOR DISCUSSION

1. How would you rate the adequacy of the official measure of unemployment as an indicator of (a) the performance of the economy? (b) economic hardship? (c) underutilization of human resources? In view of your answers, would you recommend any changes in the definition of unemployment?

2. Make a case for including discouraged workers in the count of the unemployed. Make a case against doing so. Which of these seems to you to be more persuasive?

3. The unadjusted unemployment rate fell in April 1983 while the adjusted rate rose. President Reagan cited the unadjusted figures in his public presentations, and was quoted by *The New York Times* as asserting that "statisticians have funny ways of counting." Evaluate this.

4. If there were no labor market discrimination of any kind, would there be any need for a race breakdown in human resource data? Would your answer be the same in regard to sex? What about age?

5. What are the major gaps or shortcomings in the human resource data system in the United States? What would be your major recommendations for change?

4

Trends in the Level and Composition of Human Resources

In this chapter we apply what we have just learned about the definition and measurement of human resources to explore patterns of change in the quantity and structure of human resources over time. How has the size of the labor force behaved over long periods of time, and how does it respond to short-run variations in economic conditions? What trends are discernible in the composition of the labor force by age and sex? How have the distributions of employment by industry and by occupation changed over the years? In regard to each of these topics we will be interested not only in describing trends but in accounting for them and in assessing their significance from the standpoint of human resource policy.

LABOR FORCE PARTICIPATION

Long-term trends. The quantity of human resources in any society is obviously closely linked to the size of its population. As U.S. population rose from 151 million to 226 million between 1950 and 1980, the size of the labor force grew from 64 to 109 million. For many purposes, however, it is more meaningful and useful to abstract from changes in the population by examining changes over time in the labor force participation rate—the proportion of the working age population who make themselves available for work. On this relative basis the increase over the same 30-year period was 4.3 percentage points—from 59.9 to 64.2 percent.

However, this relatively small global change in labor force participation obscures very dramatic offsetting changes among subsets of the population, as is shown in Table 4.1. For instance, among men the civilian labor force participation rate dropped 9 points (from 86.4 to 77.4 percent) while among women it rose almost 20 points (from 33.9 to 51.5 percent). As might be supposed, the lower participation of men resulted almost exclusively from decreases at the two ends of the age continuum, reflecting primarily the increased school enrollment of youth and the trend toward earlier retirement stimulated by liberalization of public and private pension programs. The sharpest decrease in participation occurred among men 65 and over—from 46 percent in 1950 to 19 percent in 1980—but a 15-point drop occurred in the 55-to-64-year age group, and even among men age 45-54 there was a 5-point decline.

In the case of women, increases occurred in virtually every demographic subgroup, reflecting a veritable revolution in the role of women in American society. Only among those 65 years and over was there no increase; the participation rate of this group remained virtually stable at just under 10 percent. Every other age group over 20 registered an increase of at least 14 percentage points, and the rise was as great as 30 percentage points in the case of women 25 to 34. The participation rate of married women more than doubled during the three-decade period, reaching exactly 50 percent in 1980. Even more indicative of the profound socio-economic change that had occurred is the fact that the proportion of mothers of preschool children who were in the labor force almost quadrupled—from 12 percent in 1950 to 45 percent in 1980.

Interesting racial differences in these trends are discernible. Among males, declining labor market participation has been more pronounced for blacks than for whites; as a consequence, whereas black and white male participation rates were about equal in 1950, a 7-point differential in favor of whites had developed by 1980. In the case of women, participation of both racial groups rose, but considerably more for whites than for blacks. As a result, the 14-percentage-point difference in favor of black women that had prevailed in 1950 shrank to only 2 points by 1980.

Correlates of labor force participation. One way of approaching an explanation of the trends in labor force participation is to seek

TABLE 4.1 Civilian Labor Force Participation Rates, by Sex, Race, and Age, 1950 and 1980

Sex and Age	Total		Whites		Blacks*	
	1950	1980	1950	1980	1950	1980
Males, total	86.4	77.4	86.4	78.2	85.9	71.5
16-17	51.3	50.1	50.5	53.6	57.4	32.1
18-19	75.9	71.3	75.6	74.1	78.2	56.0
20-24	87.9	85.9	87.5	87.2	91.4	78.3
25-34	96.0	95.2	96.4	95.9	92.6	90.2
35-44	97.6	95.5	97.7	96.2	96.2	89.8
45-54	95.8	91.2	95.9	92.1	95.1	83.9
55-64	86.9	72.1	87.3	73.1	81.9	63.5
65+	45.8	19.0	45.8	19.1	45.5	17.5
Females, total	33.9	51.5	32.6	51.2	46.9	53.6
16-17	30.1	43.6	30.1	47.2	30.2	26.0
18-19	51.3	61.9	52.6	65.1	40.6	45.7
20-24	46.0	68.9	45.9	70.6	46.9	60.0
25-34	34.0	65.5	32.1	64.8	51.6	69.2
35-44	39.1	65.5	37.2	65.0	55.7	68.1
45-54	37.9	59.9	36.3	59.6	54.3	61.7
55-64	27.0	41.3	26.0	40.9	40.9	44.9
65+	9.7	8.1	9.2	7.9	16.5	9.6

SOURCE: Manpower Report of the President (1975); U.S. President (1982b).
*Includes other nonwhites.

an understanding of the factors that operate at any moment of time to affect the likelihood of an individual's membership in the labor force. A very large number of "labor supply" studies of this kind have been made, the theoretical underpinnings of which have become increasingly complex. The earliest models had individuals allocating their time between work (the source of earnings with which to purchase goods and services) and leisure. More sophisticated subsequent versions have recognized (1) that paid employment and leisure do not exhaust the options that individuals have in allocating their time—work in the home and school attendance are alternatives; (2) that households make joint decisions concerning the allocation of the time of their members; and (3) that a truly rational approach requires a "life cycle" framework in which labor supply decisions at each stage in an individual's life are made with the view toward maximizing *lifetime* utility. The realism and/or the utility of these models need not detain us, except to note that some of the research based on life cycle theory (which requires individuals to "know" how long they will live!) has concluded that the labor force participation of men in their sixties has not been reduced by the Social Security Act (Aaron, 1982).

Nevertheless, the empirical work that has been done on the determinants of labor force participation allows us to identify its correlates with a rather high degree of confidence. While the specific variables differ depending on the particular demographic group under consideration, in general they can be subsumed under four general headings: (1) "tastes," (2) net rewards from work in the labor market, (3) net rewards for working in the home (or attending school), and (4) net resources in the absence of work (Bowen and Finegan, 1969). To illustrate by reference to married women, *tastes* would include such factors as the woman's attitudes toward work versus leisure, the relative attractiveness to her of keeping house versus working outside the home, and her perception of the appropriate role of wives and mothers.

The most obvious of the *net rewards from work* is the potential wage rate. The higher the potential earnings of a woman, other things being equal, the more likely she is to be in the labor force. But there are other more subtle influences that enter the picture. For instance, the costs of child care are an offsetting factor; the higher they are the less likely is the woman to choose to work. Health is likewise an offsetting factor in the sense that poor health makes it less likely that a woman will actually be able to obtain the prevailing wage for her type of work and thus operates to decrease the likelihood of labor force participation for any given wage level. Educational attainment bears a net positive relationship to labor force participation, either as a reflection of the more attractive jobs (aside from earnings) that are available to better-educated women or as a reflection of the stronger "tastes" of better-educated women for market work (i.e., women who are disposed to a career in the labor market are more likely than others to pursue education).

The *rewards for work in the home* are, obviously, conditioned by the size and age composition of the family. Thus, the greater the number of children the less likely is labor force participation; the presence of children under six has a more depressing effect on labor force participation than the presence of older children. *Resources in the absence of work* include the earnings of other family members (particularly the husband), family income from sources other than earnings, and net assets. For example, other things being equal, the higher the husband's income the less likely is a married woman to be in the labor force.

Some of the variables affecting the labor supply decisions of married women are more or less unique to them (e.g., cost of child care; number and ages of children). Many, however, are generalizable to other population groups. In general, empirical evidence supports the propositions that the likelihood of labor force participation (other things being equal) is positively related to potential earnings, educational attainment, physical and mental health, and is negatively related to "other" income (e.g., size of pension benefits in the case of men of retirement age).

Causal factors in labor force trends. As has been mentioned, these relationships help to explain historic changes in the labor force participation rates of specific demographic subgroups. Bowen and Finegan, in their meticulous analysis of *The Economics of Labor Force Participation* (1969), applied the regression coefficients obtained in their analyses to the actual changes that occurred over time in their explanatory variables to ascertain how much of the observed changes could be explained by the variables in their models. Table 4.2 shows the results of this type of exercise for married women and for males 65 years of age and older.

Table 4.2 tells us that of the 14-percentage-point rise in the labor force participation rate of women that occurred in the decade and a half after World War II, almost one-half is explained by the model employed by Bowen and Finegan, consisting largely of economic variables. A good portion of the remainder, they contend, can be explained by the increasing availability of part-time work, the increased availability and lower relative costs of household appliances, and increasing income aspirations of American families (pp. 226-240). For older males the model explains about four-fifths of the 19-point drop in labor force participation that occurred over the same period, the principal factor being the "increased ability to afford leisure" (p. 373). It would be a mistake to interpret these results too literally, as Bowen and Finegan themselves acknowledge. They do serve, however, to bolster confidence in our understanding of some of the major factors that affect labor force participation.

Cyclical variation in labor force participation. For more than a quarter of a century labor economists debated whether the size of the labor force varied according to the level of economic activity and, if so, in which direction. On the one hand, the "additional worker theory" argued that the labor force tended to swell during depressions as "secondary workers" (wives and working-age children) entered the labor market in an attempt to compensate for the lost income of unemployed principal breadwinners. The competing hypothesis was the "discouraged worker theory," which held that when job opportunities were limited many unem-

TABLE 4.2   Actual Versus "Explained" Change in Labor Force
Participation Rates, Married Women and Older
Males, 1948-1965

Item	Married Women, 14-54	Men, 65 and Older
Observed change in participation rate[a]	+14.2	−18.9
Attributable to demographic factors[b]	−0.4	−2.9
Attributable to income and job incentive factors[c]	+6.8	−12.3
Total explained change	+6.4	−15.2
Unexplained change	+7.8	−3.7
Explained as percentage of observed change	48%	80%

SOURCE: Adapted from Bowen and Finegan (1969: 206, 226, 354, 364).

a. Actual change in percentage points, 1948-1965.

b. Age, color and rural-urban status for both groups; presence of children under 6 for married women; marital status for older males.

c. Earnings, schooling, income of husbands (for women), other income, unemployment rate, supply of females and older males, industry mix (for women), and occupation and self-employment mix (for men).

ployed workers ceased looking for work out of a sense of futility, while potential labor market entrants would for the same reason not attempt to seek work. Thus, the additional worker theory postulated an *inverse* relationship between level of economic activity and labor force size, while the discouraged worker theory postulated a *positive* relationship.

The difference between these two views was much more than of academic significance; it had a bearing on the way in which unemployment figures were to be interpreted. In the view of the additional worker theory, as the economy moved into a recession some of the rise in unemployment was in a sense "artificial"— induced merely by the disemployment of primary breadwinners— and would disappear when the economy regained its health. In contrast, the discouraged worker theory implied that the unemployment measured during a recession understated the magnitude of the problem; there was in addition the "hidden" unemployment of those who but for their frustration would be seeking work. For example, if measured unemployment is 8 million at a time when 6 million is regarded as an acceptable level of unemployment, more than 2 million additional jobs have to be created because one can expect hitherto discouraged workers to begin to seek work as unemployment drops.

It is hard to believe that an issue as important and seemingly as straightforward as this should have remained unsettled for so long.

Nevertheless it was not until the 1960s that the empirical evidence became incontrovertible, in large measure as the result of the work of Bowen and Finegan referred to above. Their findings as well as those of a number of other investigators demonstrated that the discouraged worker theory was a better description of reality. While the additional worker phenomenon and the discouraged worker phenomenon are both evident, the latter more than counterbalances the former so that the *net* relationship between unemployment and labor force size is negative. While there is little or no controversy over the *direction* of the relationship, it has not been possible to quantify it precisely, for results are quite sensitive to methods of analyses. Based on their own work, Bowen and Finegan report estimates of hidden unemployment for the census week of 1960 ranging from 1.3 million to 386,000 depending on the method of analysis used; two other independent estimates for the same time were about 780,000 and 1.2 million, respectively (Bowen and Finegan, 1969: 495, 514-515). Thus, while one can be confident that there is "hidden unemployment" when the economy is below full employment levels, it appears to be foolhardy to attempt to specify its amount.[1]

AGE AND SEX COMPOSITION

The age-sex composition of the labor force is a function of the composition of the underlying population and of age-sex specific labor force participation rates. Thus, if the population of working age is 52 percent female and 48 percent male and if labor force participation rates of women and men are 52 percent and 78 percent respectively, then the proportions of the labor force represented by women and men will be 42 percent and 58 percent respectively.[2] As the proportions of men and women in the population do not change over time to any significant degree, trends in the sex distribution of the labor force are almost exclusively a result of changes in the labor force participation rates of women and men. These changes, which have been detailed above, have produced a dramatic shift in the sex composition of the labor force over the past 30 years. Whereas women comprised under one-third (29 percent) of the labor force in 1950, they accounted for over two-fifths (43 percent) in 1983.

Unlike distribution by sex, the age composition of the population is by no means stable over time but changes as the result of changes in birth rates, death rates, and migration rates, the first of which has been by far the most important influence. The age composition of the labor force reflects these changes in the underlying population as well as changes in age-specific participation rates.

While an extensive treatment of demographic trends is beyond the scope of this chapter, it is important to note that the long-run trend in fertility rates in the United States has been downward, interrupted by a sharp increase during the post World War II period (the baby boom). From 1910 to 1945, the birth rate dropped almost continuously from 30.1 per 1,000 population to 20.4 per 1,000, with a low of 18.7 during the Great Depression year of 1935. In the period after World War II it rose to a peak of 26.5 in 1947 but remained as high as 23.7 as late as 1960. Thereafter it declined almost continuously to 14.8 in 1976 and has remained in the neighborhood of 15 or 16 since then.[3]

These changes in fertility and a steady downward trend in mortality have produced marked changes in the age structure of the population over the past thirty years. Their implications for the long-run future remain somewhat less clear, considering that a great deal depends upon what happens to the fertility rate, and that past attempts to forecast fertility have been notoriously unsuccessful. Table 4.3 shows selected age-structure ratios for 1950 and 1976 and projections until 2050, based upon replacement-level fertility (which would involve a rise from current levels). The proportion of young persons under age 18 rose from 31 percent in 1950 to a peak of 36 percent in 1960, reflecting the baby boom. This proportion will drop perceptibly in the 1980s and reach 24 percent in the second quarter of the next century. At the other end of the age continuum, the proportion of the population 65 and over will rise from the current 11 or 12 percent to 17 or 18 percent over the same period as the baby boom generation reaches retirement age. If fertility were to remain at its current low level, these trends would be even more pronounced.

One of the favorable implications of the projected trends (Clark, 1980) is a mitigation of the unemployment problems of youth as new entrants to the labor market (age 18-24) decline as a percentage of the total age range (18-64) and even more precipitously as a percentage of those leaving the labor market (age 55-64). On the other hand, the projected increase in the old-age dependency ratio (65 and over/18-64) means that the support of retired individuals will fall upon the shoulders of relatively fewer persons of working age in the next century than currently. As we will see in

TABLE 4.3   Selected Age Structure Ratios, 1950-2050

Ratio	1950	1960	1985	2000	2025	2050
0-17/total	0.31	0.36	0.27	0.26	0.24	0.24
65 and over/total	0.08	0.09	0.12	0.12	0.17	0.18
65 and over/18-64	0.13	0.17	0.19	0.20	0.30	0.30
18-24/18-64	0.17	0.16	0.19	0.15	0.16	0.16
18-24/55-64	1.20	1.03	1.28	1.06	0.78	0.81

SOURCE: Projections for 1985-2050 from Robert L. Clark (1980: 12-13); ratios for 1950 and 1960 calculated from data in Statistical Abstract of the United States, 1975, Table 3 and 1982-1983, Table 27.

Chapter 11, this constitutes the basic long-term problem in financing social security.

INDUSTRIAL AND OCCUPATIONAL STRUCTURE OF EMPLOYMENT

The industrial structure of employment relates to the distribution of human resources according to the nature of their employer's product; occupational structure relates to composition according to the particular task or function of the employees. As the occupational composition of employment depends to a considerable degree on its industrial composition, it is logical to begin our analysis with industrial trends.

Trends in industrial structure. The most global generalization that one can make about the long-term trend in the industrial structure of the labor force is that goods production has accounted for a relatively smaller share and services production a relatively larger share of total employment. In the mid 1950s the number of workers employed in the service-producing industries (trade; transportation and public utilities; finance, insurance, and real estate; services; and public administration) for the first time equalled and then subsequently exceeded the number of workers employed in industries whose product is a tangible good (agriculture, mining, construction, and manufacturing). By 1980, about two-thirds of total employment was in services (Table 4.4).

Behind this broad generalization lies the dramatic decline in the proportion of the labor force involved in agriculture—from almost one in three in 1919 to about 3 percent in the early 1980s. Manufacturing employment declined somewhat during the period but not continuously. Both in 1919 and 1959 employment in this major industry division stood at about 25 percent of the total labor

TABLE 4.4 Percentage Distribution of Employment,
by Industrial Sector, 1919-1990

Industrial Sector	1919	1959	1979	1990
Total	100.0	100.0	100.0	100.0
Goods production	64.6	38.2	29.7	27.7
Agriculture	32.9	7.8	2.7	1.9
Mining	2.8	0.9	0.7	0.8
Construction	2.5	5.4	5.8	5.7
Manufacturing	26.4	24.1	20.5	19.3
Services production	35.4	61.8	70.3	72.3
Transportation, communications, utilities	9.2	6.1	5.3	5.1
Trade	11.2	18.8	21.4	22.2
Finance, insurance, real estate	2.8	4.1	5.3	5.7
Other services	5.6	17.3	21.0	23.2
Government	6.6	15.5	17.3	16.1

SOURCE: Data for 1919 from Wolfbein (1964: 183); data for 1959-1990 from U.S. Department of Labor (1982a: 30).

force but by the early 1980s had dropped to about 20 percent. Within the services sector the large gains were registered by the "other services" category—personal service, business and repair services, and professional services (especially education and health)—and by government. These two sectors increased continuously in relative importance, from 12 percent of total employment in 1910 to 38 percent by 1979. Needless to say, the changes that have occurred in these broad industry divisions grossly understate the total change in industrial composition of employment. One has only to think of the automobile, aircraft, and electronics manufacturing industries to recognize the dramatic shifts that have occurred *within* the manufacturing industry division since 1919.

Generating forces. The broad trends in industrial structure that have been described above are by no means unique to the United States but generally characterize the economic development of all societies and reflect the influence of two major underlying forces: variations among industries (1) in rate of growth of labor productivity, and (2) in income elasticity of demand. Labor productivity, a concept that will be examined in greater detail in Chapter 8, refers to output per unit of labor input. If a firm produces 8,000 units of product a week with a work force of 10 persons employed for 40 hours, productivity is 20 units per person hour (8,000/[10×40]). If 10 years later as a result of technological improvements, 8 workers produce 8,320 units of output in a 40-hour week, productivity is 26 units per person-hour—a productivity increase of 30 percent.

Income elasticity of demand refers to the sensitivity of consumer expenditures on a product to changes in their income. If a given percentage increase in real income results in a larger percentage increase in expenditures on a particular commodity, that commodity is said to have an elastic demand; if the percentage increase in expenditures is smaller than the increase in income, the demand for the commodity is inelastic. The dividing line between these two conditions (where demand is said to have unitary elasticity) is where the percentage increase in expenditures precisely equals the percentage increase in income. A moment's reflection will indicate that the demand for inexpensive necessities (e.g., bread) will generally be characterized by income inelasticity while expensive goods or services less crucial to survival (e.g., education) will be income elastic.

With the definitions of these concepts in mind, we can now illustrate the way in which they help to explain shifts in the industrial structure of employment. To begin with, imagine an economy with an unchanging population and labor force and with just two industries, each employing the same number of workers. Assume that productivity in each industry increases by 30 percent over a ten-year period, and that incomes increase by the same percentage with prices remaining stable. Assume further that each industry has a unitary income elasticity of demand so that the 30 percent increase in income induces consumers to increase their expenditures on the output of each industry by 30 percent. Under these very simple assumptions, output of each industry will increase by 30 percent with a constant work force and will be absorbed by the market as the result of rising incomes. There is no need for human resources to be shifted from either industry to the other.

Now, with everything else remaining the same, suppose that the demand for the product of industry A is income elastic while that for industry B is inelastic. Specifically, as incomes increase by 30 percent, consumers expand their purchases of product A by 50 percent but increase their expenditures for B by only 10 percent. Under these circumstances industry A will have to expand employment in order to produce enough output to satisfy consumers while industry B will discover that its output exceeds that which consumers wish to purchase. A shift of workers from B to A is required under these circumstances. Thus, other things being equal, industries with income elastic demands will experience increases in the proportion of the work force as productivity increases while industries with inelastic demands will register decreases.

To examine the effects of different rates of increase in labor productivity, let us now assume once again that A and B each has a unitary income elasticity of demand but that the productivity increase is only 15 percent over the ten-year period in A and as great as 45 percent for industry B, yielding an economywide average of 30 percent with a consequent 30 percent increase in real incomes. Under these circumstances consumers will wish to increase their expenditures by 30 percent on the product of each industry, but with constant work forces A would increase its output by less than this amount while B's increase would be greater than the amount consumers are wanting to purchase. Thus, with other things equal, human resources must shift from industries in which productivity growth is greater than average to those in which it is below average.

This illustration is, of course, absurdly oversimplified; but it does serve the purpose of highlighting two of the most fundamental proximate causes of shifts in the industrial structure of employment. For example, the very large decrease in the proportion of the work force employed in agriculture is explained both by higher-than-average increases in productivity in agriculture and the relative income inelasticity of demand for agricultural products. The increase in the relative importance of the services-producing sector of the economy is primarily a reflection of the lower rates of productivity increase that have prevailed there than in goods production.

Trends in occupational structure. As has been indicated, a substantial portion of the change in occupational structure that has taken place over the years is a reflection of changes in industrial structure because there is wide variation among industries in occupational mix. However, much occupational change occurs within industries as the result of changes in production methods. For instance within manufacturing industries there has been a continuous decrease in the ratio of workers directly involved in production to other categories of workers; the proportion of nonproduction workers rose from 18 percent in 1950 to 29 percent in 1980.

The broadest generalization that can be made about the long-run change in the occupational composition of total employment is that white collar employment—professional-technical, managerial, clerical, and sales—increased relative to blue collar employment—craftspersons (skilled), operatives, (semiskilled) and nonfarm laborers (unskilled). Just as services-producing workers equaled goods-producing workers for the first time in the mid 1950s, white collar employment first became as large as blue collar employment at that time (Table 4.5). It should be noted that this classification excludes two other large occupational categories—service workers and farm workers. The first of these embraces personal service (e.g., barbers, waitresses), protective service (e.g., police and fire personnel, guards), and domestic servants. The distinction between this *occupational* service category and the *industrial* service categories must also be kept in mind.

The major increases in the white collar group have occurred among professional and technical workers and among clerical workers. The former grew from under 5 percent of total employment in 1910 to over 16 percent in the 1980s. Among clerical workers the corresponding proportions were 6 to 19 percent. The managerial and sales group grew much more moderately, although the composition of the former changed substantially as salaried managers increased in relative importance and self-employed proprietors decreased.

In the blue collar group the proportion of skilled workers has remained relatively stable although its composition has obviously changed greatly. Semiskilled operatives—such as machine operators and truck drivers—increased substantially between 1910 and 1950 (from 14 to 20 percent of total employment) but then declined to 14 percent by the early 1980s. Nonskilled labor declined sharply from about 12 percent of the total in 1910 to under 5 percent currently. Reflecting the decline in agriculture that has already been noted, the occupational category of farm workers (farmers, farm managers, and farm laborers) has declined from 31 percent to under 3 percent. The proportion of service workers has risen moderately, from 10 percent in 1910 to 13 percent in 1981.

Very significant among these trends has been that of the operative group. The big increase in this relatively large occupational category between 1910 and 1950 meant that there was a large and expanding reservoir of job opportunities requiring little in the way of education or training to absorb workers displaced

TABLE 4.5 Percentage Distribution of Employment, by Major
Occupation Group, 1910-1990

Occupation Group	1910	1950	1980	1990
Total	100.0	100.0	100.0	100.0
White collar	21.5	36.6	52.2	50.9
Professional, technical	4.7	8.6	16.1	16.8
Managers, administrators	6.6	8.7	11.2	8.8
Clerical	5.5	12.3	18.6	18.6
Sales	4.7	7.0	6.3	6.7
Blue collar	38.1	41.1	31.7	31.5
Craftspersons	11.6	14.1	12.9	12.0
Operatives	14.5	20.4	14.2	13.7
Laborers, nonfarm	12.0	6.6	4.6	5.8
Service workers	9.6	10.5	13.3	15.8
Farmers, farm managers	16.4	7.4	1.5 ⎫	1.8
Farm laborers	14.4	4.4	1.3 ⎭	

SOURCE: Data for 1910 and 1950 from Wolfbein (1964: 194); data for 1980 from
U.S. President (1982b: 178); projections for 1990 from U.S. Department of Labor
(1982a: 37).

from other jobs by an advancing technology. In the past quarter of
a century, however, this category has actually shrunk in relative
importance, and the growing categories (professional and clerical)
are those with above-average educational requirements. Thus, the
process of adjusting to technological change and job displacement
has been rendered more difficult.

Before leaving the subject of occupational structure it should be
noted that the occupational classification system that has (with
minor modifications) been used for many years by the Bureau of
Labor Statistics and the Bureau of the Census was fundamentally
revamped in the 1980 census and, beginning January 1983, in the
Current Population Survey. The new classification system has 13
major categories rather than the 12 that had hitherto existed and
abandons the "white collar" and "blue collar" designations.
Occupational data for 1983 and subsequent years will therefore
not be comparable with those presented in this chapter.

Implications of historical trends. Having described and, in a
very general way, accounted for historical shifts in the industrial
and occupational composition of the work force over the past
three-quarters of a century, it is a fitting conclusion to this chapter
to reflect for a few moments on their implications. First, the
changes that have been outlined give testimony to the tremendous

flexibility of human resources as they respond to the unending dynamics of demand shifts generated by changes in the composition of the gross national product and in productive technology. To some extent the reallocation of human resources has taken place through voluntary or involuntary job changes by members of the labor force at any point in time; to some extent it has occurred through changes in rates of entry into occupations and industries by new labor force entrants. In either case it illustrates intra- or intergenerational industrial and/or occupational mobility of labor.

Second, in an age in which "robotization" creates the same fears that "automation" did a generation earlier, the trends that have been examined are a reminder that technological displacement of labor is not a new phenomenon but has been going on in one form or another since men and women first climbed down from the trees, and especially since the industrial revolution. By stretching the meaning of the term "automation" (but no more so than it has been stretched in the popular press) one may say that the dramatic decline in agricultural employment that has been described means that farmers were "automated" out of jobs.

Yet despite the very large shifts that have occurred in its composition, total employment has continued to rise and there is no evidence of the mass unemployment that some observers had feared. It is well to remember that as late as 1969, well after automation had become a reality, we had an unemployment rate below 4 percent. It is also significant that computerization has been accompanied by a continuation of the growth of clerical employment not only in absolute numbers, but in relative terms— from 15 percent in 1960 to 18.5 percent in 1981. The serious problems of structural unemployment that face the economy in the 1980s are not to be denied; nevertheless, fears of mass unemployment appear to be unwarranted. The more reasonable prediction is that "work is here to stay" (Levitan and Johnson, 1982: 113).

Third, although the historical evidence does not support the view that technological change destroys job opportunities in the aggregate, it makes clear the substantial adjustments that are required and suggests that many of these involve large human costs. Moreover, as has been observed, these adjustments have become more difficult as the result of the drying up of the reservoir of semiskilled jobs and of the fact that the growing occupational categories require above-average education and training. In any case, since the adjustments are dictated by changes that in the aggregate bring society greater volumes of goods and services, the costs that they involve ought not to fall exclusively on the unfortunate individuals who happen to be in the wrong (occupational or industrial) place at the wrong time but should be borne as widely as is possible by the entire society. Unemployment insurance and public employment and training programs are illustrative of ways in which this may be done.

Fourth, profound changes in the occupational character of the world of work have constituted great challenges to the education and training institutions of our society, which they have met, by and large, reasonably well. Nevertheless, knowing that the structure of job opportunities changes dramatically even within the lifetime of an individual suggests the desirability of two changes of emphasis in human resource development policy. First, the educational system needs to go as far as possible in building flexibility into the human agent of production. This argues for more emphasis on establishing general foundations in the schools and for greater reliance on the workplace for developing the skills unique to the particular job. Second, the idea of a once-and-for-all preparation for work needs to give way to a system that will provide educational and training opportunities throughout one's entire working life.

NOTES

1. It will be recalled that the Bureau of Labor Statistics reports the number of "discouraged workers" based upon information gathered in the Current Population Survey.

2. These figures imply that for every 100 persons in the noninstitutional population 16 years of age and over (52 women and 48 men) 64 are in the labor force—27 women ($.52 \times 52$) and 37 men ($.78 \times 48$). These are the actual proportions that prevailed in 1981.

3. A more refined measure is the total fertility rate—the hypothetical number of children a birth cohort of 1,000 female babies would produce at the same age-specific fertility rates as the current female population. The total fertility rate was about 2,200 in 1935, 3,640 in 1960, and 1,856 in 1979.

QUESTIONS FOR DISCUSSION

1. How do you account for the major trends in labor force participation rates in the period following World War II? What significance do you attach to them?

2. Evaluate the Bowen and Finegan model of labor force participation. How adequately can one measure the variables in the model?

3. Explain the significance of the major issue involved in the debate between the additional worker and the discouraged worker theories. How do you interpret the evidence on this issue, and how satisfied are you with this evidence?

4. How confident can one be of 15-year projections of the age composition of the labor force? 30-year projections? What major consequences for human resource policy do you see in the projected changes in the age structure of the population?

5. Do historical trends in the industrial and occupational structure of employment provide reliable clues to what is likely to happen in the future, or are we on the verge of a sharp break with the past?

6. What major "principles" seem to you to be supported by an analysis of the changes in the industrial and occupational composition of the labor force over the past half century?

5

The Economist's Model
of the Labor Market

The allocation of human resources takes place through the operation of the labor market. Our objective in this chapter is to develop an understanding of the concept of the labor market and to explain how it operates to allocate labor and to determine wages. For this purpose we present the economist's model of a competitive labor market. In the following chapter we raise the question of how adequately that model describes reality.

THE LABOR MARKET

Perhaps the best way to develop at least an initial comprehension of the idea of the labor market is to consider the diagram shown in Figure 5.1. In 1982, there were approximately 83 million households in the United States, in which resided about 174 million persons of working age (16 years and older). At the same time there were approximately 17 million employing establishments of all types, including national, state, and local governmental units; profit-making institutions ranging from the General Motors Corporation to tiny retail stores; agricultural units ranging from small farms employing perhaps only one farm laborer to large-scale lettuce farms in the San Joaquin Valley; and private nonprofit organizations like hospitals and a variety of social service organizations. In the average month of 1982, about 100

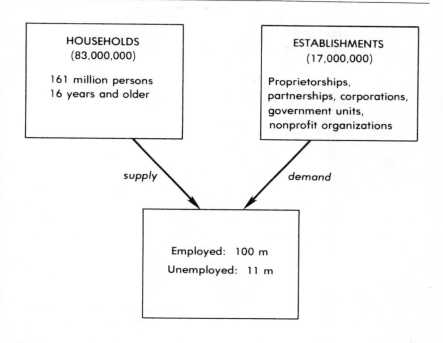

Figure 5.1:   The Labor Market

million members of the households were employed in the establishments and an additional 11 million were seeking work.

Now the labor market is the invisible institution through which these millions of household members are brought into contact with the millions of jobs in the employing establishments. It embraces all those processes through which potential workers offer themselves for (and ultimately find) jobs, and through which employers recruit workers. It is through the operation of the labor market that the total level of employment in the economy is determined, as well as its distribution among different occupations, industries, localities, and firms. It is also through the operation of the labor market that the level and structure of wage rates are determined. To use the more formal language of the economist, the labor market is the area within which the supply of labor and the demand for labor interact to determine both the level of employment and the price of labor (wages).

Labor market dynamics. While the foregoing represents a reasonable first step in exploring the concept of the labor market, it is a gross oversimplification in at least two important respects. To begin with, on the basis of what we have said thus far it would appear that household members get allocated among jobs on a once-and-for-all basis, while we know that this is not the case. Our diagram, in other words, conceals the very substantial amount of milling around that takes place within the labor market.

There is, for example, considerable movement between the households and the labor market as individuals move into and out of the labor force. The number of persons who worked at any time during the year 1981 was 117 million, in contrast with the 100 million who, on average, were employed at any one time. Thus, the number with some work experience during the year was one-sixth greater than the average level of employment. There is also considerable movement into and out of the ranks of the unemployed. About 23 million persons experienced some unemployment during 1981—a figure almost three times as great as average unemployment for the year. Finally, whether or not accompanied by unemployment, there is also a great deal of movement among jobs. Probably as many as one-tenth of all individuals who work during a year make at least one change of employer. The same proportion of employed persons change occupations during the course of a typical year, either within the same establishment or concurrently with a change of employer. Some of the interfirm movement requires a change of residence.

These kinds of dynamics are referred to as labor mobility. The types of mobility that have been illustrated are labor force mobility (into and out of the labor force), employment mobility (between employment and unemployment), interfirm mobility (from one employer to another), occupational mobility, interindustry mobility, and geographic mobility. Taken together, they represent all of the ways in which the supply of human resources can adjust to changes in the level and composition of the demand for labor. And it is through the labor market that these adjustments take place.

Geographic and occupational labor markets. The second respect in which our initial description of the labor market is an oversimplification stems from the level of aggregation that was used. If the labor market is indeed the area within which forces of supply and demand operate to determine employment levels and wages, a moment's reflection will make it obvious that at least from some points of view one has to talk about labor *markets* rather than *the* labor market.

The point can perhaps best be made by considering the extreme cases along a continuum. If one is talking about baby-sitters, supply and demand conditions prevail largely within a single neighborhood. Persons seeking baby-sitters are not likely to consider candidates who live very far from their residence; by the same token, individuals who want baby-sitting jobs generally wish to work as close to home as possible. Thus, both the supply of and the demand for baby-sitters are confined to relatively small residential areas—which is another way of saying that the labor market for baby-sitters generally consists of a neighborhood. One of the implications of this, incidentally, is that one might expect greater variation within a city in the wages paid to baby-sitters than for types of work for which the market is citywide.

At the other end of the continuum is the labor market for, say, college professors of physics. When the Department of Physics at Harvard wishes to recruit a new faculty member, it would never occur to the faculty to confine its search to the Boston metropolitan area. Similarly, a young woman receiving a Ph.D. in physics at Harvard would make her availability known to employers all over the country. Thus, on both the supply and demand sides the labor market for physicists is truly national—and, indeed, to some extent international.

Between these two extremes, most semiskilled occupations in manufacturing—or clerical or sales jobs, to take another example—have labor markets that are city- or countywide in the sense that employers generally recruit from the total local area, and residents of the area are generally willing to consider employment anywhere within it. Not only does the labor market have a geographic dimension, as the foregoing examples suggest, but it has an occupational dimension as well. That is, because labor is not a homogeneous glob, for many purposes it does not make as much sense to talk about the supply of or demand for *labor* as it does to talk about the supply of and demand for *specific categories* of human resources. Thus, one can recognize separate labor markets for nurses, librarians, janitors, typists, waiters and waitresses, and machinists.

The burden of the foregoing argument, then, is that it is more meaningful to think in terms of a multitude of labor markets than in terms of a single market for human resources. While for most purposes this is true, there is nevertheless a sense in which the notion of *the* labor market is useful. The latter concept emphasizes the point that there are linkages among labor markets that prevent any of them from being completely insulated from supply and demand forces elsewhere. For instance, while it is true that auto mechanics in Chicago ordinarily confine their search for work to the Chicago metropolitan area, if supply and demand conditions are such that job opportunities in this line of work are scarce in Chicago but plentiful in Cleveland, an unemployed Chicago mechanic may very well move to Cleveland. Indeed, even if employed the Chicago mechanic may be lured to Cleveland if wages are sufficiently higher there.

Similarly, there are links among occupational markets. Let job opportunities and/or pay rise sufficiently among sales personnel, and one can expect some waiters or typists or mechanics to make themselves available in the market for salespersons. Thus, local labor markets and occupational labor markets each tend to overlap to some degree, and the degree of overlap varies depending on geographic proximity and on transferability of skills. There is likely to be greater overlap between the New York and Philadelphia markets, for example, than between either of them and the Dallas market; similarly, the overlap between punch press operator and drill press operator is greater than between either of them and machinist. Nevertheless, there are potential linkages among all markets, at least in the long run, and in this sense one is justified in thinking about a national labor market. Perhaps the best summary of all of this is Clark Kerr's observation (1954: 92-93) that labor markets have

> vague and varying contours, but no ultimate limits short of those for American society itself . . . most labor markets are . . . indefinite in their specification of the sellers and buyers. Such a labor market is merely an area, with indistinct geographical and occupational limits within which certain workers customarily seek to offer their services and certain employers to purchase them.

THE COMPETITIVE LABOR MARKET MODEL

Having discussed the concept of the labor market, we turn now to a brief description of the traditional economic theory of a competitive labor market. It is this model that purports to describe the basic forces affecting the allocation of labor (human resources) and the determination of wages in the economy.

It is important to understand that this theory, like all other aspects of conventional economic theory, really represents simply an exercise in deductive logic. One begins with a set of assumptions relating to the behavior of employers and workers that lead to conclusions concerning both the structure of employment and the structure of wages. To provide a view of the forest before examining the individual trees, it is useful to state the two major conclusions of the theory and then to show the line of reasoning on which they are based. In brief, the theory of a competitive labor market comprises the following two propositions:

(1) Each employer will operate in such a way as to equate the marginal revenue product of labor with the marginal cost of labor.
(2) For a given type of work and for workers of a specific quality, differentials in economic rewards (i.e., wages and fringe benefits) will tend to disappear among the firms in the labor market.

The firm's demand for labor. The first of these two propositions relates to the behavior of employers and, more specifically, to the firm's demand for labor. As has been mentioned, the conclusion is simply an inference drawn from a set of assumptions, and these should therefore be made explicit. First, it is assumed that employers have perfect knowledge of the factors that affect their costs and revenues. To put this in simpler terms, the firm is presumed to know precisely how its profits would be affected by any changes that might be made in methods of production and/or in the quantity of any of the factors of production. Second, the employer is assumed to be motivated solely by the desire to maximize profits; more specifically, given the demand and supply conditions that confront the firm, the theory assumes that it will hire that quantity of each type of labor and capital that will cause profits to be as high as possible. Third, it is assumed that the several factors of production (the various types of labor and capital used in the productive process) are infinitely divisible, so that very small increments of any factor can be added. What this in effect means in the case of labor is that the employer need not choose between hiring 3 and 4 workers, but might choose to hire 3.78 workers, or— which amounts to the same thing—might vary the total number of hours or indeed minutes of labor used in, say, a week. Fourth, it is assumed, at least for purposes of convenience, that each factor of production is completely homogeneous (i.e., that there are no qualitative differences among workers in a given occupational category).

As has been said, beginning with these assumptions one can demonstrate that the employer will continuously aim to equate the marginal revenue product of labor with the marginal cost of labor (MRPL = MCL). To see why this is so, a brief review of the meaning of these terms will be helpful. The marginal physical product of labor is the addition to the total product resulting from the utilization of an additional unit of labor, holding all other factors of production constant. (The reader familiar with the calculus will recognize that the marginal physical product may be defined as dP/dL, where P is total output and L is the quantity of labor employed in its production.)

The definition of the marginal revenue product of labor (MRPL) is completely analogous: It is the addition to total *net* revenues (before the payment of wages) attributable to the utilization of one additional unit of labor (MRPL = dR/dL). Finally, the marginal cost of labor MCL is the addition to the total wage bill attributable to hiring an additional unit of labor.

The only other point that must be kept in mind before proceeding to the demonstration that employers will attempt to equate the marginal revenue product and the marginal cost of labor is the principle of diminishing marginal productivity that was described briefly in Chapter 2. This states, it will be recalled, that as additional units of, say, a particular type of labor are added to the productive process (holding all other factors of production constant), a point will be reached beyond which the marginal physical product (and marginal revenue product) will begin to decrease.

Keeping the definitions of the marginal revenue product and the marginal cost of labor in mind, it is clear that the employer will continue to add units of labor until the two are equal, since so long as MRPL is greater than MCL the employer can add more to his revenues than to his costs by adding an additional unit of labor. Table 5.1 permits us to illustrate the principle with some hypothetical figures.

Let us imagine a firm producing a product that sells for $2.00 per unit and employing assemblers in the productive process. The table purports to show what the effects on weekly output would be of employing different numbers of assemblers, all other inputs into the productive process remaining constant. For instance, the first two columns show that if the firm were to employ three assemblers, weekly output would be 400 units; if it instead chose to employ four assemblers output would be 500 units, and so on. It will be noted that the figures have been selected to illustrate the principle

TABLE 5.1   Hypothetical Marginal Productivity Calculations

Number of Workers	Weekly Output	Marginal Product	Selling Price (in dollars)	Total Receipts (in dollars)	Total Costs Except Wages (in dollars)	Net Revenues Before Wages (in dollars)	Marginal Revenue Product (in dollars)	Wage per Week
(1)	(2)	(3)	(4)	(5)	(6)	(7)	(8)	(9)
3	400	–	2.00	800	450	350	–	125
4	500	100	2.00	1000	513	487	137	125
5	590	90	2.00	1180	570	610	123	125
6	670	80	2.00	1340	620	720	110	125
7	740	70	2.00	1480	666	814	94	125

of diminishing marginal productivity. The marginal physical product of four workers—that is, the difference between weekly output with four assemblers and weekly output with only three assemblers—is 100 units; this marginal product drops as the number of assemblers increases.

Column five, which is the product of columns two and four, shows the total receipts that are associated with each level of weekly output; and column six presents a hypothetical set of cost figures that include all costs except labor. Subtracting the figures in column six from those in column five yields the series of net revenue figures shown in column seven, from which the marginal revenue product figures in column eight may be derived. Column nine tells us that the firm may hire an assembler at $125 per week and that this figure is unaffected by the number of assemblers it chooses to employ. Thus, column nine also indicates the marginal cost of labor—the addition to the total wage bill attributable to adding one additional unit of labor.[1]

Now let us inquire how many assemblers the firm would employ if the conditions shown in the table prevailed and if the firm were aware of them. One can approach the question by considering a situation in which the firm was employing only three assemblers. It would quickly become obvious to the employer that adding a fourth assembler would increase net revenues (before wages) by $137 per week, while adding only $125 per week to the wage bill, thus augmenting profits by $12 per week. The firm is thus better off with four assemblers than with three. What about adding a fifth assembler? To do so would cause a $123 rise in net revenues but would cost an additional $125 in wages, leaving the firm $2.00 per week worse off in terms of profits.

Thus, the optimal position for this firm is to hire four assemblers. It will be noted, however, that at this point the marginal revenue product of assemblers is actually greater than their marginal cost ($137 versus $125), which appears to be inconsistent with the principle enumerated at the outset—namely, that the employer would equate MRPL and MCL. A moment's reflection will make it clear that the reason for this apparent anomaly is that our illustration violates one of the assumptions underlying the theory—that the factors of production are infinitely divisible. If our hypothetical employer could have chosen to hire fractions of assemblers, it is clear that he would have had an incentive to increase the quantity so long as MRPL exceeded MCL, even if only by an infinitesimal amount. This is another way of saying that the employer would have added units of labor until MRPL and MCL were precisely equal.

Thus, granting the assumptions of the theory, it follows that every member of each category of workers in a firm gets paid its marginal revenue product—that is, precisely what any one of the category of workers in question is adding to the employer's net revenues. Under conditions of competition, this also happens to be precisely the value of the worker's product (i.e., the market value of the product that would be lost if the group of workers were to be reduced by one member). Little wonder that those who subscribe to the theory see in it an elemental kind of justice!

The supply of labor. We now turn to the second proposition with which we began our description of a competitive labor market: Rewards for identical work tend to become equal for workers of equal quality among all of the firms in the market. As in the case of the first proposition, we start by listing the assumptions that lead to this conclusion.

First, analogous to the assumption that employers wish to maximize their profits is the assumption that workers wish to maximize their "net economic advantage." Exactly what this means is not easy to specify with precision. If one could think of a labor market in which remuneration consisted solely of wages and in which conditions of employment were identical in all firms (the market for lettucepickers might be an example), this assumption would mean that workers were interested in maximizing their wage rate. It is easy enough to build the monetary value of various kinds of fringe benefits (e.g., paid holidays, medical care insurance) into the concept. Problems arise, however, when one attempts to take account of a host of other aspects of the employment relationship—

the congeniality of fellow workers, the adequacy and fairness of supervision, the pleasantness of the physical surroundings, and the like. It is possible to think of these as having monetary values to workers that they can add (algebraically) to the wage rate. Yet, realistically one knows that it is not easy—or even natural—for individuals to engage in this kind of calculation. Moreover, if one carries the idea far enough, any kind of behavior is consistent with the assumption. If a worker is observed to remain in a lower-paying job despite the availability of a higher-paying job, one can always claim that the former must have a compensating advantage over the latter; otherwise, why would the worker not have shifted? But then the theory becomes completely circular: The behavior that the assumption is supposed to predict becomes evidence for the validity of the assumption. In any case, in elaborating the theory we will for the time being assume that the wage rate is the only factor of consequence to the worker and will return later to the issue of "net advantage."

The second assumption is that workers have perfect knowledge of the labor market—that is, that they are not only aware of all alternative opportunities, but that they know enough about each to be able to figure out in which job they would be best off. Third, it is assumed that workers are perfectly mobile—that is, that where they perceive a higher-paying job (a differential in net economic advantage) they will be disposed to move into it immediately.

The process of wage equalization. Now when these three assumptions are combined with the portion of the theory relating to the employer's demand for labor that has already been explored, it is easy to demonstrate that differentials in wages for identical work will tend to disappear within a local labor market. Suppose, for example, that there are two firms employing the same category of workers (assemblers); that conditions of work are indistinguishable in the two companies; but that the wage rate for assemblers in company A is $8.30 per hour while company B pays its assemblers $7.85. One must keep in mind that in each of these companies the wage rate reflects the marginal revenue product of the number of assemblers currently employed, and that either of the firms would theoretically be willing to employ a larger number of assemblers if they could be hired at a lower wage rate. (Remember the principle of diminishing marginal productivity.)

Putting all of this together, what will happen to employment and wages in companies A and B? To begin with, workers in company B will be aware of the higher wage in A and will offer their services to that firm. The effect of the increasing numbers of employees applying for jobs at A will force the wage rate there down. Keep in mind that workers in B will prefer to work in A so long as the wage rate there is higher than the $7.85 that prevails at B. Thus, it is the competition among these workers for jobs in company A that forces the wage rate for all assemblers in that company downward. It is profitable for the company to expand employment at the lower wage rate. Thus, the movement of workers from B to A causes the marginal revenue product *and* the wage rate in A to drop as the result of the influx of workers, at the same time that the marginal revenue product and the wage rate in B rise, resulting from the departure of workers. The process continues until the marginal revenue products and the wage rates of the two firms are equalized. At that point there is no further incentive for assemblers to move in either direction.

Occupational wage differentials. Up to this point, it should be noted, we have been talking about wages for identical work (e.g., a given type of assembler). What does the theory say about wages for *different* occupations? Ought one to expect occupational wage differentials also to disappear over time? At first thought the answer seems simple. Occupational differentials between, say, janitors and machinists cannot disappear simply because low-wage janitors do not have the necessary skills to move into jobs as machinists. While this is true, it is too quick an answer, for one might argue that over long periods of time sons or daughters of janitors might be impressed by the higher earnings in the machinist trade and might therefore prepare themselves in greater numbers for machinist work than had the members of the previous generation. One could then imagine that as the result of such long-term trends, the marginal revenue product (and therefore the wages) of machinists would decline, while the marginal revenue product and wage of janitors would rise.

The theory of a competitive labor market recognizes, however, that this will not occur. For one thing, to the extent that certain innate talents are scarce, the theory points out that such scarcities could prevent enough individuals from acquiring the necessary skills for certain occupations to eliminate the wage advantage that the incumbents enjoy. In addition, and more important, the theory recognizes that occupations vary with respect to a number of factors affecting their relative attractiveness, including cost of preparation, relative cleanliness, degree of danger, and the like. Thus, occupational wage differentials are viewed as compensating for differences in these other elements of job attractiveness. In other words, the theory holds that if occupation A pays $3.50 per hour more than occupation B, that differential is exactly what is required to attract the existing number of workers into occupation A relative to the number in B. Were it any smaller, there would be fewer persons opting for A and more choosing B; were it larger, additional workers would have prepared themselves for A rather than for B.

IMPLICATIONS OF THE COMPETITIVE LABOR MARKET MODEL

We are now in a position to reflect on what the character of human resource allocation would be like if labor markets operated as the theory of a competitive labor market suggests that they do. As we have seen, workers everywhere would be paid according to their marginal productivity. Moreover, for identical work, marginal productivities and wages would become equal throughout the labor market. Any observed wage differentials for ostensibly identical work would either reflect qualitative differences among the workers of different firms (so that the wage per "efficiency unit" of labor would indeed be equal) or would merely be compensating for differences in nonwage features of jobs (e.g., fringe benefits, pleasantness of physical surroundings, etc.). So far as wages for *different* occupations are concerned, differentials would reflect either scarcities of natural endowments of individuals or differing assessments by workers of the relative attractiveness of different occupations.

All of these conditions, at least, would represent the equilibrium position of the labor market—the position toward which automatic forces would constantly be causing the market to move. In that equilibrium position, given (1) the existing technology; (2) the existing pattern of demand for goods and services; and (3) the existing pattern of workers' preferences for different types of work, every worker would be in precisely that job in which he or she was most satisfied and, at the same time, in which the greatest possible contribution to the social product (GNP) was being made. That is, given these conditions no one could increase the total output of goods and services in the economy by moving from her or his present job to any other one in the labor market. In this sense, the allocation of human resources would be optimal (ideal); moreover, the wage structure would also be optimal (ideal) in the sense of being exactly what it has to be in order to produce this optimal allocation.

Finally, human resources would continuously be flowing among alternative jobs in response to changes in social needs as reflected by the market. To illustrate, let us suppose that the saddle-making industry and the shoe-making industry are in equilibrium, with the wage rate for leather finishers in each industry being OW_1 and $O'W'_1$, respectively (Figure 5.2). Suppose, then, that a horse-riding craze develops among consumers, which is reflected in higher prices of saddles relative to shoes. As a consequence, the marginal productivity of leather finishers in saddlemaking would rise relative to the marginal productivity of the same occupational group in shoemaking (i.e., the marginal revenue product curve in saddlemaking would shift to MRP_2). This would give rise to a momentary wage differential in favor of the saddlemaking firms (W_2 versus W_1) causing leather finishers to leave their jobs in shoe factories for the higher-paying jobs in saddle manufacturing. As additional workers were employed in saddlemaking their marginal revenue product would decline (i.e., there would be a movement downward and to the right along the new MRP_2 curve) while the opposite would occur in shoe manufacturing. The process would continue until a new equality of marginal revenue products (and wages) had been achieved ($W_3 = W'_2$). As a consequence, more of society's human resources would be devoted to saddlemaking and fewer to shoemaking than had previously been the case. Employment, in other words, would have moved from E_1 to E_2 in saddlemaking and from E'_1 to E'_2 in shoemaking; and all this would have been accomplished quite automatically, as the result of the operation of market forces.

This is, indeed, an elegant system; and it is little wonder that those who believe that it describes how labor markets would operate in the absence of artificial intrusions take a dim view of government regulation of wages and of the influence of unions through collective bargaining. If unions intruded into an otherwise competitive labor market, for example, it could be demonstrated that their effect would be to distort the wage structure and to misallocate human resources.

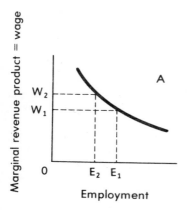 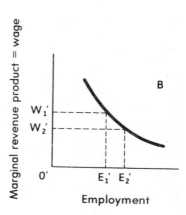

Figure 5.2: **The Reallocation of Human Resources from Shoemaking to Saddlemaking**

In Figure 5.3, let us suppose that we have two sectors of the economy in which wages for comparable labor are equal at OW_1 and $O'W'_1$. Now suppose that a union organizes sector A and forces the wage rate to OW_2. The necessary consequence of this, according to the theory, is to reduce employment in this sector from OE_1 to OE_2 as employers attempt to equate MRP to the higher level of wages. As the workers who are disemployed in sector A do not submit lightly to starvation, they make themselves available to employers in the unorganized sector B, increasing employment there from $O'E'_1$ to $O'E'_2$ and reducing wages from $O'W'_1$ to $O'W'_2$. Thus, the impact of the union is to depress wages in the unorganized sector and to cause employment shifts between the organized and the unorganized sectors. If one assumes that the labor market is competitive in the absence of collective bargaining, this clearly represents a misallocation of human resources, for any change from the optimal or ideal allocation has to be for the worse. But if labor markets are not truly competitive even in the absence of unions, the judgment is not necessarily the same. Even if one can demonstrate that unions alter the allocation of labor, the most that we can say is that the allocation is *different,* not necessarily worse. Similarly, the implication of minimum wage legislation is

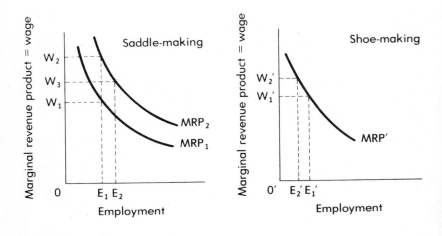

Figure 5.3: Effect of Collective Bargaining on Employment and Wages

one thing if it is introduced into a competitive labor market, but another if the labor market would not be competitive even in the absence of such legislation.

From a policy perspective, therefore, it is very important to decide how competitive labor markets really are—or would be in the absence of the intrusions of government and/or unions. This is a matter to which we turn in the next chapter.

NOTE

1. The reader familiar with microeconomic theory will recognize that columns four and nine signify that our hypothetical firm operates in both a competitive product market and a competitive labor market. The fact that selling price per unit (column four) is constant irrespective of output (and sales) means that the firm is faced with a perfectly elastic (horizontal) demand curve, the hallmark of pure competition in the product market. The fact that the wage rate (column nine) is independent of the number of units of labor hired means that the supply of labor to the firm is perfectly elastic (horizontal), which is the criterion of competition in the labor market. If the supply curve of labor to the firm sloped upward, the marginal cost of labor would differ from the wage rate but it would still be true that the profit-maximizing firm would wish to equate MRPL and MCL.

One further observation needs to be made about our example. Strictly speaking, the marginal product (and marginal revenue product) of a given factor of production (assemblers) is supposed to represent the effect on output of altering the number of units of that factor *holding everything else constant.* Under these circumstances, total costs (column six) should remain the same, irrespective of the number of assemblers employed. In this case, MRPL could be ascertained directly from column five (total receipts) and would actually equal the selling price multiplied by the marginal physical product. I have chosen in this hypothetical illustration to depart from the rigid assumptions of the theory in the interest of realism, as (except in agriculture) it is very hard to imagine output rising in response to the addition of more labor without at least adding more raw materials, which would imply an increase in costs.

QUESTIONS FOR DISCUSSION

1. Is it more useful to think of labor markets or of *the* labor market? Is the geographic scope of the labor market wider for truck drivers or nuclear physicists? Explain.

2. What is meant by "competition" in the labor market? If labor markets were perfectly competitive, what generalizations could be made about the structure of wage rates? In what sense would the allocation of labor be ideal? Describe the process through which this ideal allocation would come about.

3. How do you react to the notion that the wage differential between, say, accountants and janitors basically compensates for nonwage differences in the relative attractiveness of the two occupations?

4. What major implications for human resource policy are derivable from the model of a competitive labor market? If labor markets corresponded to the competitive model, would there be any role for government so far as human resources are concerned? If so, what would it be?

6

Real World Labor Markets

PRELIMINARY CONSIDERATIONS

How does one go about assessing the validity or usefulness of the theory of the competitive labor market that has been outlined in the preceding chapter? One way of approaching this question is to review briefly what we mean by a "theory" and what it is we expect a theory to do.

In their most elemental sense, theories are simply generalized statements of the way in which two or more variables are related to each other. We rely on them to (1) offer explanations of observed phenomena, (2) provide bases for making predictions, and (3) suggest methods of controlling the physical or social environment. If theory tells us, for example, that the relation between b and a is such that b changes if and only if there is a change in a and that the change in the former is proportionate to the change in the latter, we are in a position to (1) explain the "cause" of observed changes in b; (2) *predict* changes in b to the extent that we can predict changes in a; and (3) cause changes in b to the extent that we are able to control a. To be more specific, the theory of gravity enables us to explain why the piece of chalk I am holding falls to the floor when I open my fingers. It permits us to predict that a child who leans too far out a second story window will have an unpleasant experience; it allows us to develop the pile driver—an efficient means of sinking posts into the ground.

We are thus led to the conclusion that the criterion of a good theory is how well it performs these functions. And from this point of view, it should be noted that it does not make much sense to argue that something is "good in theory but does not work in practice" or to differentiate between the "theoretical" and the "practical." Unless a theory works in practice (at least in terms of general tendencies) it cannot be given good marks. If upon releasing the piece of chalk it moved up or sideways as frequently as it fell to the ground, it would not occur to us to assert that gravity was good in theory but did not work in practice; we would have instead sent Newton back to the drawing board. And as far as the distinction between theory and practice is concerned, it should be clear that a good theory must be "practical" in the sense of describing and/or predicting what occurs in the real world. Moreover, it is not possible to be "practical" without operating on the basis of some kind of theory. One cannot successfully cross a busy street without understanding something about vectors, velocities, and acceleration, even if the meaning of these terms is a complete mystery.

In light of all this, what requirements ought we to establish for labor market theory? It should be able to explain changes over time in the distribution of human resources among occupations, industries, and geographic locations. It should also be able to explain the pattern of wage differentials that prevails at any point in time and of changes in that pattern over time. To say this is relatively straightforward; to devise the tests and to establish the standards for determining how well the theory does these things is quite another matter, and there are profound differences among economists on these issues.

The basic problem is that no one—not even the staunchest proponent of conventional labor market theory—really expects it to correspond precisely with reality simply because there are too many confounding influences at work in the real world. (A favorite analogy offered by those disposed to defend the theory is that the law [theory] of gravity is not damaged by the observed fact that a steel ball and a feather dropped from the same height do not reach the ground at the same time; that the latter may even move sideways or upward as the result of air currents that the theory assumes out of existence.) On the other hand, no one—not even the theory's most jaundiced critic—is inclined to argue that no corresponding forces are discernible in the real world. The issue, in other words, is how useful the theory is and in what contexts it makes sense to use it as a guide to policy. To some extent this is akin to the debate between the optimist and the pessimist as to whether a glass is half full or half empty. Empirical evidence is not irrelevant, but is unlikely to settle the issue completely.

EMPIRICAL TESTS OF LABOR MARKET THEORY

It is hardly surprising that a great deal of the research that has been done by labor economists has been motivated at least in part by a desire to test the validity of one or more aspects of labor market theory. It is by no means possible to summarize even briefly all of this research, although some of it will be drawn upon in subsequent chapters. What *is* feasible is to describe in very general terms the types of studies that have been done and to sketch in bare outline what they appear to indicate about the operation of labor markets. The first part of this story is relatively straightforward and is likely to be told in substantially the same way by any reviewer of the literature, but the message conveyed by the second part will differ substantially depending on the teller of the tale.

Tests of conventional labor market theory have been of two general types: (1) those directed at assessing the validity or realism of the assumptions underlying the theory, and (2) those purporting to compare its conclusions with what is observed in actual labor markets. Illustrative of the first type are studies of workers' labor market behavior: To what extent do they make job changes and for what reasons? How do they go about finding jobs? How much do they know about alternative jobs in the labor market? What criteria do they use in evaluating jobs? Answers to questions of these types are relied on to provide clues about the degree to which workers have the kind of knowledge and make the kinds of rational calculations that will lead to the maximization of net economic advantage, as the theory assumes. In the same context, one may examine the labor market behavior of employers to see to what extent it is consistent with the premises of the theory.

The second type of study ignores the theory's assumptions and concentrates on whether its conclusions appear to be consistent with reality. Is there a tendency for wages for identical work to equalize in local labor markets? If interfirm wage differentials for comparable work are observed, to what extent are they explained by qualitative differences in the work forces or by differences in nonwage terms and conditions of employment (e.g., fringe benefits, enlightened personnel policy, etc.)? Does the movement of workers with given skills among firms, industries, and geographic locations tend to be in the direction of higher wages? Does movement of workers have the effect of eliminating or reducing wage differentials?

Before viewing the findings of studies of these kinds it is only fair to warn the reader that many economists—particularly those who are defenders of conventional microeconomic theory—argue that evidence produced by the first of these types of study is completely irrelevant. They assert that the only real test of a theory is the degree to which it permits one to make accurate predictions; and that if one can do this by an apparatus that involves assumptions contrary to fact, so much the worse for the facts. Their usual analogy is that the use of Newtonian physics to, say, calculate the trajectory of a missle cannot be depreciated merely because the theory of falling bodies is based on the assumption of a perfect vacuum.

This argument has a basic appeal, but I find it less than completely persuasive for two reasons. To begin with, while it is logically true that a refutation of assumptions does not necessarily invalidate a conclusion that is drawn from them, it at least makes the conclusion suspect—particularly if its only basis is its deduction from the (faulty) assumptions. This problem apparently bothers even some of those who advance the argument; for after claiming that the validity of assumptions is irrelevant, they frequently go out of their way to offer evidence in support of them (e.g., Rottenberg, 1956). Second, the nature of economic theory is such that it is often either difficult or quite impossible to devise a confident test of its conclusions. To take but one example, an international study of labor mobility sought to ascertain (among other things) whether shifts in the industrial composition of human resources were brought about by changes in wage differentials (in favor of the industries in which employment increased). The authors concluded that substantial reallocation of labor took place in each of the countries covered by the study without the theoretically expected alteration in wage differentials. They nevertheless felt compelled to acknowledge that this evidence was also consistent with the belief (which was in their view untenable) that the response of wages to the movement of labor was so swift that the initiating wage differentials had disappeared by the time the reallocation was observed (OECD, 1965: 16-17).

The reader is invited to make a personal judgment on this issue. However, even if the decision is to reject an appraisal of underlying assumptions as a legitimate test of theory, evidence relating to workers' behavior should nevertheless be of interest in its own right. Knowing how workers behave in the labor market and the reasons they give for the decisions they make provides interesting insights into human resource allocation that cannot be acquired in any other way.

WORKER BEHAVIOR IN THE LABOR MARKET[1]

How workers judge jobs. Conventional labor market theory recognizes that a great many factors may enter into a worker's evaluation of jobs. However, because wages are the most readily measurable facet, textbook presentations almost invariably make wage differentials central to an explanation of labor mobility. In justification of this approach, two related arguments are generally made. First, although individuals differ in how they evaluate other aspects of jobs (e.g., some people like responsibility, others seek to avoid it), there is universal agreement that the higher the wage the better. Second, it is asserted that any differences that an individual may perceive in the relative desirability of two jobs in other respects can be compensated by a wage differential between them. In this view, if a worker says that she does not like a particular job because of sexual harassment, this is simply another way of saying that the wage is too low.[2]

However one reacts to the notion that every person has a price, it is instructive to examine the factors that workers mention when asked what they like and dislike about their jobs or the reasons for having left a job and having taken another. This kind of evidence makes it clear that a large number of job characteristics are important to workers. Those most frequently mentioned can be subsumed under the following headings: (1) the intrinsic character of the work; (2) job security; (3) steadiness of work; (4) opportunities for advancement; (5) wage and fringe benefits; (6) physical working conditions; (7) the character of supervision; and (8) the congeniality of fellow workers.

There is no reason for believing that wages are any more important than the other factors on the list; depending on circumstances, any one of them can be of crucial importance to a worker. Indeed, in a more fundamental sense it is not logically possible for even one individual at one point in time to rank the attributes in order of their relative importance. A worker can hardly be expected to say whether wages or working conditions are more important to him or her unless the range of variation in these elements is specified for two actual or hypothetical jobs. To illustrate, a man who asserts that wages are more important than working conditions surely cannot mean that he would chose the higher paying of two jobs if he knew that no incumbent had been successful in living through the first shift!

The process of job search. There is considerable evidence that most workers find jobs through such informal means as direct application with employers and checking with friends and relatives. More formal methods, such as using the public employment service or private employment agencies, are considerably less common. Although some observers interpret this more-or-less haphazard method of seeking work as being at odds with the maximizing behavior postulated by conventional theory, Albert Rees (1966) has argued that the use of informal "information networks" is no indication of an absence of rationality. He maintains that given the subtle ways in which jobs differ from one another, it is probably more useful to a worker to get information in depth about a limited number of possibilities than more superficial information about a larger number.

Whether or not workers make the kinds of careful comparisons among alternatives that would allow them to maximize net economic advantage is a related issue. The amount of specific information that workers have about alternative jobs is generally insufficient to permit true maximization. The evidence on this point is somewhat difficult to summarize and evaluate; it is obviously impossible for workers to have the *perfect* knowledge that labor market theory assumes, and even the severest critics would not maintain that they have *no* information. The issue, therefore, is whether they have *enough* information to allow the market to produce something close to the optimal results implicit in the theory. Studies that have pursued this question tend to emphasize the meagerness of information at the disposal of workers. To provide but one illustration, in a study of blue collar workers in the New Haven labor market after World War II, Lloyd Reynolds (1951: 213-214) found very little correspondence between employed workers' perceptions of their wages and the actual relative position of those wages in the local labor market. For instance, although 95 percent of the employees in firms in the top half of the wage distribution thought their wage level compared favorably with others in the area, 80 percent of those in firms in the bottom half of the wage distribution had the same perception.

Of course, once a worker becomes unemployed and begins a search for work, additional information is generally acquired. However, even in most of these cases the worker appears to take the first job that meets minimum subjective requirements rather than engaging in the kind of job shopping that is implicit in the economic theory of job search.[3]

Even the decision to migrate has been found to be rather different from what might be supposed on the basis of economic theory. In their study of geographic mobility in the mid-1960s, Lansing and Mueller (1967) found that there was considerable evidence of "inertia"—planning to remain in an area despite perceived economic advantages in moving. Moreover, among those who had migrated, a third had thought about the move for less than a month prior to moving, two-thirds had not considered alternative locations, one-third had not prearranged a job in the new area (over half of whom had no information at all about jobs in the area), and less than one-half used more than one source of information to help them explore job opportunities in the new location. The authors concluded that

> most people who undertake a move to a new location and who plan to work there do inform themselves about the job situation in the new area. . . . yet the decision-making process is not as rational as the economist might wish [Lansing and Mueller, 1967: 230].

My own review of the literature on these issues led me to write as early as 1960, and to reiterate in 1970, the following:

> Labor market studies of workers' attitudes and decisions about jobs have, in short, tended to confirm the view that workers, far from being concerned exclusively—or even primarily—with "net economic advantage"—have multiple and complex goals; that their "choices" are bounded by considerable degrees of ignorance of alternatives; and that the typical worker is a "satisficing" rather than a "maximizing" man, contrary to the postulates of economic theory [Parnes, 1970: 54].

There is, to be sure, some evidence of differences in these respects between white collar and blue collar workers, with the former conforming somewhat more closely to the assumptions of the theory. However, overall it seems fair to conclude that most employed workers are not really "in the labor market" in the sense of being continuously on the lookout for more attractive alternatives. Those who become dissatisfied with their jobs may cast about for others, and unemployed workers do so out of necessity; but even in these cases interviews with workers make it very difficult to find persuasive the conventional theory of job search, according to which individuals search for work until the marginal cost of continued unemployment equals the marginal benefit of continued search.

Seniority and immobility. Before leaving this topic it is well to note that an important reason for the substantial disinterest of satisfactorily employed workers in alternatives to their current jobs is the strength of the bonds that are created between worker and job as length of service increases. These bonds are both social-psychological and economic. From the former perspective there are attachments to work associates that are painful to break, as well as the psychological comfort inherent in a familiar routine. Every job change is in a sense a leap into the unknown, for there are many crucially important aspects of a job that cannot really be evaluated until one is in it (e.g., How will I get along with the boss?).

The economic benefits conferred by seniority with a given employer are increased job security and certain perquisites (e.g., longer vacations, shift preference, etc.). The former is particularly important, and is eloquently illustrated by the response of a 50-year-old manual worker when he was asked in an interview survey whether he would accept a similar job with another employer at a 30 percent higher wage rate:

> No, I wouldn't, and if you was a working stiff rather than a college professor you'd know without even asking. Look, I'll explain it to you. I've got 22 years seniority at the plant and the place would just about have to burn down before I'd lose my job. If I take this other job I'd sure enjoy the extra money, but I'd be low man on the totem pole. First layoff, I'd be gone, and then what good would the 30 percent be doing me?

The economic implications of seniority are, of course, particularly pronounced in a unionized establishment; but even in the absence of unionization the seniority principle is rather widely accepted and is more or less rigidly adhered to in sizable sectors of the labor force.

It has been argued by some economic theorists that this influence of seniority is not really at odds with conventional economic theory, for even Adam Smith recognized that occupations differ in steadiness of work opportunities and that higher wages would therefore be paid in occupations with less steady work. However, the analogy is not a good one. In the case of the occupational differences alluded to by Smith, it can be said that carpenters in the construction industry (because of its seasonality) have less steady work than carpenters employed, say, in retail trade and thus enjoy a higher wage. In this case the difference in steadiness of work exists between two entire categories of jobs and can thus be equalized by a wage differential. In the case of seniority, on the other hand, as the greater security attaches to *an individual in a particular job*, no systematic wage differential can compensate for it. For the welder with 20 years of service in firm A, firm B would have to offer a positive differential to compensate for the difference in security; but for the counterpart welder in firm B, the differential would have to be in the opposite direction. No single interfirm differential in the wage for welders can compensate for the difference in security between the two jobs.

THE LABOR MARKET BEHAVIOR OF EMPLOYERS

The labor market behavior of workers is only one blade of the scissors in the process of labor allocation; the attitudes and policies of employers are equally relevant. Some of the practices of employers tend to reinforce and sometimes to explain the behavior of workers. For instance, informal recruitment methods tend to be the most prevalent, most employers preferring to rely on gate applications and recruitment through their existing work forces rather than on public or private employment agencies or newspaper advertisements. This means that the labor market is far removed from the competitive ideal in which all workers would be free to choose among all vacancies and all employers could select from among all candidates.

There are also other employer hiring practices that tend to "insulate" the firm from the external labor market. Among these are the formal or informal hiring specifications or preferences that many firms appear to have. Although these have been weakened by antidiscrimination legislation of the 1960s, they nevertheless may still mean that blacks, women, older person, certain ethnic groups, employees living beyond a certain distance from the plant, and workers currently employed elsewhere are barred from "competing" for certain jobs. Perhaps even more important in this context is the common employer policy of promoting from within; for to the extent that a firm were to follow this policy rigidly, there would be contact between the internal and the external labor markets only at the base of the occupational ladder. Thus, interfirm wage differentials for higher level jobs would be irrelevant from the standpoint of mobility; a worker in a low-wage firm could move to a higher-paying firm only by taking an entry job at a lower rate of pay. "Antipirating agreements" are another anticompetitive employer practice of some prevalence. These are arrangements, generally informal, under which employers in a local labor market refuse to hire workers currently employed elsewhere, at least without obtaining the consent of the current employer.

TESTING THE PREDICTIONS OF LABOR MARKET THEORY

As has been indicated, many economists argue that the appropriate test of labor market theory is not the adequacy of its assumptions but the degree to which its predictions are consistent with what is observed in real labor markets. A number of studies have taken this approach.

The direction of job movement. Conventional labor market theory predicts that the (voluntary) movement of workers will be from low-wage to high-wage firms. There is fairly persuasive evidence of such a tendency, at least on average and in general. Both in the United States and other countries there is a strong negative correlation between earnings levels and separation rates among industries. In part, this relationship results from factors that are associated in opposite directions with both wage level and turnover. For instance, industries with low wages employ relatively more women than high-wage industries, and women have historically had higher turnover rates than men. But even when these other factors are statistically controlled, there appears to be an inverse relation between earnings levels and quit rates.

When geographic mobility is considered, there is abundant evidence that net geographic migration—international as well as domestic—is generally in the direction of greater economic opportunity as measured both by differentials in employment opportunities and in income, although it seems likely that the latter is less important than the former. For instance, for the two decades from 1940 to 1960 excluding the years of World War II migration from farm to city in the United States varied *directly* with the ratio of farm wages to factory wages, which is just the opposite of what one would expect from the theory if potential wages alone are considered. However, the explanation lies in the fact that urban employment opportunities tend to be high when the farm-to-factory wage ratio is high, as both respond favorably to high levels of demand in the economy (Parnes, 1970: 59).

TABLE 6.1   Median and Interquartile Range of Weekly or
Hourly Wage in Selected Cross-Industry Occupations,
Columbus, Ohio, 1975 (in dollars)

Occupation	Median	Interquartile Range
Weekly wage		
Computer operator B (manufacturing)	178.50	150.83-206.17
Accounting clerk B (nonmanufacturing)	122.50	108.41-136.59
Hourly wage		
Tool- and diemaker	7.24	6.52-7.96
Janitor	3.97	3.39-4.55

SOURCE: Computed from data in Area Wage Survey, Columbus, Ohio, Metropolitan Area, October 1975, U.S. Department of Labor.

Labor mobility and optimal allocation of labor. The full validation of the competitive labor market model requires more than a demonstration that workers are responsive to economic differentials. A further implication of the model is that in equilibrium such differentials merely reflect either costs of movement, qualitative differences in labor, or compensating differences in the characteristics of jobs. Thus, assuming no change in the preference patterns of workers, an occupational, industrial, or geographic reallocation of labor from any equilibrium situation requires a prior change in the structure of wages. Moreover, the movement of workers induced by such changes is supposed to restore the equilibrium differential.

A number of studies have produced grounds for doubting that the interrelation between wage changes and labor mobility is as intimate as the theory suggests. Specifically, both for the United States and a number of West European countries there is evidence that substantial reallocations of labor among industries can be and have been accomplished with no corresponding changes in relative earnings. It must be acknowledged, however, that even these studies were able to cite instances in which particularly massive reallocations were accompanied by the theoretically expected wage changes.

Wage structure in a local labor market. Data on wages in a local labor market area at a particular point in time reveal substantial interfirm variation for ostensibly comparable work. Table 6.1 illustrates this point by presenting the medians and interquartile ranges of the hourly or weekly wages paid by a sample of Columbus, Ohio, employers for four quite different occupations in 1975. The interquartile range measures the values within which the middle-most 50 percent of the observations lie. In other words, taking the first row of figures as an example, the median weekly salary for all class B computer operators in a representative sample of Columbus manufacturing establishments was $178.50. However, 25 percent of all of the operators in these firms earned less than $150.83 and 25 percent earned at least $206.17.

Our purpose at this point is not to examine the relationships that exist among the four occupations, but rather to note that in each of four fairly narrowly defined and disparate occupations, the wages paid by different employers in a local labor market area are far from uniform. One would, incidentally, find substantially the same phenomenon in other labor market areas and/or at other times. Not all of the variation, to be sure, represents interfirm differences in wages because differences *within* the firms among the incumbents of each occupation are also captured by the data. However, an unambiguous measure of interfirm differences is provided by the minimum entrance salaries for inexperienced typists in 57 of the Columbus establishments. These ranged from $82.50 to $160.00 per week. There were 15 establishments that paid less than $95; 14 paid $120 or more.

How might a proponent of conventional labor market theory react when confronted with evidence of this kind? The theorist would doubtless point out at least three reasons why the observed pattern of wage differentials is not necessarily at odds with the theory. First, there may be nonwage differences in the relative attractiveness of the firms so that the observed wage differences are merely compensating or equalizing differences that actually create equality of net economic advantage. Second, the wage differences may reflect qualitative differences in the work forces of the various firms so that there is in fact equality of compensation per "efficiency unit" of labor. Third, the theory does not assert that there will be equality of net economic advantage among identical employments at any moment of time; it merely asserts that if there is not, forces will be set into motion that will produce a tendency toward equality.

It is these types of "defense" that make definitive empirical tests of the theory difficult. Nevertheless, several observations can be made fairly confidently. The most certain of these is that interfirm wage differentials, far from equalizing the nonwage attractiveness of jobs in different firms, actually reinforce them. There is abundant evidence that high-paying firms are also those most likely to have liberal fringe benefits and formalized personnel policies. With respect to quality of work force, higher-paying firms do tend to get better qualified workers, but the qualitative differences tend to explain only a small portion of the wage differentials. Most of the evidence on this point is impressionistic, but at least one carefully designed study supports the conclusion: Only 10 percent of the variation in starting salaries of typists hired through the state employment service in Illinois was explained by differences in the skills of the women as measured by screening tests administered by the employment service (Conant, 1963). Finally, so far as the tendency-toward-equilibrium argument is concerned, it is virtually impossible to collect empirical evidence that could conceivably refute the argument as the economy never "stands still" long enough for any equilibrium position to be reached. What can be said is that interfirm wage differentials in local labor markets show no tendency to shrink over time, although the relative ranking of the firms in the area wage structure may change.

AN EVALUATION OF THE COMPETITIVE MODEL

Pulling together all of the foregoing evidence on the operation of actual labor markets, what can be said about the usefulness of the competitive labor market model? How adequately would it describe the processes of human resource allocation and of wage determination in the absence of artificial intrusions by government and unions? Putting the question this way allows us immediately to spot a logical problem that has not yet been addressed. There is no way that we can know how labor markets would operate in the absence of unions and such relevant government programs as minimum wage legislation and unemployment insurance. All of the evidence that has been reviewed has been derived from labor markets in which these institutions exist.

It is possible to argue that some of the practices of unionism are responsible for deviations between the competitive model and what is actually observed in the labor market. For example, to the extent that collective bargaining emphasizes seniority arrangements it may have the effect of inhibiting the mobility of workers. Also, it is reasonably certain that unionism is at least to some extent responsible for wage differentials between unionized and nonunionized firms. On the other hand, collective bargaining has doubtless operated to reduce interfirm wage differentials within the organized sector of the economy. So far as mobility is concerned, the institution of unionism has probably operated to increase the amount of relevant labor market information union members possess. Thus, it is possible to think of ways in which unions reinforce and ways in which they inhibit market forces, and it is very difficult to know what their net effect has been.

My own view is that the observed discrepancies between the competitive labor market model and real world labor markets stem not so much from institutional restraints as from the fact that the behavior of neither workers nor employers is sufficiently close to that assumed by the theory as to yield the predicted results with the precision that most textbook presentations of the theory imply. The theory holds that competition among employers for workers and among workers for jobs creates a single wage rate for identical work (and other employment conditions) in a local labor market. Each employer must pay this wage established by market forces if the firm is to obtain and/or to keep workers. When one looks at actual labor markets one sees instead a rather broad range of wage rates that are actually reinforced by differences in other terms of employment and only in part compensated by qualitative differences in the work forces of different firms.

Nevertheless, this does not justify a complete rejection of the theoretical apparatus. The forces that it describes are indeed discernible in the labor market although they operate with considerably attenuated vigor. For instance, movement of labor is, on average, in the direction of greater economic advantage. Moreover, while a firm is confronted with a range of possible wage rates rather than a single rate, there are, after all, limits to that range. Indeed, firms that sink toward the bottom of the range frequently experience some difficulty in attracting and keeping workers. In other words (as was suggested at the beginning of the chapter), the argument between the critics and the proponents of traditional labor market theory is akin to the argument between the optimist and the pessimist as to whether the bottle is half full or half empty. The theorist has obviously never believed that there are "perfectly competitive" labor markets, nor have the critics argued that competitive forces are completely absent. The former have chosen to emphasize central tendencies while the latter have focused on the substantial deviations.

This by no means suggests that the debate is only of academic significance. Indeed, it is in the human resource policy arena that the issue is of most practical importance. For instance, if one accepts conventional labor market theory uncritically, there is really no need for any conscious human resource policy except perhaps to take those steps that are likely to result in a closer conformity between reality and the assumptions underlying the model (e.g., promoting labor market information, reducing impediments to mobility, prohibiting collective bargaining, etc.). In this view, the operation of unfettered market forces leads to the most effective development, allocation, and utilization of human resources. Moreover, any attempt to modify existing wage relationships or to encourage an allocation different from what market forces themselves effect is ipso facto bad. It is no accident that representatives of the "Chicago school" of economists, typified by Milton Friedman, have taken strong stands against collective bargaining, minimum wage legislation, human resource planning, and wage and price controls.

To take the last-mentioned as an example, among the arguments against this measure to combat inflation is that it would prevent free wage movements from performing their allocative function, and would thus result in an inefficient allocation of human resources. However, if one accepts the view that much of the allocation of labor can and does take place without the necessity of wage change, this becomes a less significant objection. With respect to collective bargaining, if one operates on the basis of an uncritical acceptance of conventional theory, any deviation from "*the* market wage" imposed by economic power is demonstrably bad. On the other hand, if one believe that market forces even in the absence of unions would produce a range of possible wage rates rather than a single rate, there is considerably less cause for alarm if a union helps an employer make the choice.

But just as it is possible to make questionable policy judgments by a blind acceptance of the competitive market model, so it is possible to go astray by not recognizing the degree to which it is valid. To support a 20 percent increase in the minimum wage over a period in which all wages have risen by 15 to 20 percent is one thing; to advocate a doubling of the minimum under these circumstances is quite another. Again, while a concern for efficient resource allocation need not preclude a policy of wage and price controls, it may indeed argue for a provision in such regulations that permits exceptions to be made when market indicators suggest the need for them.

In short, the most reasonable position regarding conventional labor market theory would seem to be an eclectic one. As in most things, moderation would appear to be a virtue. It is possible to give the theory its due and to use it within the limits to which it truly applies without assuming that it provides an exclusive and precise guide to policy.

Labor market models and the poverty problem. In addition to those illustrated above, another major policy issue that has embroiled the competitive labor market model in controversy is the poverty problem. Although this will be dealt with systematically in Chapter 9, it is convenient to discuss at this point its relationship to the issues covered in this chapter.

At the risk of some oversimplification, the way in which conventional labor market theorists look at the poverty problem—to the extent that they care to examine it at all—can be stated very briefly. Inadequate income, at least among those who can work and wish to do so, is the result of low productivity. Hence, the way to attack the poverty problem is to induce those who are disadvantaged in the labor market to invest in their human capital in order to enhance their productive skills, make themselves more attractive to employers, and thus increase the level and/or regularity of their earnings. Education and training programs are thus the prescription for those able to work. The human resource development programs that were described briefly in Chapter 1 and that will be elaborated in Chapter 10 reflect this approach.

A different perspective on the labor market that was developed during the late 1960s by Michael Piore and other economists raised doubts about the efficacy of this policy prescription (Gordon, 1972). According to this *dual labor market theory*, the labor market is not a single entity, but is in fact bifurcated—the primary market consisting of good jobs with high wages, attractive fringe benefits, and (above all) stable employment with reasonably clearly defined channels of promotion. In contrast, the secondary market is comprised primarily of low-paying, dead-end jobs with poor working conditions, characterized by employment mobility and high labor turnover. Between these two sectors there is little movement. Thus, disadvantaged individuals (especially blacks) who get channeled into the secondary market get trapped there. Moreover, within the secondary market employers tend to see all workers as homogeneous, and there is therefore little relation between productivity and earnings. Finally, the very characteristics of the secondary jobs tend to create or reinforce precisely those worker characteristics that employers find objectionable— instability and lack of incentive and motivation. To the extent that this is an accurate portrayal of the labor market, education and training are clearly not going to solve the problems of secondary workers; instead one must concentrate on restructuring jobs and/or eliminating discrimination so that secondary jobs are minimized and incumbency in them is temporary.

Although the competitive market model clearly has its deficiencies (as our earlier discussion has made clear), it is doubtful that a literal interpretation of the dual labor market theory represents an improvement (Cain, 1976). For one thing, from a conceptual point of view it is questionable whether there are two distinct categories rather than a continuum of jobs; but even when two categories are established on the basis of, say, wages and unionization, there appears to be more mobility between them than the theory suggests. Moreover, empirical evidence is inconsistent with the hypothesis that rewards within the secondary market are unrelated to the human capital characteristics of employees. In short, whatever merits the theory may have in highlighting the consequences of discrimination and the effect of unsavory jobs on the human resource characteristics of those who fill them, it does not justify any deemphasis on human resource development programs for the disadvantaged.

NOTES

1. This and the following two sections draw heavily on my previous reviews of the literature (Parnes, 1954, 1960, 1970).

2. See, for example, Rottenberg (1956). In all fairness, the specific example is mine, but it is covered by the general argument that Rottenberg makes. Sexual harassment had not become an issue when he wrote his widely cited article.

3. For the past several decades, economists have recognized that maximizing behavior does not require the individual to hold out for the best possible job, as job search requires the use of time and other resources (Stigler, 1962; Lippman and McCall, 1976). Thus, the maximizing prescription is to equate the expected gains from further search (marginal benefit) with the marginal cost of conducting it. Nonetheless, it is difficult to relate actual job search behavior as described by workers with this model.

QUESTIONS FOR DISCUSSION

1. How do you react to the assumptions underlying the competitive labor market model? So far as the validity of the theory is concerned, do you think it makes any difference whether the underlying assumptions are "realistic"?

2. "If a worker tells you that he quit a job because of poor working conditions, this is just another way of saying that the wage was too low." Interpret and evaluate this statement.

3. To what extent do you think that workers are "maximizers"? To the extent that they are, what is it that they attempt to maximize? Could you devise a research project that would provide definitive answers to these questions? What kind of evidence could possibly refute the assertion that workers attempt to maximize their total satisfaction with life?

4. What do you regard to be the most persuasive evidence relating to the validity of the competitive market model? On the basis of the evidence available to you, what is your opinion about the utility of the model as a basis for (a) understanding the operation of labor markets and (b) policy prescription.

5. Explain and evaluate the "dual labor market" theory. Do you regard this theory and the theory of the competitive labor market to be alternatives? If so, to which do you subscribe?

7

The Problem of Unemployment

In the history of industrial and postindustrial societies, there is little question that unemployment has been the most serious and most pervasive human resource problem from the standpoint both of the individual and of the society. In this chapter we examine the nature of unemployment and the types of policies that are designed to deal with it.

It is well to begin by recognizing that unemployment imposes costs on both individuals and society, and that in each case these costs are both economic and noneconomic. Focusing first on the individual, the most obvious economic effect of unemployment is the cessation of earnings with the resulting threat to the living standards of all those who have been dependent on the earnings. In addition, especially if it is sufficiently prolonged, unemployment may produce a deterioration of skills that can have long-term consequences. From some points of view the noneconomic costs are even more serious for they are more difficult to compensate. Our society still places a premium upon productive activity; as a consequence, unemployment can produce a sense of futility and frustration that may leave significant psychological and even physiological scars. There is evidence that unemployment may have adverse effects on health (Cobb and Kasl, 1977). There is also mounting evidence of a positive relationship between the unemployment rate and the incidence of suicide, admission to state mental hospitals, family discord, and homicide.

From society's point of view, the most obvious economic cost of unemployment is loss of production. For each individual who wants to work but is without a job, society is being denied that individual's potential product—a loss that can never be made up. In addition, as we do not ordinarily allow individuals to starve when they are unable to provide for themselves, those who are working must in some way support the unemployed and their dependents. In other words, the costs of unemployment insurance and some of the costs of public assistance must be included among the economic costs of unemployment.

Unemployment also contributes to social disorganization. The association between unemployment and family discord and violence has already been alluded to; in addition, if unemployment gets bad enough the entire social fabric may be threatened. Never in our national history has there been so serious an internal threat of subversion as during the depression of the 1930s when literally millions of individuals recognized no stake in the existing system. In 1932 President Hoover urged that military personnel be exempt from a 10 percent pay cut for government workers in order to preserve their morale in the event of domestic insurrection (Schlesinger, 1957: 256).

CAUSES OF UNEMPLOYMENT

Economists have classified unemployment in a variety of ways—in each case attempting to shed light on the forces responsible for it. Perhaps the most useful classification scheme involves three major categories: frictional unemployment, structural unemployment, and inadequate demand unemployment.

Frictional unemployment. Given the way in which we define and measure unemployment, a zero rate of unemployment is conceptually impossible. At all times some individuals are entering or reentering the labor force and others are changing jobs; moreover, some workers are in seasonal industries (e.g., canning, construction) in which layoffs usually occur at certain times of the year. Thus, no matter how many jobs are available, so long as some of these persons spend at least one calendar week before finding and accepting one to their liking, they will be counted as unemployed. This type of unemployment, in other words, is the inevitable concomitant of a dynamic labor market; it is frequently referred to as the "irreducible minimum" level of unemployment and is designated as frictional because it is conceived to result from imperfections or "frictions" in the labor market. That is, if workers had perfect knowledge of all jobs, if employers had perfect knowledge of all available workers, and if mobility were instantaneous, frictional unemployment would not exist.

It is clear from its definition that frictional unemployment does not constitute a substantial problem. Were it the only type of unemployment the rate would be quite low and no one would be unemployed for long, for there would be as many available jobs as unemployed workers; it would merely be necessary to bring them together. The only relevant form of public intervention would be to "grease" the labor market by improving the operation of labor market intermediaries, especially the public employment service.

Structural unemployment. Structural unemployment has sometimes been described as an especially "sticky" type of frictional unemployment. Conceptually it refers to a situation in which the problem is not the absence of jobs but the fact that the available jobs are in the wrong places or in the wrong occupations relative to the unemployed workers. Shortages of computer programmers or of medical technicians in the face of surpluses of press operators or welders would be symptomatic of structural unemployment, as would high unemployment rates of semiskilled workers in the Midwest at a time of abundant opportunities for such persons in the sunbelt.

When the occupational and/or geographic structure of job opportunities does not match that of unemployed workers, the remedy—as in the case of frictional unemployment—is reducing immobilities. Training and retraining programs and programs designed to encourage either the migration of workers or of industries are the relevant policy instruments. In this case, however, while the prescription may be clear its implementation is frequently very difficult. Structural unemployment is characterized by joblessness of long duration concentrated among particular occupational or educational categories of the labor force or in particular labor market areas.

Inadequate demand unemployment. This is the type of unemployment that is generated when the total level of spending in the economy is not sufficient to create an adequate level of employment opportunities. It tends to be broad based and to reflect an increase not only in the incidence of unemployment but in its duration.

To say that total spending in the economy is inadequate is another way of saying that total expenditures by consumers (C), by business enterprises for capital goods (I = investment), and by government (G) are not sufficient to provide jobs for all who are making themselves available for work.[1] This type of unemployment develops as the result of a recession, when the level of GNP declines; however, it can also develop as the result of the failure of GNP to grow fast enough (which is why "inadequate demand" unemployment is a better term than "cyclical" unemployment). This is an important point, and deserves a word of explanation.

Consider an economy with a labor force of 100 million persons, 96 million of whom are employed. Suppose that the labor force is growing at the rate of 2 percent per year, which means that each year an additional 2 million persons enter the labor market to seek jobs. Suppose that at the same time labor productivity is increasing by 3 percent each year—that is, the goods and services produced by employed workers increase by that amount. Under these conditions it is clear that if unemployment is not to rise above the original 4 million level, total spending (GNP) in real terms must increase by about 5 percent per year ($1.02 \times 1.03 = 1.0506$, a 5.1 percent increase) in order to absorb the new labor market entrants and the greater productivity of the employed.

Whether inadequate demand results from recession or insufficient economic growth, the symptoms are the same, as are the appropriate remedial measures. The remedies for inadequate demand unemployment include those measures that will increase the level of total spending. On the basis of our simplified formula, GNP = C + I + G, it is clear that this may be accomplished by stimulating growth in any one or more of the components without creating an offsetting decline elsewhere.

Modern governments have two principal sets of tools for accomplishing this result: fiscal policy and monetary policy. While a full account of each of these aspects of macroeconomic policy is beyond the scope of this volume, a brief and simplified explanation may be helpful. Fiscal policy relates to the actions of the federal government with regard to taxes, expenditures, and borrowing. Monetary policy relates to a set of operations available to the Board of Governors of the Federal Reserve System designed to affect the supply of money and interest rates. With regard to fiscal policy, government can increase total spending if it reduces taxes on consumers and/or businesses without at the same time reducing its own expenditures to the same extent. This will increase C and/or I while keeping G constant. Alternatively, an increase in government spending that is not financed through increased taxation will also result in an increase in total spending. Either of these approaches, of course, results in increased government borrowing.

Primarily through its ability to affect the lending capacity of the country's banks, the Board of Governors of the Federal Reserve System can affect the supply of money available in the economy and the interest rates at which it can be borrowed. By increasing the money supply and decreasing interest rates the Federal Reserve System makes it more attractive for businesspersons to borrow for purposes of investment, thus stimulating that component of total spending. Through the same means, consumer installment expenditures are also stimulated.

The foregoing is a grossly oversimplified presentation of the basic elements of macroeconomic policy measures; the reader is referred to other sources for a more detailed treatment as well as for the theoretical underpinnings (e.g., Samuelson, 1980; Barkley, 1977). In particular, I have ignored not only the universally acknowledged complexities of monetary and fiscal policy but the profound disagreements among economists concerning their use—disagreements that have become exacerbated by the record of the 1970s when high rates of inflation and unemployment coexisted. The basic point, nevertheless, remains valid; most economists recognize that some mix of monetary and fiscal policy can be relied upon to influence the total level of spending in the economy—to raise it when there is undesirable slack and excessive unemployment and to lower it when the economy is overheated and inflationary pressures are evident.

THE VOLUME OF UNEMPLOYMENT:
THE HISTORICAL RECORD

As we have seen in Chapter 3, until 1940 there were no official estimates of unemployment in the United States comparable to those that now exist. Nonetheless, it is clear that the most serious unemployment in our national history occurred during the 1930s; at the depths of the Great Depression in 1933 the unemployment rate is estimated to have been 25 percent, and more than one in three nonfarm wage or salary workers were unemployed (Lebergott, 1964: 187, 512). Since the development of the Current Population Survey, the range of unemployment rates (on an annual average basis) has been between about 15 percent in 1940 and 1.2 percent at the peak of the war effort (World War II) in 1944.

A digression on World War II. Juxtaposing these two figures highlights a fascinating bit of economic history with an important moral for employment policy. As the Roosevelt administration embarked upon its program of "relief, recovery, and reform," federal government expenditures rose dramatically and the national debt attained unprecedented levels. Although unemployment dropped from its 1933 peak, it remained stubbornly at very high levels, which led to the criticism that it was not possible for a country to "spend its way into prosperity" as the New Deal was attempting to do. Then came World War II, with government expenditures that made previous levels seem small. Budget outlays (which had been about $5 billion in 1933 and $9 billion in 1939) reached $35 billion in 1942 and over $90 billion in 1944 and 1945, and unemployment dropped to under 2 percent.

Some people respond to this record by asserting that it took the war to bring us out of the depression. This assertion has an element of validity, but it is true in a political rather than an economic sense. There is every reason to believe that equivalent expenditures in the 1930s—for example, on schools, libraries, roads, and hospitals— would have had comparable effects upon the unemployment rate. It is true, of course, that in 1944 (unlike the 1930s) there were somewhat over 11 million persons in the armed forces who were no longer "eligible" for unemployment. However, the decline in unemployment cannot be explained in any large measure on that basis; the civilian labor force was actually smaller by only 1 million in 1944 than in 1940 as millions of women, older persons, and youth entered it in response to abundant job opportunities and patriotic appeals.

It must also be recognized that a level of expenditures comparable to that of 1944 would have been inappropriate in the 1930s, for it would have been considerably greater than necessary to bring unemployment to acceptable levels and would have created inflationary pressures at least as severe as any we have subsequently experienced. Nevertheless, the World War II experience demonstrates that society can produce as low a level of unemployment as it chooses provided it is willing to pay the costs. This underscores the distinction made above between economic and political feasibility. What World War II did to the unemployment rate could, from an economic point of view, have been done in other ways; what the war did was to create a political consensus—very different from that of the 1930s—that what happened to the national debt was inconsequential. As Arthur Schlesinger (1983) observed on the fiftieth anniversary of the New

Deal, "it was not until war legitimized really effective deficits . . . that unemployment disappeared."

The post-World War II period. Since the end of World War II annual unemployment rates have ranged from a low of 3.5 percent in 1969 to a high of 9.7 percent in 1982, reaching a level of somewhat over 10 percent in the last quarter of 1982 and the first quarter of 1983. The fact that there appeared to be an upward trend in the late 1950s and early 1960s led to conflicting interpretations, the most important of which were typified by the debate between the "structuralists" and the group that attributed the problem to inadequate demand.

The structuralist view was that rising levels of unemployment were being produced by new and more rapid technological change—automation—that was altering the structure of job opportunities so profoundly that jobless individuals could not meet the skill requirements of available jobs. Massive retraining programs were the only feasible remedy.

The inadequate demand school of thought acknowledged the existence of structural unemployment but denied that it was becoming progressively worse and thus could be held responsible for the upward trend in unemployment. Their explanation was that output (total spending) was not growing sufficiently rapidly to accommodate labor force growth and increased productivity. The principal remedy, according to this view, was to stimulate the economy through conventional monetary and fiscal policy.

In point of fact, both approaches were used. The Area Redevelopment Act of 1961 and the Manpower Development and Training Act of 1962 reflected the structuralists' diagnosis; the tax reduction of 1964 was the fiscal remedy. In retrospect, it would appear that the inadequate demand theorists had the better of the argument; in any case, by the late 1960s with the economy being further buoyed by military expenditures for the Vietnam War the unemployment rate remained at a level under 4 percent for four consecutive years.

The 1970s and 1980s produced a more dismal record than the 1950s and early 1960s and even greater disagreements over policy. The recessions of 1974-1975 and 1981-1982 resulted in unemployment rates higher than any since 1940, and even nonrecession levels averaged more than 6 percent. At the same time, the rate of inflation between 1973 and 1981 averaged 9 percent and exceeded 10 percent in four years. The decision of the Reagan administration and the Federal Reserve System to break the back of inflation by generating substantial slack in the economy was successful in reducing the inflation rate to slightly under 4 percent for the 12 months ending in December 1982, the lowest level in a decade—but at the expense of an unemployment rate in excess of 10 percent.

THE ANATOMY OF UNEMPLOYMENT

Up to this point we have discussed unemployment in global terms—using a single figure to characterize the extent of joblessness during a period of one year. It is important to look behind this measure for a better understanding of the dimensions of the problem.

First, it must be recognized that the annual unemployment rate significantly understates the proportion of the labor force that experiences unemployment during a year. Because of turnover among the unemployed, the fraction of the labor force with unemployment is generally between 3 and 3.5 times as great as the average unemployment rate. For instance, during 1981, when the average number of persons unemployed was 8.3 million, almost three times that number—23.4 million—had at least one spell of unemployment. In a period longer than a year, the discrepancy is even greater. Over the 10-year period ending in the mid-1970s, the proportion of four age-sex subsets of the U.S. population who suffered some unemployment ranged between 30 percent of men 55 to 69 years of age and 68 percent of women 26 to 34 years of age (Parnes, 1982: 6).

Duration. The impact of unemployment depends in large measure on its duration. BLS data show that the duration of unemployment varies over time in the same direction as the unemployment rate. The average unemployment rate for any year is influenced by two elements: (1) the number of persons who experience unemployment, and (2) the length of time they remain unemployed. Thus, during a period of recession the unemployment rate tends to be high because both the incidence of unemployment and its average duration have risen. To illustrate, in 1969 when the unemployment rate was under 4 percent, 12 percent of the labor force experienced some unemployment, of which 13 percent were unemployed as long as 15 weeks. In contrast, when the unemployment rate was 8 percent in 1975, 20 percent of the labor force had spells of unemployment and almost one-third of these were unemployed for at least 15 weeks.

Routes into unemployment. The stereotype of the unemployed is an individual who has lost a job; in point of fact, individuals enter unemployment in several ways, the relative importance of which varies by demographic characteristics and over the course of the business cycle. The *Current Population Survey* classifies the unemployed into four categories: (1) job losers, (2) voluntary job leavers, (3) new entrants to the labor market, and (4) labor market reentrants.

In good times job losers are generally a minority of the unemployed; in recessions they grow in relative importance but do not account for much more than one-half of the total. Again we can compare 1969 and 1975 to illustrate the point. In the former year, when unemployment was quite low, 36 percent of the unemployed had lost their last jobs, 15 percent had voluntarily quit, and one-half were entering or reentering the labor market. In the recession year of 1975, job losers represented 55 percent of the total while voluntary leavers accounted for 10 percent and entrants and reentrants for 34 percent.

Labor force entrance or reentrance is a particularly prominent reason for unemployment among teenagers; in 1951 seven out of ten 16-to-19-year-old unemployed youth were looking for jobs on entering or reentering the labor market. Among adult workers (20 or older) this path into unemployment is naturally much lower, but nevertheless in 1981 accounted for about two-fifths of the female and one-fifth of the male unemployment.

Incidence of unemployment. Finally, the overall unemployment rate conceals a very substantial amount of variation by demographic characteristics, occupation and industry, and geographic location. The racial differential in unemployment is well known. The unemployment rate of blacks has been at least double that of whites in all but four or five years since 1960, and never during this period has the differential been smaller than 75 percent.

Unemployment rates vary inversely with age, being especially high among teenagers and those in their early twenties. In 1981 when the overall unemployment rate stood at 7.6 percent, the rates were about 21 percent, 18 percent, and 12 percent for persons 16-17, 18-19, and 20-24 years of age, respectively. These three age categories, comprising 23 percent of the total civilian labor force, accounted for 45 percent of total unemployment; the corresponding percentages for teenagers alone were 8 percent and 21 percent. Beyond the 20-24-year age category the drop in unemployment rates is precipitous. In 1981 the rate was 7.3

percent among those 25-34, declining to 3.2 percent among those 65 and older.

The likelihood of unemployment declines with advancing age both because of greater job security among older workers stemming from greater seniority and because of the inverse association between age and voluntary mobility. Nevertheless, older workers who do become unemployed tend to have greater difficulty finding work and thus remain unemployed longer. In 1981 the proportion of unemployed men and women between 45 and 64 years of age who were jobless for 15 or more weeks was 34 percent, as compared with 28 percent of all unemployed workers.

The sex differential in unemployment rates varies over the business cycle. The rate for females is generally higher than that of males, reflecting their greater tendency to move into and out of the labor force. The magnitude of the differential is generally larger in tight than in loose labor markets, however, because of the greater concentration of men in cyclically sensitive sectors of the economy. In 1978, when the total unemployment rate was 6.1 percent, the rate for men was almost two points lower than that for women— 5.3 percent versus 7.2 percent. In 1982, when the overall rate had risen to 9.5 percent, the differential was in the opposite direction, with rates of 9.7 percent for men and 9.4 percent for women.

The risk of unemployment varies considerably among the major occupation groups and major industry divisions. With 7.6 percent of the total labor force unemployed in 1981, the rate was as low as 4 percent among white collar workers and 10.3 percent for the blue collar group, ranging between 2.8 percent for professionals and 14.7 percent among nonfarm laborers. Among industry divisions the range was even greater—from 3.5 percent in finance, insurance, and real estate to 15.6 percent in construction.

Reflecting primarily differences in industrial structure, pronounced variation in unemployment rates prevail among labor market areas. Among the 217 major areas for which estimates are prepared from CPS data, the unemployment rate in the continental United States ranged in 1981 from a low of 3.3 percent in Oklahoma City to 14.3 percent in Modesto, California. Of the local labor markets 13 had rates at or below 5 percent, while 35—8 of which were in Michigan—were at 10 percent or higher.

THE CONCEPT OF FULL EMPLOYMENT

The several types (causes) of unemployment that have been identified are helpful in developing an understanding of the concept of "full employment." We already know that it does not mean a zero rate of unemployment, as that is not possible. But how low must unemployment be before we are satisfied that we have achieved full employment? There are several conceptual approaches to answering this question, but unfortunately none leads to a definitive operational response. One can say that full employment exists when there are at least as many job vacancies for which the unemployed can qualify as there are unemployed individuals. (We have, incidentally, no official measure of job vacancies analogous to our measure of unemployment, largely because of almost insuperable conceptual and technical difficulties in developing it.) Alternatively—and what amounts to the same thing—one can say that full employment prevails when the only type of unemployment that exists is frictional.

The reason that these approaches do not lead to an unambiguous definition of the full employment level is that the several types of unemployment that have been described are not as conceptually distinct and mutually exclusive as has been implied. Consider, for a moment, the notion of structural unemployment. We have defined it as a situation in which the qualifications of workers do not match the skill requirements of available jobs. The remedy, according to this view, is not to expand job opportunities but somehow to transform the unemployed workers through retraining programs. But suppose that at a time when there are say, 2 million "structurally unemployed" workers—the economy is stimulated by monetary and fiscal policy so that employers become desperately short of human resources of all types. Under these circumstances they may adjust their sights downward with regard to the qualifications they demand for their jobs, or may reengineer jobs so that the types of skills they had previously insisted upon are no longer necessary, or may themselves expand training activities in order to upgrade the available workers. Thus, expansion of aggregate demand would cause some of the "structural" problems to melt away.

The same line of reasoning is equally applicable to frictional unemployment. Whatever friction exists in the labor market, it is clear that the higher the level of demand for labor, the shorter the spells of unemployment and the lower the unemployment rate. It turns out that levels of frictional and structural unemployment cannot be rigorously defined even under a given set of conditions but depend upon the total level of demand for labor in the economy.

The unemployment-inflation trade-off. If this line of reasoning is valid, why not simply expand total spending until total unemployment reaches very low levels? The answer lies in the fact that as unemployment is pushed down via the expansion of aggregate demand (total spending), a point is reached beyond which inflationary pressures become severe. If all resources—human and nonhuman—were perfectly fluid and interchangeable, the economy would be much easier to manage. That is, up to the point of full utilization of resources, increases in demand would operate simply to increase output and employment with little or no effect on prices. Once the limit of productive capacity had been achieved, further increases in demand could not increase output or employment, but would have to be reflected in increased prices.

Given the fact that resources are *not* completely substitutable for one another, as demand expands beyond certain levels bottlenecks begin to appear. In the human resource arena, for instance, shortages of machinists and roofers may appear while there are still surpluses of (e.g., unemployed) assemblers and floor sweepers. Thus, as demand continues to rise, employers of roofers and machinists attempt to attract workers in these occupational categories away from one another, with resulting upward pressures on wages, costs of production, and prices. There are other factors that tend to produce the same result—for example, the greater boldness of unions as labor markets tighten—but the basic point is that beyond some level the greater the aggregate demand and the lower the unemployment rate, the higher is the probable rate of inflation.

Some years ago it was popular to formalize this relationship in terms of the so-called Phillips curve. On the basis of his study of data for the United Kingdom covering the period 1861 to 1957, A. W. Phillips (1958) found an inverse relation between the annual rate of unemployment and the annual rate of increase in money wages, and an analogous relationship has also been found between unemployment and rate of increase in the price level (inflation). The implication was that policymakers by means of monetary and fiscal policy could choose a point on the Phillips curve depending on how much inflation they were willing to accept in exchange for reducing the level of unemployment. Moreover, through a variety of labor market policies designed to reduce human resource bottlenecks (e.g., retraining), the entire curve could be shifted downward and to the left (from A to B in Figure

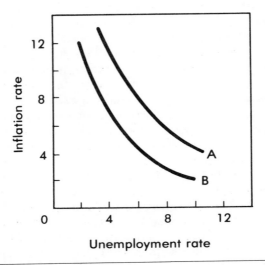

Figure 7.1:   Hypothetical Phillips Curve

7.1) so as to improve the tradeoff between inflation and unemployment (Lipsey, 1965).

The Phillips curve analysis has been challenged both empirically and theoretically. The record of unemployment and inflation in the 1970s made it clear that there is not an unchanging relationship between level of unemployment and rate of inflation. Some theorists have argued that there is a unique rate of unemployment for any set of labor market conditions that is consistent with a *stable* rate of inflation. This has been called the nonaccelerating inflation rate of unemployment, or NAIRU (Sawhill and Bassi, 1980). In any case, whether or not (or in what sense) there is a Phillips curve, no one denies that at a given point in time unemployment can be reduced by measures that increase the likelihood of inflation and that, conversely, inflation can be reduced by measures that increase the likelihood of unemployment; and in this sense there *is* a policy trade-off.

Full employment reconsidered. This proposition brings us to the "bottom line" of the issue of full employment. In the last analysis, there is no way of specifying the full employment level of unemployment except in terms of what costs society is willing to incur. In other words, we can bring the unemployment rate down as low as we wish provided that we are willing to pay the costs of doing so.

General monetary and fiscal policy may generate higher rates of inflation than we are willing to accept; attacks on structural unemployment may generate higher tax burdens than we are willing to bear; making government the employer of last resort so that everyone is literally guaranteed a job may impose costs of both these kinds and also may violate the principle held by some people that "nonessential" public employment is somehow inappropriate.

Thus, the specification of a full employment goal is in the final analysis a political rather than an economic issue. It depends essentially on the values of the policymakers and, perhaps more fundamentally, on the understanding and values of the electorate. The only other thing that can be said with some confidence has to do with the level of NAIRU. First, there is some empirical evidence that as of the early 1980s that figure—which might serve as a definition of full employment—stood in the vicinity of 5.5 to 6.5 percent (Sawhill and Bassi, 1980: 169). Second, there is virtually universal agreement that whatever the figure is, it is higher than the corresponding full employment level two decades earlier. In part this is the result of demographic changes in the composition of the labor force. The increasing proportions of women and young persons—both of whom have above-average levels of unemployment—means that any level of labor market tightness will be reflected in a higher unemployment rate than previously. Liberalization of unemployment compensation programs and other entitlements have probably had a similar effect, both by decreasing the pressures to work and by increasing the probabilities of reporting unemployment. Finally, Baily (1982) adduces evidence to show that because of increased levels of structural unemployment, the unemployment rate in the 1970s had become a misleading indicator of the extent of slack in the economy.

THE QUEST FOR FULL EMPLOYMENT

The conceptual framework outlined in Chapter 1 emphasized the point that the achievement of full employment is an overriding objective of human resource policy. From the preceding section of this chapter it is clear that a precise specification of what that goal means is not easy. Nevertheless, the remainder of the chapter will sketch the principal approaches that have been taken to reduce unemployment to acceptable levels.

The legislative commitment. The original legislative commitment to the pursuit of full employment was contained in the

Employment Act of 1946. That it was merely a qualified commitment is suggested by the fact that the adjective "full" was deleted from the original title of the bill before Congress passed it; nonetheless, it was an important law for it was the first explicit legislative recognition of the "Keynesian revolution" in economic thought. Prior to the appearance in 1936 of John Maynard Keynes' *General Theory of Employment, Interest, and Money,* the prevailing belief among economists was that any departure from full employment was temporary and self-correcting. Keynes demonstrated theoretically that this is not so—that an economy can be in equilibrium at less than full employment with no automatic forces tending to cause it to recover. Thus was provided the rationale for the use of monetary and fiscal policy to combat a recession or depression.

The act declared that "it is the continuing policy and responsibility of the federal government . . . to promote maximum employment, production, and purchasing power." It established the Council of Economic Advisers to the President and imposed on the president the obligation to make an annual economic report to Congress. It also provided for the Joint Economic Committee of the House and Senate to conduct hearings and propose legislation for meeting the objectives of the act. While the statute did not provide for any further specific means of achieving its stated aims, it made clear the government's responsibility to use monetary and fiscal policy to maintain a healthy economy.

The Employment Act was amended in 1978 by the Full Employment and Balanced Growth (Humphrey-Hawkins) Act, which restated the objectives of the earlier statute and added several others, not all of which are mutually compatible. Passed only after a four-year battle in Congress, the final version was considerably watered down from the bill as originally introduced, which had guaranteed a job to every adult who wanted one. Among the objectives specified by the statute are (1) the achievement by 1983 of an unemployment rate of 4 percent (and 3 percent for persons 20 and older); (2) a reduction of the inflation rate to 3 percent by 1983 and the achievement of price stability by 1988, provided that these goals can be met without impeding the achievement of the unemployment targets; (3) increasing productivity and real income, and achieving "balanced growth"; (4) improving the balance of trade; (5) achieving a balanced budget; and (6) reducing the ratio of federal expenditures to GNP.

To accomplish these objectives, the law mentions a number of possible methods of combatting both inadequate demand and structural unemployment but gives special emphasis to job creation programs. In this connection, the president is authorized, beginning in 1980, to create "reservoirs" of public and private nonprofit projects that will provide jobs to individuals for whom other employment opportunities do not exist. Such jobs are to be useful and productive, are to pay relatively low wages so as not to draw workers away from the private sector, and are to be designed for geographic areas of high unemployment and for the structurally unemployed.

Coordination is called for among the several levels of government and among Congress, the president, and the Board of Governors of the Federal Reserve System. More specifically, the president and Congress are to set quantitative goals each year for the reduction of unemployment, and are to develop a set of policies for the achievement of those goals. Reports from the Board of Governors of the Federal Reserve System to relevant congressional committees are also called for.

Their review of the provisions of the law lead Sawhill and Bassi (1980: 163) to characterize it as "policy without program." They observe that despite the wide range of possible strategies referred to by the act, "it is difficult to discern the specific role envisaged for each, what each is expected to accomplish, at what cost, and how each relates to the myriad of other policies directed toward similar objectives." There cannot be much question that the specific unemployment and inflation goals established by the act were unrealistic even in the light of the conditions that prevailed at the time of its passage (an unemployment rate of 6.1 percent and an inflation rate of 7.7 percent).

Pursuant to the provision that authorizes the president to recommend modification of the timetable for meeting the quantitative goals of the act, President Carter extended the timetable beyond the act's five-year planning horizon. In 1982 the five-year goals specified by the Reagan administration included an unemployment rate of 5.3 percent and an inflation rate of 4.4 percent by 1987; the administration proudly announced, however, that the statute's goal of a 20 percent ratio of federal outlays to GNP would be met in that year (U.S. President 1982a: 214).

Employment and training programs. Whereas the original Employment Act of 1946 had implicitly focused largely on inadequate demand unemployment, the Humphrey-Hawkins amendments of 1978 accorded considerable attention to the problem of structural unemployment as well. Between these two pieces of legislation was another important statute whose principal emphasis was on combatting structural unemployment—the Manpower Development and Training Act (MDTA) of 1962. Just as the Employment Act had recognized the responsibility of the federal government to assure an adequate total level of demand for labor, so the MDTA imposed the responsibility of exercising surveillance over the labor market in order to assure an effective match between the supply of and demand for human resources. Just as the Employment Act had imposed on the president the obligation to present to Congress an annual *Economic Report,* so the MDTA called for an annual *Manpower Report* (later called *Employment and Training Report*). The MDTA was replaced in 1973 by the Comprehensive Employment and Training Act (CETA) and again in 1982 by the Job Training Partnership Act (JTPA).

Because MDTA and its successors are important elements in U.S. policy directed toward the attainment of full employment, they clearly fall within the purview of this chapter. However, as the legislation's major thrust was the provision of vocational and labor market skills, it is also appropriately classified among human resource development policies. Accordingly, the principal review of this legislation and its implementation is reserved for Chapter 10. However, there is one component of employment and training programs—public service employment (PSE)—that requires some straining of language to be considered an example of human resource development policy but that is clearly a means of achieving full employment. In the remainder of this chapter, then, we focus not only on PSE but on other methods of direct job creation as well.

Direct job creation. The phrases "direct job creation" (Haveman, 1980) and "selective employment policy" (Solow, 1980) have both been used to describe programs designed to create employment opportunities in specific areas or for particular categories of individuals as distinguished from expanding employment generally through stimulative monetary and fiscal policy. The two chief mechanisms for achieving this end are public service employment and wage subsidies to private employers for specified categories of employees.

Solow (1980: 129-130) perceives three possible reasons why direct job creation may be thought to be preferable over more general economic stimulation: (1) greater efficiency ("more bang for the buck") in the sense of creating more employment per dollar of expenditure; (2) greater equity, in the sense that whatever employment is created will go disproportionately to those who need it most; and (3) less inflationary, in the sense that stimulation of demand for workers among whom unemployment is higher than average will exert less upward pressure on prices than an equivalent expansion of jobs in the labor force generally.

The first use of public service employment (PSE) to combat unemployment occurred during the Great Depression, with the establishment of the Works Progress Administration (WPA). At its peak, the WPA had over 3 million workers on its rolls, ranging from engineers, statisticians, artists, and musicians to unskilled laborers on construction projects. The WPA introduced millions of people to band concerts that they otherwise would have had no opportunity to hear, resulted in a substantial amount of useful research (the Current Population Survey was developed originally by a WPA project), and left monuments in the form of public parks and buildings that are still being used. Nevertheless, its critics equated it with "leaf raking" and "made work"—images that continue to condition attitudes toward PSE programs.

The WPA was terminated in 1943, and it was not until 1971 that PSE again made an appearance in the United States. In that year President Nixon, despite an earlier veto of amendments to the MDTA because they included provisions for such a program, signed the Emergency Employment Act. This authorized a two-year public employment program (PEP), which employed over 400,000 persons between August 1971 and June 1973. Although PEP was discontinued, authorization for PSE programs in areas of substantial unemployment was provided by the Comprehensive Employment and Training Act (CETA) of 1973. In the following year a contracyclical PSE program was added to CETA in response to a deepening recession. Outlays for PSE programs increased sharply, from $1.3 billion in FY 1975 to a peak of $5.8 billion in FY 1978. Thereafter the program was curtailed and finally was eliminated entirely by the Job Training Partnership Act of 1982.

PSE programs potentially serve several employment-related objectives as well as the social service objective of providing for unmet public needs (Nathan, 1980; Johnston, 1980). *Countercyclical* PSE, exemplified by the WPA, PEP, and Title VI of CETA, is aimed at reducing unemployment in times of recession. PSE directed at *structural* problems is designed to provide jobs, employment experience, and income to the disadvantaged, with the expectation that such experience will enable them to move into "regular" jobs. This approach is illustrated by Title II of CETA, which provided transitional public sector jobs to the disadvantaged, and also by the so-called work experience programs—Operation Mainstream, Neighborhood Youth Corps, and the CETA Summer Youth Employment Program—that placed persons in low-skilled jobs as a means of allowing them to establish work records and to gain experience in a work environment. Finally, the most ambitious form of PSE would involve government as *employer of last resort*—in effect, guaranteeing a job to every adult who wants one. Nathan (1980: 62) estimates that such a program would require 15 to 20 million jobs and would cost in the neighborhood of $100 billion.

One of the most controversial aspects of PSE funded by the federal government is the extent to which it actually results in a net increase in employment rather than simply the substitution of federal for state and local funds for the supported programs. In response to a congressional mandate, the National Commission for Employment Policy commissioned a study of this issue by the Brookings Institution. The study found a substitution rate of about 20 percent—well under the estimates yielded by other studies, which ranged as high as 100 percent after two years. Because the Brookings estimate was based upon interviews with the officials of state and local government agencies that were administering PSE programs, it may be low. Nevertheless, the investigators discerned at least three interests of the officials to whom they talked that would argue against substitution—(1) concern about the legal prohibition of such use of the funds; (2) "pragmatic concerns about the PSE program because of the uncertainty surrounding the future funding"; and (3) a sincere dedication to "the national objectives of reducing unemployment and aiding the disadvantaged" (Nathan, 1980: 63-64).

The second major approach to direct job creation is through subsidized employment—in the United States, principally by means of tax credits. The earliest example of this approach was implemented in the early 1970s in the Work Incentive (WIN) program—an effort to move certain categories of welfare recipients into paid employment. The New Jobs Credit, enacted in 1977 as a countercyclical measure, involved the broadest application of the technique. Employers were granted limited tax credits for the portion of their wage bill in excess of 102 percent of that of the previous year up to a specified maximum. In the following year this was replaced by the Targeted Jobs Tax Credit, which as its name suggests is designed to stimulate the employment of specified categories of individuals, including economically disadvantaged youth, Vietnam veterans, and exconvicts; handicapped individuals under vocational rehabilitation programs; and the recipients of certain categories of welfare payments. The tax credit is the same as that under the WIN program—50 percent of the first $6,000 of annual wages during the first year and 25 percent during the second. An additional program applicable to disadvantaged youth 16 to 17 years of age during the summer months became effective in 1983. It allows a tax credit equal to 85 percent of the wages paid to each youth up to a maximum of $300 for the summer.

Unlike the PSE programs, subsidized employment has bene-fitted very few individuals. For example, only 4 percent of the eligible target groups were hired under the Targeted Jobs Tax Credit program during its first 18 months, and many of these would obviously have been employed even in the absence of the program (Saks and Sandell, 1980). The Reagan administration's Council of Economic Advisers has attributed the limited participa-tion to "administrative problems [in] . . . determining program eligibility, . . . reluctance . . . of eligible recipients to use the tax credit as a self-marketing tool, and employers' reluctance to let government programs influence hiring decisions" (U.S. President, 1982a: 45).

In the pursuit of full employment, how useful are direct job creation methods as compared with general stimulation of the economy by means of monetary and fiscal policy? Solow (1980), admitting the absence of conclusive empirical evidence, believes that selective policies are marginally advantageous from the efficiency and price stability points of view and clearly so from the equity perspective, provided that the programs in fact reach the intended population (which is not always the case). With respect to efficiency, concentration of the programs on low-wage workers means that each dollar buys more employment and also has a greater multiplier effect than if spent in other ways; however, the first of these advantages is to some extent offset by the substitution or displacement that occurs, and the second by the high marginal implicit tax rates faced by many low income people (e.g., welfare recipients). With respect to price stability, the idea that selective policies are less inflationary rests on the commonsense obser-vation that a given expansion of employment will create less competitive pressure for higher wages when confined to population groups among whom unemployment is high than if it is general.

Solow's careful analysis makes it clear that *if* direct job creation can be targeted on the intended beneficiaries and *if* there is little or no displacement, it is precisely the approach to be used for combatting structural unemployment in an economy where inflationary pressures threaten. On the assumption that structural unemployment problems will continue to plague the American economy—or, indeed, become worse—this suggests that direct job creation will become an almost indispensable tool if we as a society wish seriously to pursue the dual objectives of full employment and price stability.

NOTE

1. The fourth component of total spending is net exports (F=foreign trade), which will be ignored in this discussion. The sum of these four elements equals the gross national product (GNP).

QUESTIONS FOR DISCUSSION

1. Do you see any way of quantifying the total costs of unemployment either to the individual or to society as a whole? If not, is there any rational way of deciding what measures society ought to be willing to take to prevent unemployment or to alleviate its burden?

2. Seasonal and technological unemployment are terms frequently encountered in the literature. How would you fit them into the classification of unemployment presented in this chapter?

3. What are the most significant conclusions to be drawn from an examination of the historical record of unemployment over the past half century?

4. What meaning do you attach to the concept of "full employment"? Does a sensible answer to this question today differ from what it would have been 15 or 20 years ago?

5. How do you interpret and react to the following statement from the text: "In the last analysis, there is no way of specifying the full employment level of unemployment except in terms of what costs society is willing to incur."

6. What schools of thought do you discern regarding the relation between unemployment and inflation?

7. Under current conditions, what additional measures, if any, ought the federal government pursue to reduce the unemployment rate? Under either current conditions or those that you believe are likely to prevail in the future, what role do you see for direct job creation measures?

8

Productivity, Wages, Hours, and Prices

We learned in the last chapter that unemployment may be generated in the economy by inadequate spending and, on the other side of the coin, that excessive spending may generate inflationary pressures. In this chapter we examine more closely the phenomenon of inflation as it relates to the general level of wages. In the process we discuss the fundamental relationship between labor productivity on the one hand and wages, hours, and prices on the other.

SOME CONCEPTS AND DEFINITIONS

Before embarking on this analysis, it is necessary to explore the meaning of three concepts: labor productivity, inflation, and *real* wages.

Labor productivity. It will be recalled from the discussion in Chapter 4 that labor productivity refers to a ratio between output and some measure of labor input, generally person-hours of work. The concept may be applied to an individual firm, to an industry, or to the economy as a whole. As there must be a common metric for measuring output, in all but the simplest cases it is expressed in terms of dollar values. For the economy as a whole, the appropriate measure is the gross national product (GNP)—the total value of all final goods and services produced in a year.

Whether the reference is to the economy at large or to some subdivision thereof, we are generally interested not in the absolute level of productivity but in its change (in percentage terms) over some period of time. Thus, when we say that labor productivity in the private sector of the United States economy increased by 22 percent between 1966 and 1980, this means that on average one person-hour of work produced over one-fifth more goods and services in the latter than in the former year.

What are the basic factors that have produced the long-term upward trend in labor productivity? Historically, the most important has been an increase in the amount of physical capital with which human resources cooperate in the productive process. The substitution of calculators for pencils and paper involves a substantial increase in the amount of capital used by statistical clerks and results in large increases in their output per hour. Qualitative improvements in capital equipment without any increase in the value of resources involved can have the same effect, as is illustrated by the substitution of electronic for the old electric calculators.

Improved organization and management can also result in greater output per person-hour. For example, the specialization of labor that is permitted by the modern supermarket produces increases in labor productivity as compared with the old corner grocery store over and above what can be accounted for by increased capital investment alone. Qualitative improvements in human resources—increases in the quantity of *human* capital— are another important source of increase in labor productivity. Finally, changes in the industrial structure of employment may also change the average level of productivity in the economy as a whole. Thus, the shifting of human resources out of agriculture, where the value of output per person-hour is relatively low, into other sectors of the economy has resulted in a rise over time in the average level of productivity.

Inflation. Inflation refers to a rise in the average level of prices. There are several measures of changes in the price level; the one that is best known and that is most relevant to assessing the welfare of individuals is the Consumer Price Index (CPI). The CPI is based on a monthly survey of prices of a large variety of goods and services in several hundred representative communities throughout the United States. The items that comprise the index are weighted according to their relative importance in the expenditures of urban consumers.[1] The index expresses the relationship of the average level of prices at that time to the average that prevailed in a base year (currently 1967). Thus, the CPI of 289.1 in 1982 meant that consumer prices were almost 2.9 times as high in 1982 as they had been in 1967.

What causes an increase in the general level of prices? The classic explanation of inflation has been described as "too much money chasing too few goods"—that is, a situation in which total spending in an economy is increasing faster than the output of goods and services, with a resulting bidding up of prices. This has been described as a "demand-pull" inflation; in contrast, some economists refer to a "cost-push" inflation in which the initiating factor is a rise in production costs that forces prices upward. This has generally been regarded to result from too rapid a rise in wages, although the experience of the 1970s demonstrated that such external "shocks" as increases in the price of imported oil could also generate an increase in the general level of prices. Some economists—the "monetarists"—believe that the distinction between demand-pull and cost-push inflation is fallacious. Their view is that the only cause of inflation is an excessive rate of growth in the money supply, and that even rises in production costs cannot generate inflation unless the monetary authorities choose to "underwrite" them by increasing the supply of money.

Wages. On the surface, the term "wages" is more generally understood than either of the other two concepts we have just examined, yet there are several aspects of the term that deserve elaboration. Although popular usage differentiates between the "wages" of blue collar workers and the "salaries" of white collar workers, the former term is used here in a generic sense to refer to compensation for any human effort used in the productive process.

There are several measures of wages that are useful in different contexts. The *wage rate* is the basic payment guaranteed to the worker per unit of time. *Average hourly earnings* is a measure of total wages received over a period of time divided by the number of hours worked. The average hourly earnings of a blue collar factory worker might be higher than his or her wage rate as the result of one or more of a number of factors: (1) the use of an incentive system in which the wage rate is the basic guarantee with the expectation that the worker will normally earn more than this; (2) the inclusion in average hourly earnings of "overtime" for which a

premium of one-and-one-half times the base rate has been paid; or
(3) the inclusion of bonuses of various kinds. *Total employee
compensation* is the most comprehensive measure of wages, and
therefore the broadest measure of the total *labor costs* of the
employer. It embraces virtually all payments made by the employer
in the worker's behalf including paid vacations, holidays, and
leaves; employer contributions to pension and insurance systems;
and unemployment compensation and social security taxes.
Reflecting the growth of "fringe benefits," total employee compensation per hour has grown more rapidly than average hourly
earnings in recent decades. For the private nonfarm economy as a
whole in 1974 pay for time worked constituted 78.2 percent of
total compensation per hour. Of the remainder, 8.2 percent
consisted of other direct payments to workers (e.g., paid vacations
and holidays) while 13.6 percent represented wage supplements
of various kinds (Douty, 1980: 9-10).

Any of the concepts of wages that have been reviewed above
may be expressed in *money* or in *real* terms. Real wages refer to the
actual goods and services that can be purchased with money
wages. Thus, in measuring a change in real wages over time, the
change in money wages must be adjusted for whatever change in
the price level occurred over the period. This is accomplished by
means of a "deflation technique" in which the CPI is used to
express wages for different time periods in dollars of constant
purchasing power. The process consists of dividing the money
wage figure by the CPI for the corresponding time period and
multiplying by 100.

The following example will make the procedure clear. As the
data in Table 8.1 show, average hourly earnings of production or
nonsupervisory workers in the private nonfarm economy were
$4.53 in 1975 and $7.67 in 1982, an increase over the seven-year
period of 69.3 percent. The price level, as measured by the CPI,
rose from 161.2 to 289.1 over the same period—an increase of
79.3 percent. Real wages, therefore, expressed in terms of 1967
dollars *decreased* from $2.81 to $2.65—a drop of 5.7 percent.

The productivity-wage-inflation connection. The preceding
exploration of the concepts of productivity, inflation, and wages
allows us now to make clear certain very fundamental relationships
among them. First of all, it is important to recognize that increases
in productivity are the most fundamental source of increases in
real income, of which wages are by far the most important

TABLE 8.1   Change in Money and Real Average Hourly Earnings,
Production and Nonsupervisory Workers, 1975-1982

Measure	1975	1982	Percentage of Change
(1) Average hourly earnings, current dollars	4.53	7.67	+69.3
(2) Consumer Price Index (1967 = 100)	161.2	289.1	+79.3
(3) Average hourly earnings, 1967 dollars ([Row 1/Row 2] × 100)	2.81	2.65	-5.7

SOURCE: U.S. President (1983: 206, 221).

component—accounting for about three-fourths of total national income. As Kendrick (1977: 1) has noted, "since resource inputs seldom grow much faster than population, . . . the main way that output per capita can be raised is by the growth of productivity."

Second, it should be noted that wages (total employee compensation per hour) cannot for long increase faster than labor productivity is increasing without resulting in inflation. If employee compensation per hour increases at a faster rate than labor productivity, this means that labor costs per unit of output are rising with a consequent upward pressure on prices.

Third, if total employee compensation per hour increases at the same rate as labor productivity, the wage increases are not inflationary whether viewed from a demand-pull or a cost-push point of view. From the cost-push vantage point, if employee compensation per hour in a particular firm increases by, say, 5 percent over a two-year period and output per person hour increases by the same percentage, then labor cost per unit of output remains unchanged. From the demand pull point of view, if an economy's resources are being fully utilized and wages (and other incomes) are increasing at the same rate as output, the increase in potential spending is being exactly matched by an increase in the volume of goods and services available to be purchased with no resulting pulling up of prices.

Finally, it is important to recognize that if increases in wages (employee compensation per hour) occur at the same rate as labor productivity is increasing, other income shares (e.g., profits) can increase at the same rate with no necessary inflationary consequences. Thus, for wages to increase at the same rate as labor productivity does not mean that all of the productivity gains are being reaped by labor. The hypothetical data in Table 8.2 illustrate

TABLE 8.2   Hypothetical Productivity and Revenue Change
Over a Five-Year Period, ABC Widget Company

Item	Year t	Year t + 5
Person-hours per week	4,000	4,000
Number of widgets per person-hour	10	11
Employee compensation per hour (dollars)	7.00	7.70
Labor cost per widget (dollars)	0.70	0.70
Other costs per widget (dollars)	0.30	0.30
Selling price per widget (dollars)	1.20	1.20
Output per week (number of widgets)	40,000	44,000
Revenues per week (dollars)	48,000	52,800
Total costs per week (dollars)	40,000	44,000
Profit per week (dollars)	8,000	8,800

these points. As labor productivity and wages both increase by 10 percent in this widget manufacturing company, unit labor costs remain constant at \$.70 per widget. On the assumption that other costs per unit remain the same,[2] selling price can remain unchanged at \$1.20 per widget. Weekly profits rise from \$8,000 to \$8,800— an increase of 10 percent.

THE HISTORICAL RECORD

The data in Table 8.3 show the changes over the post-World War II period in the variables we have discussed. Real GNP (in 1972 dollars) increased from 470 billion in 1947 to 1.5 trillion in 1982. This means that the total volume of goods and services that the economy produced was slightly over three times as large in the latter as in the former year. The next four rows of figures in the table are increasingly refined measures of human resource inputs into the productive process. The fact that the relative increase in population was only about half as great as the increase in output means that per capita income almost doubled over the period. As a measure of potential human resource input, it also suggests that the major explanation of the tripling of output over the period was increasing labor productivity. This is confirmed by the fact that the number of person-hours devoted to productive activity was only 0.3 times higher in 1982 than in 1947 while output per person-hour was 2.3 times as high.

Turning next to the several measures of wages, it will be noted that average hourly earnings in current dollars rose from \$1.13 to

TABLE 8.3   Selected Data on Real GNP, Labor Inputs, Productivity, and Real Compensation: 1947-1982

Item	1947	1966	1982	1966/ 1947	1982/ 1966	1982/ 1947
GNP (billions of 1972 dollars)	470.3	984.8	1475.5	2.09	1.50	3.14
Population (millions)	144.1	196.6	232.0	1.36	1.18	1.61
Civilian labor force (millions)	59.4	75.8	110.2	1.28	1.45	1.86
Civilian LFPR	58.3	59.2	64.0	1.02	1.08	1.10
Average weekly hours	40.3	38.6	34.8	0.96	0.90	0.86
Person-hours (1967 = 100)	90.5	100.0	118.8	1.10	1.19	1.31
Average hourly earnings (in dollars)	1.13	2.56	7.67	2.27	3.00	6.79
Average weekly earnings (in dollars)	45.58	98.82	266.92	2.17	2.70	5.86
CPI (1967 = 100)	66.9	97.2	289.1	1.45	2.97	4.32
Real hourly earnings (in 1967 dollars)	1.69	2.63	2.65	1.56	1.01	1.57
Real compensation/ person-hour (1967 = 100)	54.0	97.6	113.7	1.81	1.16	2.11
Output/person-hour	53.0	97.8	122.4	1.85	1.25	2.31

SOURCE: U.S. President (1983).

$7.67—an increase of 579 percent. (This was larger than the increase in average weekly earnings because average weekly hours of work had declined over the period.) The fact that prices, as measured by the CPI, had risen by 332 percent means that the increase in real average hourly earnings was a much more modest 57 percent. This is nevertheless an impressive gain; the amount of goods and services that could be obtained by an hour's work increased by almost three-fifths for the average production or nonsupervisory worker over the 35-year period. The increase in total compensation per hour was even larger: In real terms this more than doubled, reflecting the relatively larger increase in fringe benefits than in direct wages.

The last two rows of figures in the table are the most important in illustrating the basic underlying relationship between gains in productivity and gains in real wages. There is a rather close correspondence between the percentage increase in output per person-hour (labor productivity), and the percentage increase in total compensation per person-hour not only over the entire

35-year period but also within each of the two subperiods that are shown. These two subperiods, it will be noted, differ substantially from each other. The economy was considerably healthier during the first than during the second. The percentage by which prices rose was 4.4 times as great during the 16 years from 1966 to 1982 as during the 19 years from 1947 to 1966; at the same time, the productivity gain was less than one-third as great. The average annual rate of productivity growth between 1947 and 1966 was 3.1 percent in contrast to only 1.3 percent between 1966 and 1982. Between 1973 and 1982 the average rate of productivity increase was below 1 percent, and productivity actually declined from the preceding year in 1974, 1979, and 1980.

No confident explanation of the slowdown in productivity growth can be offered (Adler, 1982) although a number of factors have been cited as possible contributors to the phenomenon (Kendrick, 1977). Among these are (1) the increasing proportions of women and youth in the labor force who are, on average, employed in lower productivity jobs; (2) a decrease in the ratio of expenditures for research and development to GNP; (3) the diversion of resources from productive uses induced by rising rates of inflation; (4) the effects of a variety of social ills, including increased drug abuse and crime; and (5) increased regulation of industry, especially by the Environmental Protection Agency and the Occupational Safety and Health Administration, which increased the required inputs into the productive process without affecting measured outputs (improvements in the purity of air and water and in the health and comfort of workers are not reflected in the measurement of the GNP).

IMPLICATIONS OF INCREASING PRODUCTIVITY

It is not possible to be confident about the future trend in productivity. Forecasts for the late 1970s and early 1980s made as recently as 1977 by authorities on productivity change (Kendrick, 1977: 98-99) have proven to be wildly optimistic. Nevertheless, the most reasonable assumption is that most of the forces that have produced the long-term historic growth in labor productivity will continue to operate in the future. While the growth rate in excess of 3 percent that prevailed in the two decades after World War II may prove to be exceptionally high (as it was historically relative to the first half of the century), it seems likely that we can look forward to rates of at least 2 or 2.5 percent in the future. Even the lower of these leads to a doubling of productivity (and thus of potential per capita income) over a 35-year period. It is therefore worthwhile to take a more careful look at the implications of improvements in labor productivity for human beings in their productive roles.

Increases in labor productivity *necessarily* mean higher real incomes and/or increased leisure. This is not a matter of economics but simply expresses the arithmetic or definitional relationships among the terms. Consider Robinson Crusoe on his desert island, surviving by catching fish and garnering coconuts. As the number of fish and coconuts he can acquire with an hour's effort increases, either because he becomes more skilled (improvement in human capital) or because he fashions crude nets and ladders (increases in physical capital), one of two things happens (or some combination of the two). Either Crusoe continues to work as long as he had previously, in which case he enjoys more fish and coconuts (increased real income); or he decides to take it easier, devoting more time to basking in the sunshine or contemplating life under a coconut tree (increased leisure).

What is true of Robinson Crusoe is equally true of a modern society except that the mechanisms for translating improvements in labor productivity into higher incomes or more leisure are considerably more complex. Theoretically, the higher real incomes can come about either through falling prices (resulting from decreased costs of production) with wages remaining constant; through increases in money wages with constant prices; or through any combination of change in which wages rise faster (or fall more slowly) than prices. During most of the twentieth century the pattern has involved increases in both prices and money incomes with the latter outstripping the former, and this is the most likely pattern for the future as well.

Increases in leisure can occur in a variety of ways—through a reduction in the number of weekly work hours, increases in holidays or vacation time, later entrance into or earlier departure from the labor force. Historically, the first of these was the principal means of taking increased leisure in the United States until about 1940. Between 1890 and 1940 the scheduled workweek in manufacturing dropped from 60 to 40. Except for an increase during World War II, actual hours have hovered around that level ever since. In all nonagricultural industries combined, however, average weekly hours have dropped from a level of about 40 in the immediate postwar period to about 35 in the early 1980s.

reflecting primarily the increasing proportion of (voluntary) part-time workers in many nonmanufacturing industries.

Annual hours of work have continued to decline since 1940 largely as the result of the increasing prevalence of paid vacations and paid holidays. Prior to World War II these benefits were virtually unheard of among blue collar workers. Today paid vacations of from one to four weeks are the norm, and the period of service required to qualify for them continues to be shortened. Paid holidays have increased from an average of two in 1940 to nine in the early 1980s. As a consequence, average annual hours of work declined from 2,252 in 1940 to 1,836 in 1980—a drop of 18 percent (Levitan and Johnson, 1982: 58-59).

It is thus clear that historically we have chosen to take the fruits of increased productivity in the form of both increased real incomes and increased leisure. What is the mechanism through which the choice is made? How is it determined in what proportions these two rewards will be reaped? To some extent the decision is made in the same way that Robinson Crusoe made his—that is, by individual workers as they make decisions about the kinds of jobs they take (e.g., part time versus full time; school teacher versus manager) and whether or not to "moonlight." To this extent, the normal operation of the labor market provides an answer to the question.

To a considerably greater extent, however, the answer is provided by collective decisions, and the instruments for making them are government and collective bargaining. For example, when the Fair Labor Standards Act of 1938 required that hours in excess of 40 per week be compensated at a premium rate of 150 percent, this in effect represented a collective decision in favor of relatively more leisure. Similarly, child labor legislation and school attendance laws ensured later entrance into the labor market, while the Social Security Act encouraged (or at least permitted) earlier departure therefrom. Of even greater significance is the institution of collective bargaining. Each time a union and management negotiate an additional paid holiday or a liberalized vacation plan they are making a collective decision in favor of more leisure rather than higher real incomes for the workers covered by the contract.

There is just one additional point that needs to be made in this context, which has to do with the criteria in terms of which social decisions regarding income and leisure rationally should be made. Some people—particularly trade union representatives—appear to believe that in the face of rapid technological change mass unemployment can be avoided only by a reduction in hours. While there may be some merit to the notion that hours reduction as an alternative to improvements in real weekly earnings may help to preserve jobs *in a particular industry*, there is no reason to believe that this is a legitimate approach for the economy as a whole. There are effective policies for pursuing full employment irrespective of the quantity of human resource input, and these have been explored in the preceding chapter. Increases in leisure ought never to be chosen simply as a mean of increasing the total volume of employment in an economy; rationally, such a choice should be made only if it is believed that needs for additional goods and services *of any types* (e.g., education, playgrounds, and better water as well as more conflakes or motor boats) are less important than more time away from work.

WAGES AND PRICES: INCOMES POLICIES

The final policy issue relating to the subject of this chapter concerns the relationship between wages and prices and the possibility of avoiding or mitigating inflation by means of what has come to be known as "incomes policies." We have seen that increases in total hourly compensation in the economy as a whole are not inflationary so long as they do not exceed the economywide rate of increase in labor productivity. If this is so, and given the fact that in major sectors of the economy wages and prices are administered rather than being determined exclusively by automatic market forces, is there some way in which wage and price decisions can be influenced in order to reduce the probability that they will generate inflationary pressure?

To enable us to think through this question, imagine for a moment an economy in which there are only three industries, which are of equal importance in terms both of employment and of contribution to the GNP. In industry A the annual rate of productivity growth is 6 percent; in B, 3 percent; and in C, 0 percent—for an economywide average of 3 percent. According to what we have already seen, if the firms in each of these industries increased the hourly rate of employee compensation by an amount equal to the rate of productivity increase in that industry, unit labor costs would remain unchanged and real incomes would increase by *an average* rate of 3 percent for the economy as a whole—precisely equal to the average rate of productivity increase.

A moment's reflection, however, will indicate that a process of this kind would be both inequitable and unworkable. From the standpoint of equity, it would mean that after some years secretaries in industry A might be receive twice the income of those doing identical work in industry C. Equity considerations aside, the labor market—even with all its imperfections—could not operate with such disparities.

Suppose instead, then, that the prescription is for an increase in compensation of 3 percent in *each* industry. Under these circumstances labor costs per unit of output, and therefore prices, could be expected to rise in industry C, fall in industry A, and remain stable in industry B. For the economy as a whole, while some prices would rise and others would fall, the general price level would remain constant while real incomes would rise by 3 percent.

It is precisely this line of reasoning that underlies "incomes policies" that have been implemented in several European countries and also in several different forms in the United States. The so-called "wage-price guideposts" of the Kennedy and Johnson administrations called for increases in total employee compensation per person-hour equivalent to the trend rate of increase in labor productivity; and for price stability in industries with average rates of productivity growth, price increases in those with below-average productivity gains, and price decreases in those with above-average gains. There were no explicit means of enforcement; reliance was placed on "jawboning."

A more formal system of controls was instituted by the Nixon administration in the period 1971-1973, and the Carter administration introduced a program in 1978. Needless to say, the specific formulation of the guidelines or controls has depended upon the rate of inflation that has prevailed at the time of their introduction. That is, the specification of the Kennedy-Johnson guideposts assumed the existence of price stability to begin with. If a rate of inflation of, say, 5 percent exists when an incomes policy is formulated, the appropriate wage guideline would obviously have to be somewhat higher than the trend rate of productivity increase.

Prior to the inauguration of the Reagan administration, which has taken a dim view of any type of wage or price controls (or guidelines, for that matter), the most recent development relating to incomes policy was the idea of using tax incentives or penalties to induce compliance with wage-price guidelines (U.S. President, 1981: 57-68)—the so-called tax-based incomes policy (TIP).

There is, however, substantial disagreement among economists about the potential usefulness of any type of incomes policy in combatting inflation. Neoclassical economists and especially the monetarists are particularly hostile. One of the principal arguments against this approach is that it prevents the labor market from performing its allocative function. A uniform percentage increase in employee compensation each year would mean that existing percentage wage differentials would be "frozen"; thus, changes in wage differentials—which theoretically are relied upon to reallocate human resources—could not occur. The cogency of this argument, of course, depends on the degree to which one believes the labor market operates according to the competitive model. Moreover, even if one believes that effective allocation of human resources depends upon flexibility in wage differentials, it would be possible to provide for exceptions to wage guidelines where labor supply considerations dictated them, as has actually been done.

An even more fundamental objection to wage-price controls or guidelines is that they attack symptoms rather than causes. As has been seen, monetarists argue that the only real cause of inflation is too rapid a rise in the money supply; attempting to influence wage and price decisions, therefore, is not only pernicious but irrelevant. It is probably true that a majority of economists believe either that an incomes policy is dangerous or that it is not likely to be effective. Nevertheless a number of respected members of the profession including John Kenneth Galbraith, Robert Solow, and James Tobin have professed to see some merit in the approach. No one believes that an incomes policy alone can prevent inflation or indeed that it can be helpful in the face of a substantial excess of aggregate demand. However, there is reason to believe that accompanied by appropriate monetary and fiscal policies such a policy can moderate inflationary pressures and improve the tradeoff between inflation and unemployment.

NOTES

1. There are actually two versions of the CPI, one based on the expenditure patterns of blue collar and clerical workers and the other on the patterns of all urban consumers.

2. Actually, this is a conservative assumption, as the fixed costs per unit would be expected to fall as output increases.

QUESTIONS FOR DISCUSSION

1. "Real wages depend basically on labor productivity. Therefore, the most objective basis for determining how much wages should be raised in a particular firm in a given year is the increase in output per person-hour that the firm has experienced." Explain the sense in which real wages are governed by labor productivity. Do you agree with the remainder of the statement?

2. How do you account for the substantial decline in the rate of productivity growth during the past decade and a half? What are the prospects for a resumption of the earlier trend?

3. Explain and quantify the several ways in which society has historically reaped the fruits of increased labor productivity. What would you like to see happen in this regard in the future? What do you think is most likely to happen?

4. Make the case for and the case against an incomes policy. State and defend your own position on the issue.

5. "If average employee compensation per person-hour in the economy increases at the same rate as labor productivity, workers capture all of the benefits of rising productivity even though they have not been basically responsible for it." Discuss.

9

Equity and Efficiency in the Labor Market

The Problems of Poverty and Discrimination

The vast majority of individuals in the United States derive their livelihood directly or indirectly from the labor market. Almost 90 percent of American families have at least one earner (wages or self-employment income), and somewhat over one-half have more than one. Nonetheless, for one reason or another—physical or mental incapacity, emotional problems, responsibilities for child care, lack of skills, lack of motivation—some persons cannot or will not participate in these types of gainful activity. Others try, but suffer unemployment. Moreover, among the majority of labor market participants who work steadily at full-time jobs, there is great variation in earnings, and some are employed at wages so low as not to yield a decent standard of living for them and their families. As a consequence of all these factors there is substantial inequality in family income, and some families earn incomes below the level at which society can comfortably allow its members to live.

This creates a dilemma for a democratic free-enterprise society. On the one hand, a free enterprise economy relies upon economic rewards and penalties to induce its members to exert productive effort and thus to achieve economic efficiency—getting the most out of given inputs. On the other hand, large variations in levels of living—especially when some individuals are commonly acknowledged to be living at indecently low levels—violate the egalitarian principles of a democratic society.

EQUALITY VERSUS EFFICIENCY: THE BIG TRADEOFF

Thus is created the necessity for a compromise between equality and efficiency, perhaps nowhere more eloquently analyzed and evaluated than by the late Arthur Okun in his *Equality and Efficiency: The Big Tradeoff* (1975). How one reacts to particular policy measures designed to affect the distribution of income depends, of course, not only on one's perception of its effects on each of these two variables but on the relative importance attached to each. Okun describes his own value orientation and his perception of the fact of a tradeoff in the following words:

> I have dozens of good questions about the fairness of market-determined incomes. But I don't claim to have any good answers. The appraisal is obviously a matter of personal judgment. In mine, incomes that match productivity have no ethical appeal. Equality in the distribution of incomes (allowing for voluntary leisure as a form of income) as well as in the distribution of rights would be my *ethical* preference. Abstracting from the costs and the consequences, I would prefer more equality to less and would like complete equality best of all. This preference is a simple extension of the humanistic basis for equal rights. To extend the domain of rights and give every citizen an equal share of the national income would give added recognition to the moral worth of every citizen, to the mutual respect of citizens for one another, and to the equivalent value of membership in the society for all.

> Nonetheless, my preference for one person, one income, is not nearly so strong as that for one person, one vote. Equality in material welfare has much lower benefits and far higher costs than equality of political and civil entitlements. . . . [W]hile the provision of equal political and civil rights often imposes costs on society, . . . the attempt to enforce equality of income would entail a much larger

sacrifice. In pursuing such a goal, society would forgo any opportunity to use material rewards as incentives to production. . . . Any insistence on carving the pie into equal slices would shrink the size of the pie. That fact poses the tradeoff between economic equality and economic efficiency. Insofar as inequality does serve to promote efficiency . . . I can accept some measure of it as a practicality . . . But that is a feature of the universe that I regret rather than enjoy [pp. 48-49].

The inefficiencies that inhere in income redistribution schemes lie in their administrative costs and in the adverse effects they may have on the economic incentives both of those from whom income is taken and those to whom it is given. But Okun points out that not all efforts to promote greater equality are necessarily at the expense of efficiency. In particular, improving the productive capabilities of persons with little or no skills may lead to both greater equality and greater efficiency. To the extent that labor market discrimination exists, its elimination also promotes increased efficiency as well as increased equality.

When equality and efficiency do collide, Okun argues for a compromise between them.

In such cases some equality will be sacrificed for the sake of efficiency, and some efficiency for the sake of equality. But any sacrifice of either has to be justified as a necessary means of obtaining more of the other (or possibly more of some other valued social end) [p. 88].

Not all social scientists, of course, share Okun's values, and even those who do may have differing perceptions of the effects of specific programs on both equality and efficiency. Nevertheless, any consideration of policy issues requires one to grapple with the issues that Okun raises. It also requires a familiarity with the facts relating to income distribution and the extent of labor market discrimination. Most persons would probably not regard complete income equality as the *ethical* ideal (as Okun does), but whatever ideal one holds in this regard needs to be laid up against the existing distribution of income. Moreover, in deciding upon appropriate policy measures it is clearly necessary to be able to differentiate between income differentials that reflect differences in productivity and those that result solely from labor market discrimination.

The remainder of this chapter, therefore, provides a factual foundation for our subsequent discussion of human resource development policy (Chapter 10), income maintenance policy (Chapters 11-13), and antidiscrimination policy (Chapter 14). We examine first the distribution of income in the United States, then turn to the definition and measurement of poverty, and conclude with an examination of the evidence relating to the extent of discrimination based on race and sex.

INCOME DISTRIBUTION

In March of each year the CPS collects information on the amount and sources of money income of the members of its representative national sample of households. The resulting data permit us to know what proportions of families and of unrelated individuals fall within specific intervals of income, or alternatively, what proportion of all income is received by units in various segments (e.g., deciles, quintiles, etc.) of the income distribution. The data in Table 9.1 show one such distribution for 1981. In that year median family income was $22,388. One-fifth of all families had incomes under $10,900, while another one-fifth had incomes of more than $37,500. At the apex of the pyramid, 1 family out of 20 enjoyed an income of $58,500 or more. This top 5 percent of the families received almost as large a proportion of the total income as the 40 percent of the families at the bottom of the distribution.

The data appear to be completely straightforward, yet their evaluation requires attention to a number of considerations. First of all, data obtained from household surveys tend to understate certain types of income—especially that derived from property. When adjustments are made on the basis of other sources of information, average income rises by as much as 10 percent, the share of the top 5 percent of recipients increases, and changes occur in the mean income of certain demographic groups—most notably a rise in the income of families headed by persons 65 or older (Radner, 1981: 16-17).

Second, it is not clear how the extent of income inequality should be measured. Boulding (1975: 17) has demonstrated that among several different sets of unequal numbers, alternative measures of inequality produce different rankings of the degree of inequality. Actually, the most widely used measure for this

TABLE 9.1   Income Level and Percentage of Aggregate
             Income Received by Each Fifth and Top
             5 Percent of Families, 1981

Income Group	Percentage of Income	Level of Income (in dollars)
Lowest fifth	5.0	10,918
Second fifth	11.3	18,552
Third fifth	17.4	26,528
Fourth fifth	24.4	37,457
Top fifth	41.9	–
Top 5 percent	15.4	58,554

SOURCE: Statistical Abstract of the United States (1983: 435).

purpose is the Gini coefficient, which is derived from the so-called Lorenz curve illustrated in Figure 9.1.

The horizontal axis of the graph measures cumulative percentages of households arranged from those with the lowest to those with the highest incomes. The vertical axis measures the cumulative percentage of total income. If all families had exactly the same income, a given percentage of families would represent exactly the same percentage of total income, so that all of the points on the Lorenz curve would lie on the solid diagonal line. At the other extreme, complete inequality (where, say, one family received all of the income) would result in a Lorenz curve that follows the bottom and right-hand borders of the graph. Thus, the greater the bow in the curve from the diagonal, the greater the inequality. The Gini coefficient, which conceptually ranges between 0 (complete equality) and 1 (complete inequality) is calculated by dividing the area under the bow (A in the diagram) by the total area under the diagonal (A+B).

Equity versus equality. The third, and by far the most difficult problem in evaluating the distribution of income in the United States lies in deciding how much income inequality is desirable or is to be expected. "Despite their phonetic similarity and philological connections" (Bronfenbrenner, 1973: 10), the terms equality and equity mean quite different things. The number of Americans who would *oppose* an *equitable* distribution of income must be at least as small as the number who would *favor* an *equal* distribution. But,

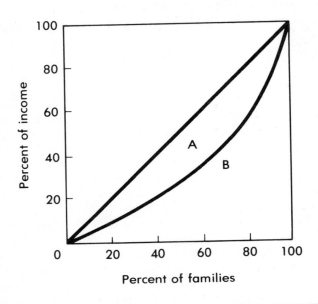

Figure 9.1:   A Lorenz Curve

while a more equitable distribution of income is generally construed to mean a more equal distribution, just how much equality equity requires is surely subject to wide disagreement.

This is an issue that facts cannot resolve; nevertheless some of the *sources* of inequality in the distribution of family income need to be kept in mind in addressing the equity issue. A sizable portion—perhaps as much as one-third—of the inequality in income that is measured in any one year reflects age differences that would exist even if lifetime incomes were completely equal. In 1980 the mean income of families headed by an individual under 24 years of age was $14,696, as compared with $30,279 for families in which the head was 45-54. Moreover, even aside from age differences, an accounting period as short as a year tends to magnify inequalities because of transitory windfalls or temporary periods of adversity that would average out over longer periods.

Inequalities of family income may also result from variation among families in the number of income-earners, a matter that is at least to some extent subject to choice. One-earner families in 1980 had an average income of $17,724, as compared with $23,746 for two-earner families and $35,414 for those with four or more earners. *Family size* also makes a difference from the standpoint of the welfare implications of incomes of different levels. From this point of view the data on family income understate the degree of inequality in economic welfare; while total income bears a moderately positive relationship with family size (between two and five members), per capita income falls continuously as family size increases—from $10,297 in two-member families to $3,511 in those with seven or more persons.

Even allowing for the kinds of factors that have been discussed, there remain very large differences in incomes to individuals that result from differences in extent of property ownership and differences in labor market status and experience. Income-yielding wealth is particularly unequally distributed. The richest 1 percent of the population owns over one-half of all stocks and bonds and about one-fourth of all assets. About half of all property income goes to the top 5 percent of income recipients.

As wages and salaries account for about three-fifths of all personal income, it is clear that the labor market accounts for a major portion of income inequality. Among year-round full-time male workers, median earnings in 1978 were $15,730, but 14 percent earned less than $9,000 and 16 percent earned $25,000 or more. Including women workers would increase the spread considerably. Among them the median was $9,350; 16 percent earned less than $6,000 and 13 percent earned $15,000 or more.

It should be kept in mind that the data on income distribution include cash transfer payments such as social security and welfare benefits (but not in-kind transfers like food stamps). On the other hand, they do not reflect the effects of taxes. The best available evidence suggests that when all types of taxes are considered, the tax burden is roughly proportional to income through most of the income range (except at the very highest levels) and thus has relatively little effect on the distribution of income (Pechman and Okner, 1974). However, because transfer payments go disproportionately to low income groups, they have a major effect.

Considering only income and employment taxes, Okner (1975: 65) calculated Gini coefficients for distributions of 1966 income (1) before taxes and (cash) transfers, (2) after transfers, and (3) after transfers and taxes—.4595, .4155, and .3998 respectively.

Thus, the reduction in income inequality attributable to transfers was $(.4595-.4155)/.4595 = 9.6$ percent, and the total reduction attributable to transfers and taxes was $(.4595-.3998)/.4595 = 13.0$ percent. Transfer payments, in other words, accounted for about three-fourths of the total reduction in inequality (i.e., $9.6/13.0$) while taxes accounted for one-fourth. Transfers were found to be particularly important in reducing income inequality among the aged. In two-person families headed by an individual 65 or older, the pretax and pretransfer Gini coefficient was reduced by 29.3 percent by transfer payments and by 32.5 percent by transfers and taxes combined.

From the foregoing, it is clear that income distribution data like those in Table 9.1 show less inequality than would prevail in the absence of government intervention. According to Hoagland's (1982: 63) estimate of the distribution of pretax and pretransfer income, if only market-determined income were considered, the share going to families in the lowest quintile in 1980 would have been 0.6 percent and the share of the top quintile would have been 48.2 percent. After taxes and transfers (in-kind as well as cash) the corresponding percentages become 6.5 and 39.8.

The Bureau of the Census has been producing data on the distribution of income since 1947, and over that period of time there has been little change in measured inequality. There is reason to believe, however, that the distribution was somewhat more equal after than before World War II with a reduction in the share going to the top 5 or 10 percent of the families but no change in the share going to the lower half (Lampman, 1973: 83).

In any case, Lampman notes that Americans have a high degree of tolerance for the degree of inequality that prevails. He quotes James Tobin as follows:

> Americans accept and approve a large measure of inequality; the differential earnings of effort, skill, foresight, and enterprise are seen as deserved, just so long as the earnings were legitimately and fairly won.

It seems fairly clear that as a society we are less interested in achieving greater equality of income distribution than in making certain that there is a floor below which we do not allow individuals to fall. This brings us, then, to a consideration of the poverty problem.

THE PROBLEM OF POVERTY

The definition and measurement of poverty. A war on poverty requires identification of the enemy. It was not until the declaration of that war in 1964 by the Johnson administration that the United States had an official definition of poverty. Developed by the Social Security Administration, the measure was based on economy food budgets for families of different sizes. These budgets had been prepared by the Department of Agriculture to represent the minimum expenditures that "would supply all essential nutrients using food readily purchasable in the U.S. market." To arrive at the "poverty line," the food budget was multiplied by three because a 1955 survey had indicated that expenditures for food averaged about one-third of family income. The resulting poverty thresholds for families of different sizes are updated each year to reflect changes in the Consumer Price Index. For a family of four, the poverty threshold in 1982 was $9,862.

The poverty index and the data that emerge from its application are subject to a number of criticisms. On the one hand, it has been argued that official data overstate the extent of poverty because they are based only on money income and thus do not include in-kind transfer payments such as food stamps and Medicaid benefits. Adjustments for such benefits can be made, but it is not clear how the benefits should be valued; including them at market value, for example, would mean that a destitute family would be pulled out of poverty by an expensive operation!

On the other hand, there are reasons to believe that the official measures provide an unrealistically low measure of the extent of poverty (Schulz, 1980: 35-37). The food budgets on which the thresholds are based were not necessarily intended to be adequate for long periods of time. Furthermore, the factor of three by which allowances for food were multiplied is somewhat arbitrary; a survey made in the early 1960s by the BLS indicated that urban families spent approximately one-fourth, rather than one-third, of their incomes for food.

Finally, and most fundamentally, it is questionable whether *any* definition of poverty that is expressed in terms of an *absolute* level of real income makes sense. Poverty, after all, is a relative matter; families who are today in the bottom fifth of the income distribution probably live better in absolute terms than those in the middle of the income distribution in 1800, yet this does little to mitigate the sense of deprivation that they feel and that their more fortunate contemporaries recognize. It is worth noting in this connection that since 1960 the official poverty threshold has dropped from a little over one-half to somewhat over one-third of median family income.

As a substitute for the existing system of defining and measuring the extent of poverty, the University of Wisconsin Institute on Poverty has proposed a four-tiered set of standards using as a reference point the "prevailing family standard," which would be defined as the median actual expenditures of a two-parent family of four. The "social minimum" would then be one-half, the "lower living standard" would be two-thirds, and the "social abundance standard" would be one-and-one-half times the prevailing family standard. Adjustments would be made for differences in size and type of family (Watts, 1980).

Because of the limitations described above, it would seem to be unwise to use the official statistics uncritically as a measure of the extent of poverty or even as indicators of trends over time in the number of "poor" people. However, they do serve to point up variations in the incidence of poverty among demographic subgroups of the population.

Progress in eliminating poverty. A useful set of adjustments to the official poverty statistics has been made by Danziger and Plotnick (1982), which allow a reasonably good assessment of the degree of progress that has been made in the war on poverty. They calculate the number of persons in poverty between 1965 and 1978 using four income concepts and a relative as well as an absolute measure of poverty. The income measures are (1) pretransfer income, (2) prewelfare income, (3) posttransfer income, and (4) adjusted income. The first of these is pretax income exclusive of any transfers; the second includes social insurance transfers (e.g., unemployment compensation) but not cash welfare payments; the third, which is the official measure, includes all cash transfers; and the fourth takes account of both taxes and in-kind welfare benefits, and also adjusts for the underreporting of certain types of income. For each of the first three income measures, the *relative* poverty line was computed by maintaining the same relationship to median family income as prevailed in 1965.

Table 9.2 shows the percentage of the population in poverty in 1965 and 1978 according to each of the eight criteria. Note that according to the official measure (posttransfer income) the poverty population declined from 16 to 11 percent over the

TABLE 9.2 The Incidence of Poverty Among Persons, 1965 and 1978 (in percentages)

Income Measure	Absolute		Relative	
	1965	*1978*	*1965*	*1978*
Pretransfer	21.3	20.2	21.3	23.9
Prewelfare	16.3	12.6	16.3	16.5
Posttransfer	15.6	11.4	15.6	15.5
Adjusted	12.1	4.1*	–	–

SOURCE: Danziger and Plotnick (1982: 40).
*Figure is for 1980.

13-year period. (If one uses 1960 as the starting point, the decline is more impressive, for the proportion of the population in poverty in that year was 22 percent.) Between 1978 and 1982, however, the downward trend in the incidence of poverty was reversed as the result of the deep recession and the curtailment of welfare expenditures. The poverty rate was 14 percent in 1981 and 15 percent in 1982.

Virtually none of the decline between 1965 and 1978 can be attributed to a change in the way the market distributed incomes, for the incidence of pretransfer poverty was virtually as great at the end of the period as at the beginning. When in-kind as well as cash transfers are included in income, the poverty rate declined from 12 to 4 percent—a decrease of two-thirds. Thus, most of the decline in poverty over the period is attributable to the fact that transfer payments per recipient increased considerably more than real average family income.

Another way to look at the data in Table 9.2 is to examine, for 1978, the reduction in the incidence of poverty attributable to the several forms of transfer payments. Social insurance benefits reduce the poverty rate from 20.2 to 12.6 percent, thus removing from poverty about 38 percent of the pretransfer poor. Cash welfare benefits cause an additional drop of 1.2 percentage points, or about 6 percent of the poor. The final adjustment reduces the poverty rate to 4 percent (in 1980), removing an additional 36 percent from poverty. The major element (but not all) of this adjustment is the addition of in-kind welfare benefits, which are estimated to pull about 28 percent of the original poor above the poverty line. Thus, transfers of all kinds are responsible for shifting out of poverty almost three-fourths (72 percent) of those who would be poor on the basis of market incomes alone.

The very low (4 percent) adjusted poverty rate is the basis for the claim by some that the scourge of poverty has been all but eliminated. However, when one keeps in mind how the poverty lines are obtained, this seems to be an unduly optimistic view. In particular, it is instructive that when poverty is defined in relative terms, its incidence on the basis of market incomes was more than 10 percent greater in 1978 than in 1965. Even when one includes all cash transfers—which have had such a dramatic effect in reducing absolute poverty—relative poverty remains about as great as it was more than decade ago.

Variation in the incidence of poverty. As would be expected, there is a very great degree of variation in the incidence of poverty among demographic subsets of the population. The most dramatic differences are those by race and by family structure. In 1980, when the official poverty rate for the total population was 13.0 percent, the rate was 10.2 percent among whites and 32.5 percent among blacks. For persons living alone the rate was almost exactly twice as high as for those living in families—22.9 percent versus 11.5 percent. In families headed by a woman, the rate was 36.7 percent, as compared with 7.4 percent in families with male heads. Number of family members is also a critical variable. The poverty rate increases monotonically from 8.6 percent in two-person families to 27.9 percent in families with seven or more members.

Contrary to what seems to be generally believed, the rate among persons 65 and older is not substantially greater than for the population as a whole—15.7 versus 13.0 percent. This is largely a reflection of the important role played by social security old age benefits, for on the basis of market incomes alone the poverty rate of the aged approaches 50 percent. Even when transfers are included, the poverty rate among aged individuals living alone is far above average—24.4 percent for men and 32.3 percent for women. Families headed by young people (15 to 24 years of age) have a poverty rate more than twice as high as the average for all families.

Finally, it comes as no surprise that there is a pronounced relationship between educational attainment of family heads and the incidence of poverty. About one-fourth of all families headed by a person with less than eight years of education are in poverty, as contrasted with 8 percent of families headed by a high school graduate and 4 percent where the family head has had some college.

There is another, and from some points of view better, way of answering the question, "Who are the poor?" That is by identifying those groups who are most likely to be in poverty on the basis of their market incomes—that is, prior to transfers (Institute for Research on Poverty, 1981-1982). Among the almost 21 million poor households whose market incomes put them in poverty (1976), the largest component—46.8 percent—are those headed by a person 65 or older. The next largest single group are households headed by a disabled individual—12 percent of the total. Households headed by a woman with a pre-school-age child make up an additional 7 percent of the total. These three categories, consisting of households in which the heads are unlikely to be working or even to be expected to work, together account for almost two-thirds of the total.

An additional 21 percent of poor households are headed by persons who work less than full time, and 7 percent have heads who are full-time workers. Finally, 5 percent are headed by students, whose poverty is generally destined to be short-lived and in many cases results solely because interfamily transfers or loans are not included in measured income. Thus, it would appear that conventional labor market policies are potentially relevant to only a minority of all poverty-stricken families.

LABOR MARKET DISCRIMINATION

Among the most obvious and persistent characteristics of the system of rewards that prevail in the American labor market are the inferior positions of blacks relative to whites and of women relative to men. Among full-time, full-year wage and salary workers, the earnings of blacks are four-fifths as high as those of whites; the earnings of women are three-fifths as high as men's. From a policy perspective, it is important to know to what extent these differentials reflect differences in productivity and to what extent they reflect labor market discrimination. Economists have given a great deal of attention to this issue in recent years, and it is useful to summarize the generalizations that seem to be warranted by their research findings.

The meaning of labor market discrimination. The fact that two categories of individuals are accorded different rewards in the labor market is obviously not in itself indicative of discrimination. If on average they differ in regard to education, training, health, or vigor, one would expect corresponding differentials in rewards just as one expects such differentials based upon individual differences *within* each of the categories. Moreover, if, for whatever reason, the members of one of the categories systematically ignore more favorable labor market opportunities, the less favorable rewards that result cannot be attributed to labor market discrimination. In either of these cases, however, the explanation could lie with discrimination elsewhere in the society—for example, differences in educational opportunities that produce differentials in productivity, or differences in socialization processes that are responsible for different labor market "choices."

Neoclassical economists like Gary Becker and Kenneth Arrow have developed elegant definitions and models of discrimination, and dual labor market and radical economists have offered competing formulations (Marshall, 1974). For our purposes a simple definition will suffice—labor market discrimination exists when an identifiable group of individuals are systematically rewarded less favorably than others and there are no corresponding differences in productivity. Differential rewards may be in the form of hiring, compensation, promotion, or any other condition of employment.

This definition, it will be noted, makes *motive* irrelevant. The discriminating employer may have a "taste for discrimination," to use Becker's (1971) term; may mistakenly believe that there are indeed differentials in productivity that require differential rewards; or may simply be following mindlessly patterns that have become traditional. In any case, the problem lies in the *behavior* of employing establishments and not in the characteristics of the category of individuals against whom the discrimination prevails.

It should also be noted that this definition makes discrimination exceedingly difficult to document. The way in which economists have generally approached the question has been to see whether, in a multivariate framework, race or sex differences in some aspect of labor market experience or status (e.g., average hourly earnings, annual earnings, unemployment, occupational status) can be completely explained by differences in characteristics that are known to bear a relationship to productivity (e.g, education, training, health, employment experience, etc.). To the extent that there are residual unexplained differences, the existence of discrimination is inferred. In view of the large number of characteristics that can affect productivity and for which good measures do not normally exist, it is hardly surprising that most careful researchers have acknowledged that unexplained race or sex differences that they have found do not necessarily *prove* the existence of discrimination.

Racial differences in labor market experience. In virtually every aspect of labor market experience, blacks fare less well than whites. They tend to be disproportionately concentrated in lower-level occupations. Almost one in three is a service worker or a laborer as compared with less than one in five whites; the proportion of black professional and managerial workers is less than one-third that of whites (7 percent versus 24 percent). The unemployment rate among blacks is generally at least twice that of whites. As a consequence of these factors, wage rates and annual earnings of blacks are substantially lower than those of whites. These racial differences in earnings are greater among men than women. For full-time, full-year wage and salary workers, the black/white median annual earnings ratio in 1978 was .77 for men and .92 for women. In some major occupation categories (e.g., clerical, operatives, and service), black women had average annual earnings about as high or higher than those of white women.

Blacks suffer numerous disadvantages relative to whites prior to entering the labor market, and it would be surprising if these were not reflected in their employment experience even in the absence of discrimination in the labor market. However, despite the difficulties in generating conclusive statistical evidence on racial discrimination, there appears to be no reasonable doubt about its existence—which, of course, should hardly be surprising to anyone who has any knowledge at all about American society.

The availability during the past decade of rich longitudinal data banks such as the National Longitudinal Surveys of Labor Market Experience (NLS; Parnes, 1975) and the Panel Survey of Income Dynamics (PSID; Morgan, 1975) has increased the confidence with which this assertion can be made. They have provided not only a large number of measures of labor market experience, but— what is more important—measures of psychological variables related to productivity (e.g., intelligence, initiative, commitment to the work ethic) that can be used as statistical controls in multivariate analyses in order to isolate "pure" racial differences.

Studies in which such controls have been introduced (in addition to the more conventional human capital variables) do not eliminate racial differentials in favor of whites in wages, occupational status, incidence of unemployment, or upward occupational mobility (Daymont and Andrisani, 1983). This evidence is consistent with the conclusion drawn by Stanley Masters (1975) on the basis of his study of black-white income differentials among males. Masters's analyses, based on census and survey data, use years of education and scores on the Armed Forces Qualifying Test as "proxies" for productivity. They lead to the conclusion that the major portion of the earnings differential between blacks and whites results from differences in productivity, but that at least 30 percent is unexplained by these variables and is presumably the result of labor market discrimination.

It would seem unwise to draw any conclusion about what proportion of the difference in labor market status and experience of whites and blacks is attributable to labor market discrimination. Different studies have produced different estimates depending upon the particular dependent variable used, the sample of individuals studied, and the explanatory variables used in the analysis. However, to reserve judgment about the *existence* of race discrimination pushes scholarly caution beyond realistic bounds.

There is evidence that the extent of discrimination has lessened over the past decade or two, presumably as the result of the civil rights movements, including the antidiscrimination efforts of government. Daymont (1981a, 1981b) has shown that even when one controls for labor market conditions and the improved human capital characteristics of black men relative to white men, there was improvement between the mid 1960s and the mid 1970s in the earnings of blacks relative to whites. Masters's data likewise show that the trend toward narrowing income differentials in the period following World War II increased significantly after passage of the Civil Rights Act of 1965.

Sex differences in labor market experience. The occupational distributions of men and women differ far more than do the distributions of blacks and whites. About four-fifths of all women in the labor force are employed in ten categories of work, each of which is predominantly female—nurses, teachers, librarians, social workers, salespersons, health technicians, service workers, and textile and clothing workers. There has been little change in these stereotypically women's jobs over long periods of time, although the effects of the women's liberation movement are discernible in recent years in the increasing proportion of women in traditionally male strongholds. During the decade of the 1970s, for instance, as the number of lawyers almost doubled and the number of physicians increased by more than one-half, the proportion of women grew from 5 percent to 14 percent in the former case and from 9 percent to 13 percent in the latter. As the number of computer operators more than tripled, the proportion of women in this occupation jumped from 29 percent to 55 percent.

Not only are women concentrated in occupational categories characterized by relatively low wages, but they tend to earn less than men even when they are employed in the same occupational category. In this case, however, the earnings differentials are much smaller—perhaps in the neighborhood of 10 percent, as compared with 40 percent when all full-time men and women workers are considered together.

It is easier to detail these differences in the labor market positions of men and women than to offer completely confident explanations for why they occur. Sex discrimination is even more difficult to document than race discrimination, as it is less clear in the case of sex than of race that differences in occupational distribution result from employer practices rather than from the educational and job decisions that the "disadvantaged" have been conditioned to make long before their entrance into the job market. It is clear that there is pervasive sex discrimination in the entire culture, and that much of it is benign in intent however damaging it may be in effect. Every time a doting father brings home a nurse's set for his young daughter and a doctor's set for his young son, he is practicing sex discrimination that may have significant implications for the later labor market activity of his offspring.

Nevertheless, when differences in occupational distribution are ignored and earnings are related to determinants of productivity, the disadvantage of women relative to men is even greater than that of blacks relative to whites. Duncan et al. (1983: 135-150) have looked at this issue utilizing the rich PSID data base, which affords the opportunity to control for a wide variety of variables that are presumed to be related to productivity, including education, duration and continuity of work experience, self-imposed restrictions on work, and absenteeism. All of these factors explain less than one-half of the wage gap between men and women, suggesting to the researchers that "we need to turn more attention to the alternative explanations of socialization effects and discrimination."

As in the case of racial differentials, it is hard to avoid the conclusion that at least some of the differences in the rewards garnered by employed men and women result from labor market discrimination. For one thing, there is no reason to believe that the sex distinctions that have been so firmly rooted in the culture affect the personnel decisions and choices made by employers any less than they affect the educational and occupational choices of women. For another, the disparity in pay between men and women in the same occupations (with productivity measures controlled) cannot very well be explained on the basis of culturally conditioned occupational choices.

POLICY OPTIONS

There are three policy approaches to the problems that have been considered in this chapter. The most unambiguous is to attempt to root out whatever discrimination prevails in the labor market; successfully doing so eliminates inequities at the same time that it promotes greater efficiency. This policy measure is described in Chapter 14.

Beyond this, there are basically two means of achieving greater equality in the income distribution. One is to increase equality of *opportunity*, largely by improving the productive capabilities of individuals whose earnings are low or nonexistent. This is the role of human resource development policies that are considered in the next chapter. The second is to operate on the income distribution directly through income maintenance (transfer) programs, the subject of Chapters 11-13. The two approaches are clearly not mutually exclusive alternatives, for, as we have seen, a large proportion of the pretransfer poor are not expected to work.

QUESTIONS FOR DISCUSSION

1. Explain the issue of "equality versus efficiency" in the labor market. To what extent is there a necessary trade-off between these two values, and to what extent may they be complements? To the extent that there is a trade-off, how does your value orientation compare with that of Arthur Okun?

2. Comment on the difference between the concepts "equity" and "equality." What is your personal view on how much and what kinds of inequality are "equitable?"

3. In your view, what is the most realistic way of defining "poverty?" In the light of your response, how do you evaluate the official measure of the extent of poverty in the United States? What modifications, if any, would you recommend?

4. What would you suggest as an appropriate definition of labor market discrimination? Can you devise a definitive empirical test of its existence? How do you assess the empirical evidence relating to (a) race, and (b) sex discrimination in the labor market?

5. What is the strongest case you can make for the desirability of eradicating poverty? What about its feasibility as a policy objective? Given a commitment to the objective, what combination of policy measures do you recommend?

10

Human Resource Development Policy

Human resource development embraces all the processes that create skills and know-how relevant to success in the labor market. These processes are numerous, varied, and only poorly understood. The *institutions* that play a role in human resource development are also numerous and are not readily classifiable. From many points of view the most fundamental is the family, but except for acknowledging this fact we will have little more to say about the family's role or about ways in which it might be made more effective.

For our purposes, the important institutions of human resource development can conveniently, even if somewhat arbitrarily, be classified into three major categories: (1) "regular" schooling; (2) "adult" education and training, exclusive of federally financed employment and training ("manpower") programs; and (3) the federal employment and training programs. The first of these categories includes primary, secondary, and higher education; the second and third together embrace all other education and training, and are separated only because of the relatively recent appearance of the latter and of the major role played in it by the federal government.

"REGULAR" EDUCATION[1]

We can speak rather confidently about the extent and character of the education and training that takes place in the "regular" school system, for the National Center for Educational Statistics in the United States Department of Education collects and publishes current data on formal education in both public and private schools.

Elementary and secondary education. About 46 million students between the ages of 5 and 17 were enrolled in public and private schools in 1981—almost one-third of whom were in grades 9 through 12. Private schools accounted for slightly more than one-tenth of total enrollments—about the same proportion at both the primary and secondary levels.

Public primary and secondary education is financed largely by state and local governments. Of a total expenditure of $12 billion in 1982, only 8.6 percent came from federal funds. The role of the federal government has been largely restricted to providing financial assistance to schools in areas with high concentrations of low income families or in areas burdened by federal activities (e.g., military installations); strengthening instruction in specific subjects important to national defense (e.g., science, mathematics, foreign languages); helping to finance vocational education; and improving equality of educational opportunity for minorities and for women.

A veritable educational revolution has occurred in the United States during this century (Mare, 1979). The average (median) person born in its early years completed only 8.6 years of schooling; those born at midcentury achieved an average of 12.8 years. Whereas in 1910 about three-fifths of all persons 5 to 19 were in school, by the mid-1970s the proportion had reached about nine-tenths. Between 1940 and 1980 the proportion of persons 25 years and older with less than a high school education dropped continuously—from 76 percent at the beginning of the period to 45 percent in 1970 and 30 percent in 1981. By the end of the period three-fourths of all 17-year-olds were graduating from high school and nearly half of the graduates were going on to college.

There were other signs of progress as well. Between 1966 and 1981 the proportion of public school teachers with graduate or six-year professional degrees rose from 15 to 45 percent at the elementary level and from 32 to 54 percent at the secondary level. Expressed in terms of dollars of constant (1980) purchasing power, total expenditures on public primary and secondary education rose between 1960 and 1980 from $41.2 billion to $96.0 billion. This represented almost a doubling on the basis of per capita of total population (from $230 to $424) and exactly a doubling on the basis of per-pupil expenditure (from $1,247 to $2,494). Average teachers' salaries rose by 22 percent, as compared with a 5 percent increase in average weekly earnings of production and nonsupervisory workers in private industry.

Nevertheless, public education in the early 1980s appeared to be in deep trouble, and had been for some time. The remarkable quantitative improvements were accompanied by—and perhaps even helped to produce—serious qualitative deficiencies. Two reports issued in 1983 highlighted indicators of its inadequacies. With respect to results, the first of these (National Commission on Excellence in Education) called attention to the facts that (1) 13 percent of 17-year-olds are functional illiterates; (2) on 19 academic achievement tests administered in 21 countries, American youth were in last place on seven and in first or second place on none; and average Scholastic Aptitude Test (SAT) scores of college-bound seniors dropped by 50 points on the verbal component and 36 points on the math component between 1963 and 1980.

With respect to the content of education and the character of the educational process, the second report (Goodlad, 1983), which was based on an eight-year study that included systematic classroom observation in 13 communities, noted that the average instructional day in a junior or senior high school includes 150 minutes of talking, of which only 7 are initiated by students; that the extent of student involvement declines as they advance from grade to grade; and that there is in most classrooms an "emotionally flat" atmosphere that causes students to "put their minds on hold."

The most dramatic and eloquent indictment was that of the National Commission on Excellence in Education (1983):

> Our nation is at risk. The educational foundations of our society are presently being eroded by a rising tide of mediocrity. If an unfriendly foreign power had attempted to impose on America the mediocre educational performance that exists today we might well have conceived it as an act of war.

The commission's principal recommendations were for (1) more demanding high school graduation requirements, including three years of math, science, and social studies; one semester of computer science; and (for the college-bound) two years of foreign language; (2) higher achievement standards for graduation and for admission to four-year colleges; (3) increased time for basic academic studies, either through a reallocation of existing time or through a longer school day or school year (noting that the average in the United States is 180 six-hour days as compared with 220 eight-hour days in Great Britain); (4) better training and pay, and 11-month contracts, for teachers; and (5) increased citizen involvement in schools.

A third report, by the Carnegie Foundation for the Advancement of Teaching (1983), was somewhat less pessimistic. It suggested that the worst was behind us; that public concern in the late 1970s had helped to produce some modest improvements in test scores and high school curricula and a lifting of college admission standards. The report observed that schools had met a number of new challenges, serving more students from different racial and cultural backgrounds, educating many handicapped students who had previously been excluded, and developing new experimental programs. Nevertheless, it acknowledged a remaining "large, even alarming gap between school achievement and the task to be accomplished."

The need to upgrade teaching in elementary and secondary schools is almost universally recognized but there is less consensus on how this should be done. The problem has been of long standing, and there is some evidence that it has become more serious in recent years. In 1973 high school seniors intending to enter colleges of education had SAT scores on the verbal and math components 59 points below the national average; by 1980 the gap had widened to 80 points. One proposed remedy, in addition to raising teachers' salaries generally, is to introduce salary differentials based on merit rather than solely on the basis of seniority and advanced degrees. However, teacher organizations tend to be fearful that this type of salary system would simply allow implementation of favoritism rather than leading to more effective teaching. A perhaps even more obvious need is for differentials by field of specialization that reflect the realities of the labor market.

More radical proposals for change are designed to force public schools to compete with other educational institutions and/or among themselves. These include tuition tax credits that would, in effect, allow parents to send their children to private schools in part at public expense, and voucher systems, which would provide parents with educational "chits" that they could use at the school of their choice. One problem with these proposals is their uncertain constitutionality as applied to church-affiliated schools. But in addition, critics of these "market" approaches—and especially the investment tax credit—argue that they would lead to greater inequality of educational opportunity by encouraging flight from the public schools of precisely those families who are sufficiently concerned and active to press for reform, leaving behind larger concentrations of the disadvantaged.

The most effective strategy for educational reform will doubtless continue to be debated during the remainder of the decade. One of the issues will be whether the view of the Reagan administration on the appropriate role of the federal government shall prevail. After two decades of increasing federal involvement aimed especially at equalizing educational opportunity, President Reagan argued that education should be returned to the exclusive control of the state and local governments. Total federal budget authority (in real terms) was to drop 43 percent between 1981 and 1983 and by an additional 26 percent between 1983 and 1985. As of the end of 1983 the proposal had not been implemented.

Vocational education. The vocational curriculum at the secondary level is ostensibly the most relevant to preparation for employment, yet studies that have assessed the effectiveness of this curriculum as compared with the general curriculum have not produced evidence of its general superiority for those students who do not go on to college (Grasso and Shea, 1976). Specifically, such studies show that males enrolled in vocational programs are neither less likely to drop out of school nor more likely after graduation to do better in the labor market than comparable students in the general curriculum. On the other hand, it appears that female students in business and office vocational programs are more likely to graduate and to obtain higher-paying jobs than women in the general curriculum, although the advantage tends to disappear after 10 years of labor market experience.

Higher education. At the beginning of academic year 1981-1982, 12 million persons were enrolled in institutions of higher learning, about one-third of whom were in two-year colleges or degree-granting vocational-technical institutes. Total enrollment was more than three times as large as in 1960 as the result of two factors—the baby boom cohort's achievement of college age and increases in age-specific enrollment rates. Between 1960 and 1981 enrollment rates increased by 11 percentage points for 18-to-19-year-olds (from 38 to 49 percent), by 12 points for those

20-21 years old (from 19 to 32 percent, and by 7 points for the 22-24-year age group (from 9 to 16 percent). In relative terms the increase for older age groups was even larger—from 4.9 to 9.0 percent for those 25 to 29 and from 2.4 to 6.9 from those 30 to 34.

Enrollment increases over the past two decades have been particularly pronounced among women and blacks, causing the disparity between the sexes to disappear and the disparity between whites and blacks to shrink. In 1960 women comprised about one-third of all college students; by 1981 they represented one-half. Over the same period, the proportion of black college students rose from slightly under 6 percent to about 10 percent. There was also an influx of women into areas of specialization that have traditionally been strongholds of men. Women's share of the total number of degrees rose from 5 to 23 percent in medicine, from 1 to 13 percent in dentistry, from 2 to 30 percent in law, and from 0.3 to 8.7 percent in engineering. Of the total number of two-year degrees, the proportion going to women rose between 1970 and 1981 from 44 to 54 percent. The rise was from 28 to 40 percent in natural science, from 36 to 50 percent in data processing, from 54 to 64 percent in business, and from 6 to 26 percent in police and corrections work.

Total expenditures of institutions of higher education amounted to $73 billion in academic year 1981-1982, of which 14 percent came from the federal government, 31 percent from state governments, 2.5 percent from local governments, and the remaining 52 percent from other sources—largely tuition payments and private school endowments. Governmental funds financed four-fifths of the expenditures of public institutions, but only one-fifth of those of private institutions. The private schools, incidentally, accounted for about one-fifth of all enrollments in higher education.

Institutions of higher education produce a large number of potential incumbents of high level occupations each year. In 1980 there were almost one million bachelor's degrees conferred and one-half million degrees below the bachelor's level. At the postbaccalaureate level there were about 300 thousand master's degrees, 33 thousand doctorates, 15 thousand degrees in medicine, 5 thousand in dentistry, and 36 thousand in law.

A college degree has long been recognized as a ticket of admission to the more attractive and higher-paying jobs offered by the labor market. Among all employed civilians 25 to 64 years of age in March 1983, two-thirds of those with 4 or more years of college were in managerial or professional occupations, as compared with one-eighth of those with only 12 years of education. Median income of males with 4 years of college was $22,173 in 1980, 52 percent above the median for men with only a high school diploma. For women the differential was even larger—$10,119 versus $6,080, or 66 percent.

However, largely as the result of increasing supplies of college graduates and of some slowing down in the rate of growth of managerial and professional jobs, the relative income advantage of college graduates has declined in recent years and the economic return to higher education, calculated by the methods described in Chapter 2, has declined (Freeman, 1976).

Nonetheless, as the foregoing figures demonstrate, the absolute advantage is still great. Moreover, as Haveman and Wolfe (1983) have pointed out, there are a number of advantages of schooling both to the individual and to society that are not captured by earnings differentials and that are thus not reflected in calculations of rates of return. From the individual's perspective these include the greater fringe benefits and better working conditions that are available in the jobs to which higher education permits access. Improvement in the quality of leisure and the quality of the choices that an individual makes must also be considered, as well as the benefits that are reflected in the development of one's children. Haveman and Wolfe conclude that conventional benefit-cost estimates have captured only about three-fifths of the benefits conferred by higher education.

"ADULT" EDUCATION AND TRAINING[2]

No one knows how much education and training activity takes place after formal schooling ends. Recent estimates of the number of persons engaged in such activity have ranged from 12 percent to virtually 100 percent of the population 17 years of age and older, depending on the breadth of the definition of learning experience. The narrowest estimate, based on NCES statistics, counts only part-time instruction in schools. The broadest, based on sample surveys, includes any type of learning experience, including a trip to the library for needed information.

Not only is it difficult to know what to include, but there is no commonly accepted term that embraces the wide variety of education and training activities that can contribute to the development of job skills once formal education ceases. For convenience, let us use "adult education and training" for this purpose. The most careful and comprehensive recent catalogue of these kinds of activities has been prepared by Paul Barton (1982), who describes the "organized learning" activities in which adults engage during their working lives (i.e., after the termination of formal education). The essential criterion for inclusion, in other words, is the "*resumption* of education after a substantial interval." We should note, however, that following this definition leads us to some double counting, because some of the adult education that Barton describes takes place in institutions of higher learning among workers who return to school some time after entering the labor market.

The principal components of this adult education and training network, together with the best available estimates of the number of individuals annually served by each, are the following: (1) adult education in elementary and secondary schools (1.6 million); (2) adult participation in postsecondary vocational or business schools (1.5 million), two-year colleges and vocational institutes (2.8 million), and four-year colleges (3.3 million); (3) classroom education and training in private industry, including tuition-aid programs (6.3 million); (4) military training (1.6 million); (5) armed forces voluntary education programs (0.6 million); (6) other employee training programs offered by government employers (1.6 million); (7) apprenticeship programs (0.5 million); (8) education programs offered by community organizations (10.9 million); and correspondence instruction (3.9 million). Even these do not exhaust the list; not included are the relevant activities of the cooperative extension service (United States Department of Agriculture) and of professional associations, and workers' education programs sponsored by labor organizations.

The estimates of "enrollments" in these programs are exceedingly crude. An indication of the extent of our ignorance is the fact that a 1973 survey of institutions offering correspondence courses reported approximately 4 million students, while a 1975 adult education survey conducted by the NCES found only about 600 thousand individuals who reported taking such courses! Barton laments the fact that we know "only that somewhere between 38 and 84 million people are engaged in organized learning" and recommends the appointment of a National Commission on Education and Training Statistics to "identify gaps in statistical information and . . . to assemble a picture of the whole as well as the parts" (1982: 32).

Training in industry. There is not much question that employing establishments themselves are the most significant sources of work skills among individuals who have terminated their formal schooling. Most of what we know about training practices within industry comes either from surveys of firms or surveys of workers. The most recent worker survey based on a representative national sample is now 20 years old. Of the 86 percent of all workers between the ages of 22 and 64 who had less than three years of college, about two-fifths reported having acquired some formal training for their jobs, including company courses (6.6 percent) and apprenticeships (8.2 percent). When asked about training on their present jobs, 30 percent reported some formal training, but 45 percent had just "picked up" the job and 8 percent said that no training was necessary.

Putting together bits and pieces of information gleaned from a number of employer surveys, one can conclude that formal training is provided by less than one-half of all firms but by more than four out of five of those with 500 or more employees. The proportion of workers involved in any one year may be as high as one-fifth in large firms, but smaller for industry generally. Much of the formal skill training is aimed at managerial and other white collar workers; manual workers receive a disproportionately small share.

However unsatisfactory are the measures of formal training in industry, we are even less able to quantify the far more pervasive *informal* on-the-job training (OJT) that takes place. There are virtually no records of informal training, and estimates have had to be made indirectly on the basis of rather heroic assumptions. The most definitive work of this kind is that of Jacob Mincer (1962), who estimated that American males invested $13.5 billion in OJT in 1958 (by accepting wages below their marginal productivities) in comparison with an investment of $21.6 billion in regular education.

Apprenticeship. The institution of apprenticeship extends back into the Middle Ages when artisans learned their trades under the tutelage of a master craftsman. Only a small proportion of skilled workers today acquire their skills through apprenticeships, which are generally arranged jointly by employers and unions. About half a million workers are enrolled in such programs, about three-fifths of whom are registered with the Bureau of Apprenticeship and Training (BAT) in the United States Department of Labor or with a BAT-approved state apprenticeship agency. The remainder are in unregistered programs.

To meet the requirements of the National Apprenticeship Act of 1937, a program must have a minimum age of at least 16, must include a definite schedule of class instruction and work experience under adequate supervision designed to create competence in the trade, must provide for a progressively increasing schedule of wages and for periodic evaluation of apprentices, and must be open to men and women without regard to race, creed, color, national origin, or physical handicap.

At the end of fiscal 1981 there were about 52,000 registered programs. BAT has been placing emphasis on expanding apprenticeship outside of the industries in which it has been traditional. As the result of recent promotional campaigns, for example, there were about 500 apprentices in the finance, insurance, and real estate industry in 1982. The proportion of all apprentices accounted for by the construction industry dropped from 60 percent to 54 percent between 1980 and 1982. Programs have been developed for persons in the armed forces, where 24,000 individuals were being trained in 72 occupational categories that are found in the civilian economy. Programs have also been inaugurated among prison inmates in order to develop employable skills and thus reduce the likelihood of recidivism upon release. In 1982 there were 27 federal correctional institutions in which 650 inmates were receiving training.

The distribution of adult education and training. Given the data limitations that have been described, it is hardly surprising that we cannot make confident generalizations about the characteristics of individuals who participate in adult education and training activities. However, if the NCES survey data on adult education (narrowly defined) are at all indicative, it would appear that such participation is quite uneven and that it tends to be concentrated in those groups who, even without it, enjoy superior positions in the labor market. For example, in 1978 when the NCES measure of the incidence of adult education was 11.6 percent for the adult population at large it was 3.3 percent among those with less than 12 years of education and 26.5 percent among those with four or more years of college. The rate of participation was twice as high among whites as among blacks (12 versus 6 percent), and more than three times as high among persons with incomes of $25,000 as among those with less than $5,000 (17.5 percent versus 5.3 percent).

It is this kind of evidence that has led to the charge that adult education "is probably more elitist on socio-economic indicators than today's undergraduate education" (Cross, 1978), and that leads Barton to call for systematic efforts to equalize opportunities, including improved information and counseling services and experimental and demonstration programs designed to make it easier for the underrepresented groups to participate in education and training. It is precisely these groups that have been the principal targets of the federal employment and training programs, the subject of the following section.

FEDERALLY FINANCED EMPLOYMENT AND TRAINING PROGRAMS

It should be kept in mind that the amount of space to be accorded in this section to the federally financed training programs is disproportionate to their share in the total human resource development effort in the United States. As of the beginning of the decade of the 1980s they accounted for only about 7 cents of each training dollar; elementary, secondary and postsecondary education accounted for 73 cents, private business and industry for 15 cents, and government civilian and military training for 5 cents (Johnston, 1981: 83). In a sense, the federal programs have emerged to compensate for failures in other parts of the system.

The origins of employment and training programs. The entrance of the federal government into postschool training for employment was largely a result of the unemployment experience of the 1950s that generated the inadequate demand-structural unemployment debate (described in Chapter 7). The earliest legislative response to what some perceived as a problem of technological unemployment was the Area Redevelopment Act of 1961, which provided for industrial development assistance to economically depressed areas, as well as training programs in such areas for unemployed workers. In the following year the Manpower Development and Training Act (MDTA) was passed, establishing a more general program of retraining throughout the country. Unemployed workers were to have opportunities for classroom training and subsistence allowances, or for on-the-job training to the extent that such opportunities could be arranged with private employers. The program involved a partnership at the federal level between the Department of Labor and the Department of Health, Education, and Welfare, and at the state and local levels between the public employment service and vocational education administrators.

It was not long before experience indicated that the original MDTA had misconstrued the nature of the unemployment problem; the principal need was not for retraining technologically displaced "mainstream" workers but rather for training individuals who had no useful skills to begin with, many of whom needed basic literacy training and other forms of assistance if they were to be able to compete successfully in the labor market. As early as 1963 MDTA was amended to increase the permissible proportion of youth from 5 percent to 25 percent of total enrollment, and the program became increasingly targeted upon the economically disadvantaged and upon those groups suffering discrimination in the labor market.

There were two other sources of federal involvement in employment and training programs. One was the Economic Opportunity Act (EOA) of 1964, the legislative embodiment of the Johnson administration's war on poverty; the second was the 1967 amendments to the Social Security Act. Under the EOA two youth programs were inaugurated—the Neighborhood Youth Corps and the Job Corps. The former involved work experience in public service jobs for in-school and out-of-school youth, as well as a summer jobs program. The Job Corps was a residential training program for youths from seriously deprived homes and neighborhoods. Beginning in 1968 Job Opportunities in the Business Sector (JOBS) was begun as a joint responsibility of the Office of Economic Opportunity (OEO) and the Department of Labor. Under the aegis of the National Alliance of Business (NAB), a committee of prestigious business leaders, the cooperation of private industry was to be enlisted to provide subsidized employment to the disadvantaged.

The Social Security Amendments of 1967 established the Work Incentive Program (WIN), designed to make welfare recipients employable and to get them off the welfare rolls. Adult recipients of Aid to Families with Dependent Children (AFDC) were required to register for work or training opportunities as a condition of continued receipt of benefits. The program offered a variety of services for improving employability, including basic education, institutional or on-the-job vocational training, and day care for children. A later (1971) amendment to the Internal Revenue Act provided for tax credits to employers hiring participants in the WIN program.

The Comprehensive Employment and Training Act. By the early 1970s, "manpower" programs (the pre-women's liberation term for employment and training programs) had become a firmly entrenched component of human resource policy in the United States. Outlays for federal programs, which had totaled less than $250 million in fiscal year 1961, had grown to more than $3 billion in fiscal year 1970. Literally hundreds of evaluations of the programs had been made by academic researchers, and although the methodology generally left a great deal to be desired, the verdict was generally favorable (Perry et al., 1975).

Nonetheless, there was dissatisfaction with several aspects of the administration of the programs. For one thing, there was a lack of coordination, and indeed outright competition among the federal agencies involved in administering the programs—Labor, HEW, and OEO. For another, there was not only a bewildering proliferation of programs at the local level, but a rigidity in their definition that frequently inhibited adequate adaptation to local conditions and local needs. These criticisms led to calls for "decentralization" and "decategorization"—that is, conferring greater responsibility upon local agencies for deciding upon the appropriate mix of services and providing funds unearmarked for specific programs. Partial moves in these directions occurred during the 1960s even without legislative authorization. The Concentrated Employment Program (CEP), for example, utilized MDTA and EOA funds to operate a single office in each of about 80 areas to which applicants could come for assignment to the specific program most relevant to their needs. The Cooperative Area Manpower Planning Sytem (CAMPS), inaugurated cooperatively by the federal funding agencies, encouraged state and local agencies involved in program administration to develop joint manpower plans for federal approval. Arrangements of this kind were consistent with the "New Federalism" philosophy of the Nixon administration, which called for block grants to state and local governments with substantial discretion over how they were to be used. And so, by late 1973 there were human resource planning staffs in every state and in over 100 cities.

Passage of the Comprehensive Employment and Training Act (CETA) in 1973 formalized the decategorization and decentralization of employment and training programs. The act provided that units of local government with populations of 100,000 or more might apply to become "prime sponsors." After approval by the Department of Labor of an employment and training plan prepared by the prime sponsor, funds would be allocated that were to be spent for the types of services specified in the plan. Areas within a state that did not become prime sponsors were included in a "balance-of-state" prime sponsorship under the authority of the governor. By 1982 there were a total of 476 prime sponsors. In addition to the provisions for comprehensive services to be administered through the prime sponsors, CETA continued the Job Corps as a responsibility of the Department of Labor and also continued to vest responsibility in the Department of Labor for funding research and demonstration projects and for operating national programs for certain groups with special labor market disadvantages—e.g., migrant workers and American Indians. Finally, the act established the National Commission for Manpower Policy (later the National Commission for Employment Policy) to study policy issues and to report to the President and Congress.

Significant amendments to CETA were enacted in 1974, 1977, and 1978. The first of these authorized a sizable countercyclical public service employment (PSE) program (see Chapter 7). In 1977 the Youth Employment Demonstration Projects Act added a major series of programs for youth. The 1978 amendments restricted all CETA programs to the economically disadvantaged and long-term unemployed, and added a $5 billion Private Sector Initiative Program (PSIP) under the control of Private Industry Councils (PICs) to promote the employment of the disadvantaged in private industry.

Thus, as CETA stood in 1981 it provided for comprehensive services, administered through state and local governments, to improve the employability of the disadvantaged or unemployed, including public service employment (PSE) for the structurally unemployed (Title II); special employment and training programs for youth, including the Job Corps, as well as work experience programs and special demonstration projects designed to keep youth in school (Title IV); a countercyclical PSE program when unemployment exceeded 4 percent of the labor force (Title VI); PSIP, designed to test the effectiveness of alternative approaches to involving the business community in employment and training activities (Title VII); a Young Adult Conservation Corps providing up to one year of employment for out-of-school unemployed youth 16 to 23 years of age (Title VIII); and the special federal responsibilities described above (Title III).

Expenditures on these programs in fiscal year 1979 amounted to about $9.5 billion, of which over one-half was accounted for by public service employment—19 percent under Title II and 35 percent under Title VI. An additional one-fifth of the expenditures were for general services under Title II, and a roughly equal proportion for the youth programs under Titles IV and VIII.

Despite a rising national unemployment rate, federal expenditures for CETA dropped sharply between 1979 and 1983, from over $9 billion in the former year to under $4 billion in the latter. Reductions were made in all of the programs except PSIP, but the most drastic change was the complete elimination of PSE programs, which had attracted a considerable amount of criticism and which President Reagan strongly opposed. The PSE program—especially during its very rapid build-up from 300,000 to 750,000 jobs in 1978—was accompanied by instances of inefficiency and fraud that soured many people on the program and on CETA in general. For this as well as other reasons, the political consensus that had for almost 20 years provided solid support for the employment and training effort disappeared (Mangum, 1981).

In addition to controversy over the substance of the program—especially concerning the relative emphasis to be placed on providing training versus providing jobs and income—there was continuing disagreement over the respective roles of the federal, state, and local governments and over the division of responsibility between the government and the business community in planning and administering the programs (Guttman, 1983).

The Job Training Partnership Act. With the approaching expiration of CETA's authorization, compromises on these issues were finally worked out after months of debate, and the Job Training Partnership Act (JTPA) was passed late in 1982 as the successor to CETA. The new act vested much greater responsibility in the state governors, ceding to them many of the functions that the Secretary of Labor had performed under CETA, and gave substantially increased authority to the private industry councils (PICs) in planning and administering employment and training programs. With respect to substance, JTPA ruled out PSE programs and placed greater emphasis than had CETA on training as compared with other forms of support and service.

More specifically, JTPA provided that funds would flow from the Department of Labor to the states on the basis of their relative levels of unemployment and numbers of economically disadvantaged persons. The state governors designate "service delivery areas" (SDAs) within the state (analogous to CETA's prime sponsors) with the stipulation that any unit of government (or consortium of contiguous governments) with a population of 200,000 or more must be so designated if it wishes. Each SDA must have a PIC, of which the chairperson and a majority of members represent the private sector, and whose other members represent educational agencies, organized labor, rehabilitation agencies, community-based organizations, economic development agencies, and the public employment service.

The PIC is responsible, in partnership with the appropriate local official (e.g., mayor) for developing a two-year job training plan that describes the services to be provided and the procedures for identifying and selecting participants and the providers of services; establishes performance goals; and contains a budget. On approval of the plans of the SDAs by the governor, state funds are apportioned among them largely on the basis of the same criteria used for allocating funds among the states.

So far as program is concerned, the federally administered programs that existed under CETA are retained (Title IV) and the SDAs are authorized to provide a variety of training and other employability-promoting services to the economically disadvantaged (Title II) and to "dislocated" mainstream workers (Title III). At least 40 percent of the Title II funds are reserved to serve youth under age 22. PSE is prohibited; and emphasis on training versus income and other types of support is achieved by the requirement that, except for summer youth programs, 70 percent of the funds must be used for training with no more than 30 percent being devoted to administration and other forms of supportive services. However, the restriction is not completely rigid, as half of the costs of a training-related work experience progam may be counted as training costs, and SDAs are permitted to exceed the 30 percent limit under specified conditions.

The provisions of JTPA became effective October 1, 1983, with the preceding 12 months constituting a transitional period. The Reagan administration's 1984 budget requested $3.6 billion for JTPA programs, a reduction of about $100 million from the 1983 level. Almost three-fourths of the total ($2.625 billion) was for Title II programs, including $725 million for summer youth programs; $240 million was for programs for displaced workers (Title III); and $793 million was for federally administered programs, including $586 million for the Job Corps.

What effects the new legislation will have remain to be seen. Many hold great hopes for the increased involvement of private industry in the planning and administration of the programs, especially in view of the acknowledged fact that most job opportunities are in the private sector. However, the PSIP experience under CETA creates some grounds for skepticism, even though the PICs had less power under PSIP than they do under JTPA. A study by the General Accounting Office (1983) that compared PSIP with traditional training efforts under CETA found a somewhat higher percentage of placements in the PSIP programs, but very little difference when other "positive outcomes" are also considered. However, there was evidence of "creaming" in the

PSIP programs; as measured by education and age they served a more advantaged clientele than other programs.

Evaluation of employment and training programs. Verdicts about the usefulness and degree of success of employment and training programs vary considerably. It is easy to find allegations in the popular press that they have failed. The studies of careful scholars, on the other hand, provide fairly strong evidence of the utility of at least some types of programs. One of the problems in arriving at confident conclusions lies in the methodological difficulties that beset attempts to evaluate the programs (Borus, 1979). For one thing, a complete evaluation requires examination of a large variety of dependent variables in addition to employment and earnings, many of which are difficult if not impossible to measure. Second, simple before-and-after examinations of a relevant variable (e.g., earnings) are unsatisfactory, for earnings may be expected to rise even in the absence of training as the result of maturation and inflation not to mention the phenomenon of regression toward the mean among those at the bottom of the income distribution. Finally, in the absence of a truly experimental research design there must be a carefully selected control group if the independent effects of the training program are to be isolated. Otherwise, what might appear to be an advantage created by the program might result, for example, simply from the fact that workers with above-average initiative gained access to it.

On the basis of his review of some of the more sophisticated evaluations of employment and training programs Michael Borus (1980) has concluded that classroom, on-the-job, and work experience training programs have tended to justify their costs; that there is no evidence of the greater effectiveness of training for women versus men, or for blacks versus whites, or for any other educational or age group; and that short classroom training courses and programs with high completion rates are more likely than others to yield improvements in earnings.

On the basis of more recent (and probably better) evidence than was available to Borus, the General Accounting Office (1982) has also concluded that CETA programs have benefited their participants, although their detailed findings differ somewhat from those of Borus. Citing an analysis of data for CETA participants drawn from the Department of Labor's Continuous Longitudinal Manpower Survey (CLMS) and for a control group of individuals drawn from the CPS, the GAO noted that CETA participation increased the 1977 earnings of participants by an average of $300 to $400—a 7 percent gain over the comparison group. Gains for women were found to exceed those of men, and persons whose pre-CETA earnings were very low experienced especially marked improvement.

Perhaps the best evidence of the potential value of certain types of training programs for the disadvantaged is that provided by the Supported Work Experiment—a transitional work experience program administered by the Manpower Demonstration Research Corporation with funding from private foundations as well as federal agencies, including the Employment and Training Administration of the Department of Labor (Gueron, 1980). A total of 10,000 persons were employed in 15 locations over a four-year period beginning in 1975. Four groups were represented— unemployed ex-offenders, former drug addicts, female welfare (AFDC) recipients, and young school dropouts. One of the unique aspects of the project was its experimental design; participants and members of a control group were selected by random assignment. The work environment was designed to emphasize peer support, close supervision, and a gradual increase in the demands placed upon participants.

The effects of the program were found to be clearly positive for the welfare recipients and the ex-addicts. With respect to these two groups, "society as a whole receives benefits in the form of useful goods and services, reduced criminal activity, and increases in future employment that are considerably in excess of program cost" (Gueron, 1980: 8).

Conclusion. In my judgment, there is no more fitting appraisal of the federal employment and training effort than that provided in late 1979 by Eli Ginzberg, a lifelong student of human resource policy and Chairman of the National Commission for Manpower (Employment) Policy from its formation in 1973 until 1982. Acknowledging the limitations of data and analyses, Ginzberg (1980: 186-187) offers the following judgments of the role and the potential of employment and training programs:

> An advanced economy such as that of the United States must continue to experiment with manpower policies and programs for the reason that it cannot rely solely on the self-corrective forces of the market to assure optimal employment opportunities. . . .

> The destructive effects of gross inequalities in opportunities and rewards reach across generational lines. The children of the poor, the unskilled, and the undereducated are likely to enter adulthood ill prepared to cope with the roles of work and citizenship . . . It is not easy for manpower programs . . . to compensate for the cumulative

deficits ... [b]ut as the Job Corps experience underscores, a multifaceted effort directed at remedial education, skill acquisition, and job placement can make a real difference. ...

The most favorable method for assisting low-skilled persons to improve their long-term occupational status and income is to provide them with training that leads to a desirable job. ...

A society with a large number of adults in need of jobs and income that the regular economy fails to provide, even under conditions of rapidly expanding employment such as existed during most of the 1970s, has every reason to experiment with public service employment. ...

A beginning has been made ... to raise the contribution of the educational system to the occupational skills and goals of the student body and, more broadly, to improve linkage among the schools, employers, labor, and the manpower authorities.

Once a democratic society becomes cognizant of gross inequities and inefficiencies, as it did in the 1960s, with respect to the long-term neglect of minorities and the poor, it does not have the luxury of turning its back on its newly acquired knowledge and insight. Response is imperative ... political tensions and social unrest would have been much greater had the federal government not demonstrated a concern and had it failed to act. Manpower programs may have fallen far short of what was needed, but they surely were preferable to a policy of indifference and neglect.

NOTES

1. This section draws heavily on Johnston (1981).
2. Much of the material in this section is taken from Barton (1982).

QUESTIONS FOR DISCUSSION

1. On the basis of your own experience or the experience of relatives and friends, what appear to be the principal means through which work skills are acquired?
2. When you were in high school, to what extent did you view the educational process as being relevant to your future success in the labor market? Would it be useful if this connection were emphasized more than it is?
3. In retrospect, what were the greatest strengths and the greatest limitations of your own secondary school experience? From the vantage point of human resource development, in what ways do you think that the educational process might be strengthened?

4. In general terms, what should be the respective roles of "regular" schooling, on-the-job training, government employment and training programs, and other forms of adult education in creating and maintaining skills and know-how for the world of work?

5. In your opinion, what are the most significant changes in public policy effected by the substitution of JTPA for CETA? Do you believe that the changes are likely to be for the better?

6. What problems arise in appraising the effectiveness of employment and training programs? On the basis of the evidence available to you, what are your conclusions about the desirability of such programs?

11

Income Maintenance

Overview and OASDHI

Modern governments have developed a variety of public programs designed to provide protection against loss of income or against certain risks that may impose substantial burdens on income (e.g., medical care). The term "social security" in its very broadest sense has been used to encompass all such programs (Burns, 1954). It is worth noting that, so defined, the concept of social security is sufficiently comprehensive to embrace public education even though we are accustomed to thinking about education very differently from the way in which we think about, say, unemployment compensation or Medicare.

Social security schemes fall into two major categories: social insurance and public (social) assistance programs. The former pay benefits as a matter of right to individuals who meet the statutory eligibility requirements, irrespective of their financial circumstances; the latter provide benefits only to those who can demonstrate financial need. Thus, even a millionaire can qualify for unemployment compensation or for old age benefits under the Social Security Act, while public assistance (welfare) payments under Aid to Families with Dependent Children are payable only to families whose income falls below stipulated levels. A second difference between social insurance and public assistance in the United States is that the former programs are generally financed by payroll taxes on employers and/or workers, while the latter are financed out of general revenues. In the remainder of this chapter we present a bird's-eye view of the social security system in the United States and then examine in detail the Old Age, Survivors, Disability and Health Insurance (OASDHI) program. The following chapter describes unemployment compensation and workers' compensation, while Chapter 13 deals with public assistance.

Social insurance versus private insurance. Before describing the contours of social security in the United States it is worthwhile to take a moment to examine the character of social insurance— and particularly its similarities to and differences from private insurance. There is one basic respect in which social and private insurance are similar: Both involve a pooling of risk. Consider fire insurance as an example. While we know with considerable confidence what the total cost of fires will be in the United States next year, we do not know where they will strike. Fire insurance is an arrangement whereby individuals can incur a small but certain loss (premium) in order to avoid a much larger but uncertain one. In precisely the same way, social insurance programs accumulate funds through payroll taxes on all workers (and/or their employers) in order to make payments to those individuals who actually experience the loss against which the program provides protection.

There are, however, several respects in which social insurance differs fundamentally from private insurance. To begin with, it is generally compulsory rather than voluntary. Moreover, the rights that social insurance programs confer are provided by statute rather than contract and thus are subject to change or indeed even abrogation by legislation. Third, whereas private insurance adheres rigidly to the principle of "equity," social insurance generally compromises that principle in the interest of "adequacy." In other words, the benefits in private insurance for a given category of risk are generally strictly proportionate to the premiums that have been paid; social insurance, on the other hand, in order to provide an adequate "safety net," typically provides a subsidy in favor of low income individuals so that the ratio of benefits to payroll taxes is higher for low-wage than for high-wage workers.

Finally, and in many respects most important, the criterion of financial soundness differs as between private and social insurance programs. To be "actuarially sound," a private insurance company must have reserves at least equal to its accrued liabilities. In simpler terms, this means that a life insurance company must have sufficient assets to pay off all of the benefits that its current policy holders are entitled to. In contrast, authorities on social security generally agree that because a social insurance program is based on the taxing powers of government, it is financially "safe" so long as the scheduled tax rates are sufficient to pay the estimated benefits under the program as far into the future as one can foresee.

In the light of these differences, are social insurance programs truly "insurance"? The reader is invited to arrive at an independent judgment on this issue. Whatever the decision, it is important to recognize that names *do* make a difference. Proponents of old age insurance and unemployment compensation were frequently eager to emphasize the insurance aspects of the programs—in part, at least, as a means of selling them to the American public at a time when opponents characterized them as dangerous steps toward socialism. The approach was successful but has been responsible for a way of viewing the programs that may have constrained their development and that has certainly provided ammunition to their opponents, who have reveled in pointing up departures from "sound" insurance principles.

To illustrate the importance of how one is conditioned to perceive a social security program, contrast the way in which the American public views public education with the way in which it views old age pensions under the Social Security Act (Parnes, 1983: 10-11). Public education is widely perceived as an institution that serves a vital social purpose and therefore demands compulsory public support irrespective of the degree to which a specific individual or family uses it. Property owners without children pay the same school taxes as those with children. When the baby boom generation flooded the elementary schools in the 1950s and 1960s, adults, while perhaps lamenting the required increase in taxes, did not bemoan the fact that they were having to "put in" more than they had (previously) "gotten out" of the educational system.

In contrast, most Americans view social security as an arrangement in which one pays in premiums while working in order to withdraw a monthly pension in retirement. As a consequence, a "baby bust" generation not only laments the increase in taxes required to support a baby boom generation in retirement, but regards this as a manifestation of an "intergenerational inequity." Needless to say, there is nothing inherent in the program that *requires* it to be viewed in this way. Even if eligibility for and level of benefits are related to lifetime work experience, there is no reason why the collection of revenues—whatever their source—could not be viewed as an independent process. The support of retired workers, in other words, would be seen as an essential social objective (like public education) requiring broad social support.

The social security "system." Social security in the United States is the product of a variety of state and federal statutes that have been adopted at different times over the past three-quarters of a century. It is, as a consequence, anything but "systematic"; its major elements may be described as follows.

The principal *social insurance* programs are OASDHI, unemployment compensation, workers' compensation, and temporary disability compensation. OASDHI, a completely federal program that was introduced in 1935, will be described in detail in the next section. Unemployment compensation, a product of federal and state legislation of the mid-1930s, pays cash benefits to individuals who have lost their jobs. Workers' compensation provides cash and medical benefits to workers who have been injured on the job or who suffer occupational diseases; it is almost exclusively a product of state laws, the earliest of which appeared in 1911 and the last of which was passed in 1948.

Temporary disability compensation pays cash benefits for limited periods of time (26 weeks at most) to individuals unable to work as the result of a non-work-connected illness or injury. It exists in only a handful of states (Rhode Island, New York, New Jersey, California, Alaska) and, by virtue of federal law, for railroad workers. The cash benefits under all of the social insurance programs are designed to provide partial compensation for income loss, and are accordingly related to previous earnings.

As has been observed, social assistance programs are designed to aid the needy, providing both cash benefits and "benefits in kind" (i.e., goods and services). The major cash assistance programs in the United States are Aid to Families with Dependent Children (AFDC), Supplemental Security Income (SSI), and general assistance. The first of these is a federal-state program that is available to families in which children have been deprived of parental support. SSI, a federal program, pays benefits to individuals over age 65, to the blind, and to the permanently and totally disabled. All of these are called "categorical" assistance programs because they are available only to specified categories of needy individuals. In contrast, general assistance, which is financed exclusively at the state and local levels, provides aid on an unrestricted (but much less generous) basis.

In addition to the cash assistance programs, there are those that make goods or services available to needy individuals. The most important of these are the food stamp program, the medical assistance program (Medicaid), and subsidized housing. The social assistance programs will be described in detail in Chapter 12.

Role of the Social Security Act. Despite its diverse origins, the social security mosaic in the United States owes a great deal to the Social Security Act of 1935. It was that statute that established the pension system out of which has emerged the OASDHI program. As will be seen in the next chapter, it also was instrumental in inducing the states to enact unemployment compensation laws. Finally, it provided for the categorical assistance programs that were originally financed jointly by federal and state governments.

OASDHI: HISTORICAL DEVELOPMENT

OASDHI—or, more specifically, the program of retirement benefits that it provides—is what the person in the street generally calls "social security." As initially passed, old age pensions at age 65 (OAI) were the only benefits provided. Over the years the law was amended to provide benefits to dependents of retired individuals (1939); to dependent survivors of individuals who die, irrespective of age at death (SI, 1939); and to the permanently and totally disabled and their dependents (DI, 1956). In 1965 health insurance (HI or "Medicare") was added for individuals 65 and over and for the recipients of disability benefits.

Not only has there been an expansion of the risks covered by the program, but coverage of individuals has also expanded considerably. Originally confined basically to wage and salary workers in the nonagricultural profit sector of the economy, the law covered only about 60 percent of the labor force. Coverage has been expanded to more than 90 percent of the labor force. As of the early 1980s, the only significant exclusions are federal civil servants;[1] farm workers and domestics with very irregular employment; about 30 percent of state and local government workers employed in jurisdictions that have not elected coverage; and railroad workers, who are covered under a separate Railroad Retirement Act that is coordinated with OASDHI.

Finally, liberalization has also occurred in the level of benefits paid under the program. The average retirement benefit increased by 55 percent in real terms between 1960 and 1981. Provisions that were added to the law in the 1970s assure (1) that retirement benefits for successive cohorts of retirees will rise proportionately with increases in wage levels so that the ratio of benefits to preretirement earnings will remain constant; and (2) that the benefits awarded to recipients will maintain their purchasing power, despite upward movements in the price level. Total benefits under the program grew from $31.6 billion in 1970 to $120 billion in 1980—an increase of 280 percent.

OASDI

With the foregoing introduction, we will turn our attention now to the retirement, disability, and life insurance aspects of the program, reserving for later a discussion of Medicare. Our examination of OASDI will be facilitated by calling attention at the outset to certain basic features of the program.

Some basic characteristics. Like all social insurance programs, OASDI is compulsory. Needless to say, the compulsion occurs with respect to financial support of the program, not with respect to its benefits. From this point of view there is less compulsion involved here than in the case of public education, where school attendance laws require individuals to avail themselves of the supported services (or their equivalents). Second, benefits payable under the program are related to prior earnings and are thus to be construed as compensating for income loss. However, the relationship between benefits and prior earnings is not rigid. A number of provisions of the program are designed to assure adequacy of protection at the expense of strict equality. Specifically, provision for dependents' and survivors' benefits means that a covered worker with a family will normally enjoy a higher return than one without dependents. In addition, the benefit formula is weighted to yield a relatively larger proportion of low than of high wages, and the existence of a minimum benefit has the same effect.

Third, the program is financed by payroll taxes levied on both the worker and employer. While the tax paid by each party is the same (with the self-employed paying a rate three-fourths of the combined employer-employee rate), it does not follow that the actual burden of supporting the program is divided equally between workers and employers. Economists recognize the possibility that employers may shift the burden of the payroll tax forward to consumers in the form of higher prices or backward to the workers in the form of lower wages than they would otherwise be receiving. While it is difficult to be certain which (if either) of these alternatives occurs, the consensus appears to be that most of the burden of the payroll taxes is borne by the workers (Brittain, 1972).

Fourth, the OASDI program is not designed to provide complete financial protection against the risks that it covers. Instead, it is conceived to provide merely a basic "floor of protection," with additional support to be provided by other means. Much of the literature on old age security, for instance, refers to a "three-legged stool"—one of which is represented by social security benefits, a second by employer-provided pensions, and a third by individual savings.

Fifth, the OASDI program pays benefits as a matter or right, without reference to need. The "retirement test" under the program, which reduces benefits if earnings exceed specified levels, appears at first blush to contradict this principle. Its rationale, however, is as a criterion of the individual's meeting the risk for which protection is provided—specifically, *retirement*. Thus, income from sources other than earnings do not limit benefits.

Eligibility requirements. Eligibility for benefits under the OASDI program depends upon an individual's having achieved the "insured" status, of which there are three categories. Each of these is defined in terms of a specific number of "quarters of coverage," which are calendar quarters in which an individual has earned a specified minimum (e.g., $340 in 1982) in a job covered by the social security tax.

To be "fully insured," an individual must have one quarter of coverage for each year that elapses between age 22 (or 1950, if later) and the year in which the individual (1) achieves age 62, (2) becomes disabled, or (3) dies. There must be a minimum of 6 quarters of coverage; once 40 quarters have been achieved the fully insured status is permanent. Thus, so far as retirement benefits are concerned, eligibility is normally achieved by serving for at least ten years in covered employment. It must be emphasized that being "fully insured" tells us nothing about the amount of benefits an individual will receive; the determinants of the benefit level will be described below. The "currently insured" status—which is relevant to death benefits payable to children of the deceased and their surviving parent—requires 6 quarters of coverage out of the 13 ending with the death of the insured.

The "disability insured" status—which is required for receipt of disability benefits—requires an individual to be not only fully insured but to have at least 20 quarters of coverage out of the 40 preceding the onset of disability. (A somewhat less restrictive rule applies to workers under 31 years of age.) Disability is defined as the "inability to engage in any substantial gainful activity by reason of . . . physical or mental impairment." The individual must have been disabled for at least 5 months, and the disability must be expected to last for a total of at least 12 months (or until death). Determinations of disability are made by state vocational rehabilitation agencies, subject to review by the Social Security Administration.

Benefit amount. All of the benefits payable under OASDI are related to the "primary insurance amount" (PIA), the monthly retirement, disability, or death benefit that is calculated on the basis of the insured worker's prior earnings. The procedure for calculating the PIA will be described in the context of the retirement benefit; for disability and death the principle is the same, except that the period over which earnings are averaged ends with the onset of disability or with the death of the insured.

The first step involves the calculation of the average indexed monthly earnings (AIME)—that is, the individual's average earnings adjusted to reflect wage and salary levels near the time of retirement rather than over the entire work career. To arrive at this figure, the earnings of the individual (up to the maximum subject to the social security payroll tax) for each calendar year between age 22 (or 1950, if later) and age 60 are listed, and the figure for each year is adjusted upward by the percentage by which average annual earnings for all workers have increased between that year and the year the individual achieves age 60.[2]

To illustrate, consider T. Johnson who retired at age 62 in 1980. Below are shown (1) his earnings for selected years, (2) average earnings of all workers in those years, and (3) Johnson's indexed earnings:

Year	Johnson's earnings	Average annual earnings	Johnson's indexed earnings
1951	$ 3,600	$ 2,799	$13,577
1960	4,800	4,007	12,645
1978	25,900	10,556	25,900

The indexed earnings for 1951 are obtained as follows: $3,600 × ($10,556/$2,799) = $13,677.

Next, the five years of lowest earnings are discarded and those for the remaining years are summed and divided by 12 times the number of years. The PIA is then calculated by the application of the benefit formula to the AIME. For 1982, this formula was as follows:

$$PIA = 90\% \text{ of first } \$230 \text{ of AIME } +$$
$$32\% \text{ of next } \$1158 \text{ of AIME } +$$
$$15\% \text{ of excess over } \$1388$$

Each year, the "bend points" in the formula (i.e., the dollar amounts in each of the lines above) are increased by the percentage increase in average annual earnings (with a two-year lag).

The PIA as thus calculated is the monthly benefit for an individual who retires at age 65. For retirements at earlier ages the benefit is proportionately reduced, down to 80 percent at the minimum age of 62. For retirement at ages between 65 and 72 there is a premium of 3 percent per year, which is scheduled to rise to a maximum of 8 percent by 2010. Finally, the resulting figure is adjusted upward by the percentage rise in the CPI between the time of the calculation (age 60) and the time at which retirement actually takes places.

Stepping back from the detail for a moment, it is useful to consider several aspects of this procedure and to understand what they accomplish. First, note that a number of values are geared to annual changes in economywide average wages: (1) the individual's own earnings record, (2) the bend points in the benefit formula, and (3) the maximum earnings subject to the social security tax. These three factors, in combination, mean that the ratio of the retirement benefit to earnings in the years immediately preceding retirement (replacement rate) will remain constant for successive cohorts of retirees. In other words, if the replacement rate is approximately 50 percent for an 1982 retiree whose AIME is equal to the average monthly wage of all workers, then a retiree in, say, 2015 who occupies the same relative position in the earnings distribution will also have a 50 percent replacement rate. Thus, if the historic patterns of increasing real wages prevails in the future, successive generations of retirees will be increasingly well off in real terms.

Second, the effect of the benefit formula is to create a higher replacement rate for an individual whose earnings have been low than for a person higher up in the earnings distribution. To illustrate, application of the 1982 benefit formula to an AIME of $1,550 yields a benefit of $601.90, for a replacement rate of 38.8 percent; for an AIME of $800 the corresponding PIA is $396.80, for a replacement rate of 49.6 percent. Finally, once an individual becomes a beneficiary, the real benefit is maintained during his or her lifetime by virtue of the cost-of-living adjustment.

Types of benefits. As has been indicated, all of the benefits provided for by the OASDI program are based upon the insured individual's PIA, which has just been described. Certain categories of dependents of retired or disabled benefit recipients are entitled to benefits equal to 50 percent of the PIA: (1) a spouse, or unmarried divorced spouse of the insured worker is entitled to the benefit at age 65 (actuarially reduced if taken between 62 and 65; (2) each unmarried child of the insured is entitled to a benefit if the child is under 18 (or 19 if a full-time high school student), or, if disabled, with the disability having been incurred prior to age 22; (3) a spouse, irrespective of age is entitled to a benefit if he or she is caring for a child under age 16 or for a disabled child whose disability began prior to age 22.

Specified survivors of insured workers who die either prior or subsequent to retirement are also eligible for benefits. (1) The widow or widower or unmarried divorced spouse of an insured worker is entitled to a benefit equal to 100 percent of the PIA at age 65 or, if disabled, at age 60 (actuarially reduced if taken as early as age 60 or, if disabled, age 50). (2) An unmarried spouse or divorced spouse who is caring for an unmarried child under 16 or with a disability that began prior to age 22 receives a benefit equal to 75 percent of the PIA. (3) Each unmarried child under age 18 (19, if a full-time high school student) is entitled to a benefit equal to 75 percent of the PIA. (4) A dependent parent receives a benefit equal to 82.5 percent of the PIA (or 75 percent to each of two parents). Finally, there is a lump sum funeral benefit of $225 that is payable to a surviving spouse.

Despite the variety of potential monthly benefits that might go to the members of a single family, there is a maximum benefit that can be paid with respect to any one insured worker's account. This is established by a formula that yields a maximum ranging between 1.5 and 1.9 of the PIA.

The earnings test. The limitation on earned income has already been referred to in the context of the retirement benefit. The same limitation applies to all of the cash benefits provided by the law. When earnings reduce (or eliminate) the benefits of the insured worker, all of the dependents' benefits are automatically affected. In addition, each recipient of a dependent's or survivor's benefit is individually subject to the earned income restriction. The earnings restriction applies only to persons under age 70. As of 1982, earnings in excess of $6,000 for persons 65 or older (or $4,400 for those under age 65) result in a benefit reduction of $1 for every $2 of excess earnings. The earnings limits are increased each year to reflect the annual increase in average wages.

Benefit levels and beneficiaries, 1982. As of the end of 1982 there were about 36 million recipients of OASDI monthly payments—approximately 31.5 million on OAI and 4.5 million on D.I. Retirement benefits were going to about 20 million individuals and disability benefits to 2.8 million. The remaining 13 million beneficiaries were either dependents of these two categories or survivors of insured workers who had died.

The average monthly retirement benefit was about $400. Perhaps more meaningful than this figure are illustrative benefits that would be payable to 65-year-old workers at different income levels who retired in 1982. Table 11.1 shows these values, as well as gross and net replacement rates for hypothetical workers at three levels of preretirement earnings: (1) the maximum subject to social security taxes, (2) the average for all workers, and (3) the legal minimum wage on a full-time basis. For each case, two different family situations are depicted: one for a single worker and one in which there is a 65-year-old spouse entitled to a spouse's benefit.

The monthly social security benefit ranges from $330 for the single minimum wage worker to $940 for the married worker who has had the maximum earnings subject to tax. Expressed as ratios to preretirement earnings, the replacement rates for married couples are about 38 percent for the maximum earners, 65 percent for average earners and 85 percent for the minimum wage earner. When the replacement rates are calculated on the basis of preretirement *disposable* rather than gross income (taking into account taxes and work expenses) they rise to a range of 58 to 96 percent. Schulz (1980: 179) has cautioned that the 87 percent shown for the "average" earner cannot be interpreted as indicating that the average retiree enjoys a replacement rate this high. The

TABLE 11.1 Illustrative Benefits for 65-Year-Old Retirees in 1982

Item	Maximum Earner		Average Earner		Full-Time Minimum Wage Earner	
	w/Spouse	Single	w/Spouse	Single	w/Spouse	Single
Gross monthly earnings, 1981	2,475	2,475	1,129	1,129	581	581
Plus food stamps	0	0	0	0	42	0
Minus taxes and work expenses	859	1,048	276	339	96	133
Disposable income	1,616	1,427	853	790	527	448
SS benefit, 1982	940	627	739	493	495	330
SS benefit/ preretirement earnings	38%	25%	65%	44%	85%	57%
SS benefit/ preretirement disposable income	58%	44%	87%	62%	96%	74%

SOURCE: Adapted from Tables 1-2 in Report of Social Security Advisory Council (1979).

reason is that average earnings are calculated for all workers, irrespective of age; workers who are on the eve of retirement have earnings considerably above the all-employee average.

HEALTH INSURANCE (MEDICARE)

Medical insurance was not among the recommendations made by President Roosevelt's Committee on Economic Security, whose report became the basis for the Social Security Act. The omission was attributable at least in part to the fear that such a proposal would jeopardize the other elements of the program. However, health insurance was one of the earliest forms of social insurance to have developed elsewhere, and pressures for its adoption in the United States, which had begun early in the century, intensified after 1935. After a number of unsuccessful attempts to inaugurate comprehensive programs, Medicare—designed for persons 65 and over entitled to OASI cash benefits—was adopted in 1965. In 1972 it became applicable also to recipients of disability benefits who had been on the rolls for at least two years (and their dependents or survivors if over 65) and to insured persons with chronic kidney disease requiring dialysis or kidney transplants.

The Medicare program, officially known as Health Insurance for the Aged and Disabled, differs fundamentally from the other components of OASDHI in two related respects: (1) It provides medical services rather than cash benefits and, as a consequence, (2) benefits are not related to prior earnings. A third difference is that nongovernment agencies—Blue Cross, Blue Shield, and insurance agencies—play the major role in administering the program.

There are two components of the Medicare program, which are financed in very different ways. Hospital Insurance (HI) covers hospital and posthospital services and is financed by a portion of the OASDHI payroll tax; Supplementary Medical Insurance (SMI) covers physicians' services and a variety of other medical costs (e.g., diagnostic tests, x-rays, rental of oxygen tanks, etc.) and is financed by premiums paid by the individual plus federal government contributions from general revenues that are at least equal to the premiums. (These two components are frequently referred to respectively as Medicare Part A and Medicare Part B.) SMI has thus been characterized as "a voluntary individual insurance program with government subsidy that is underwritten and administered by the government, using private carriers to assist with the administration (Myers, 1981: 396).

HI benefits. Certain forms of medical service are not covered by Medicare, the most important of which are out-of-hospital prescription drugs, routine physical examinations, prescription and furnishing of eyeglasses and hearing aids, inoculations, cosmetic surgery (except to repair an injury), and custodial care (e.g., nursing homes).

HI benefits cover inpatient hospital care, posthospital services in a skilled nursing facility (SNF) and posthospital home health (HH) services. For each spell of illness, inpatient hospital benefits cover the first 90 days, in addition to which the individual has a "lifetime reserve" of 60 days that can be used after a 90-day spell has been exhausted. A "spell of illness" begins with admission to the hospital and ends when the individual has not been an inpatient in a hospital or SNF for 60 consecutive days. A portion of the costs must be paid by the beneficiary—(1) an initial deductible ($204 in 1981) that rises each year with increases in hospital costs, and (2) a daily charge equal to 25 percent of the deductible after the first 60 days of the 90-day benefit period and 50 percent for any of the 60 lifetime reserve days that are used.

SNF services are designed for individuals who need medical attention (as distinguished from simple custodial care) but who can be served in less costly facilities than hospitals. To be eligible for SNF benefits, an individual must have spent at least 3 consecutive days in a hospital and have been admitted to the SNF within 30 days after discharge. The first 20 days of SNF service are free of charge to the individual; each of the next 80 days requires a payment equal to one-eighth of the initial (hospital) deductible. HH services, for which there is no cost-sharing requirement, include visits by nurses and therapists, part-time services of health aides, and the costs of medical appliances.

SMI benefits. SMI benefits are available, by and large, to all persons 65 and older who elect to pay the premiums, irrespective of whether they are covered by HI. They are also available to disabled individuals eligible for HI who elect coverage. Individuals who fail to elect coverage when first eligible may enroll later but only at a higher premium rate. This is to discourage the adverse selection of risk that might occur if individuals could without penalty delay coverage until the probability of illness was higher.

Beneficiaries are entitled to reimbursement of 80 percent of reasonable charges for physicians' and other allowable medical services, after a deductible of $60 per calendar year. There is no dollar maximum on covered services, except for psychiatric services outside of hospitals and for service of independent physical therapists. Doctors may be paid directly by SMI for covered amounts if they agree to this procedure, in which case the doctor then bills the patient for the remainder (the deductible plus the 20 percent). More typically, the doctor is paid directly by the patient, who then submits the doctor's itemized bill to the insurance carrier (typically Blue Shield) for reimbursement. All funds for payment of benefits and for the administrative expenses of the carriers come from the SMI Trust Fund in the Treasury Department. This fund consists of the premiums paid by those who elect coverage plus appropriations from the Treasury for the government subsidy, plus interest earnings. Premium rates are determined each December and become effective during the 12-month period beginning in the following July. They rise automatically in proportion to increases in hospital costs. The rate for the year ending June 30, 1982, was $89 per month—up from $33 for 1973-1974.

FINANCING OASDHI

The OASDHI program is financed by a payroll tax on employers and employees that in 1982 stood at 6.70 percent of the first $35,700 of wage or salary income for each worker. The tax rate for self-employed individuals was 10.05 percent. Each year the maximum earnings subject to tax rises by the percentage increase in average wages two years earlier. The tax rate is scheduled to rise in stages to a maximum of 7.65 percent in 1990. Of the total tax, a portion is allocated by the statute to each of the three programs; in 1982 the rates were 4.575 for OASI, .825 for DI, and 1.30 for HI. Three separate trust funds have been established in the Treasury, into which the respective tax revenues flow and from which benefits are paid. (As explained in the preceding section, there is also an SMI Trust Fund for Part B of Medicare.) Excess funds are invested in U.S. government obligations.

Some basic relationships. Before considering some of the financial problems that OASDHI has and will continue to face, it is useful to consider how the characteristics of the program that have been described affect its financing. To begin with, any retirement program that bases eligibility on work experience but that allows individuals to qualify for benefits after relatively short periods of covered employment will experience steep increases in costs from the time of its initiation until it "matures." In 1940, when OASI benefits first became payable, only a minute fraction of all persons 65 and over were eligible to receive them, as the overwhelming majority had already retired and could thus not achieve eligibility. As a consequence there were 50 taxpaying workers for every beneficiary in 1945. In contrast, in 1980 even persons 100 years of age would have been only 56 at the time social security taxes first became payable; virtually all persons 65 and over were thus potentially eligible for benefits. As a consequence, the number of taxpayers per beneficiary (which had been about 14 in 1950) dropped to 5 in 1960, 4 in 1970, and 3 in 1980.

To put all of this in other terms, benefit costs as a percentage of covered payrolls would necessarily increase under these circumstances, even if average benefits conferred by the program had remained constant relative to average earnings. Given that basic fact, there are two ways in which the rising costs might have been met: (1) The payroll tax might have started out very low and have risen each year sufficiently to yield the revenues required by that year's benefit costs—a so-called pay-as-you-go system. (2) The tax might have been fixed at a level sufficient to pay the long-run costs of the program, being higher than necessary at the outset and building up a reserve invested in government securities; in later years, the payroll tax would have been below the actual current benefit costs, the difference being provided by interest earnings on the reserves. Although a modified reserve plan was originally contemplated, the tax rate increases that it called for were not put in place, and so the OASDHI program has been financed largely on a pay-as-you-go basis.

It is sometimes argued that this results in shifting the burden of supporting retirees from the generation for whom the payroll tax is low to the later one that pays the higher rate. In point of fact, the argument is specious. The only difference between a pay-as-you-go and a reserve system of financing social security is the *form* of the tax burden *within* each generation. With a reserve system the earlier generation pays a higher payroll tax than it otherwise would but lower taxes of other kinds, as the surplus social security revenues that are invested in government securities are available for other governmental purposes. After the program matures, the reserve system allows lower payroll taxes, but the interest on the government securities held by the trust fund must be raised by other forms of taxes. Thus, there is no escaping the economic truism that the costs of supporting each generation of retired workers *must* come out of current production. The goods and services that retired persons consume, in other words, must be produced by those who are then at work.

Analogous to the long-run increases in the OASDHI costs that have been produced by the maturing of the program are those that are forecast for the future because of demographic changes. As we learned in Chapter 4, the surge in the birth rate after World War II and its subsequent decline resulted in a population bulge—the baby boom—the first of whose members will reach retirement age in the second decade of the next century. Although there are considerable uncertainties concerning the future course of fertility rates, this factor along with increases in longevity is expected to reduce the number of taxpayers per beneficiary from the current level of three to two by the year 2030.

In addition to the factors that can produce long-run changes in the costs of OASDI there are factors that can have effects in the very short run. Changes in the level of unemployment and in rates of change in wages and prices are particularly important. As unemployment rises tax revenues obviously decline, and benefit costs may rise if individuals 62 years of age and older retire as the result of job loss. Increases in wages have the immediate effect of increasing revenues; increases in prices, by virtue of indexing, cause benefits to rise. When wages are rising faster than prices—which is the historic pattern—income into the OASDI trust funds tend to increase faster than outgo. Should this pattern be reversed—as it was during much of the 1970s and early 1980s[3]—a drain on the trust funds tends to occur.

OASDI financing problems The foregoing discussion should make it easy to understand the financial crisis that the social security system faced in the early 1980s. In April 1982, the Trustees of the OASDHI trust funds (Secretaries of Health and Human Services, Labor, and Treasury) announced that (1) without some action the program would be unable to pay benefits by mid-1983; (2) scheduled payroll tax increases in 1985, 1986, and 1990 would create a favorable trust fund balance until 2010; but (3) thereafter and particularly from 2030 to 2055 there would be a "substantial deficit under all but the most optimistic assumptions." Over the total 75-year planning period the average deficit would be 1.52 percent of payrolls under intermediate assumptions and 6.17 percent under pessimistic assumptions.

The short-run problem was essentially a product of unfavorable economic conditions—high unemployment rates and rates of inflation that outstripped increases in money wages. The long-run problem was a product of the demographic factors that have been described.

To meet these problems, a variety of measures to increase the income and/or to reduce the payments from the OASDI trust funds were debated (Munnell, 1983). Among the principal suggestions for increasing revenues were (1) advancing the scheduled increases in payroll tax, (2) financing part of the cost of the program from general revenues, (3) extending coverage to federal employees and to the employees of state and local governments and nonprofit organizations that had not elected coverage, and (4) taxing a portion of social security benefits, with the proceeds to be transferred to the OASDI Trust Funds. Proposals to reduce the projected levels of benefits included (1) modification of the cost-of-living adjustment, (2) gradually increasing the age for normal retirement, and (3) changing the procedure for calculating AIME so that replacement rates would gradually decline. The latter two suggestions, of course, were relevant to the long-run financial problem.

The rationale for several of these proposals may be explored briefly. Those who favored modifying the cost-of-living allowance pointed out (1) that social security beneficiaries had fared better than employed wage earners in keeping up with inflation during a period in which prices had risen faster than wages, and (2) that the way in which the CPI treated housing had resulted in an overstatment of the rise in living costs, especially for older people, among whom home ownership rates are high. The argument for raising the retirement age rested largely on the achieved and prospective increases in life expectancy and on the likelihood that future cohorts of older persons would be healthier and better educated with correspondingly improved opportunities for employment. Proponents of the change pointed out that in the first half of the next century the average individual would have as many years of life remaining after age 68 as did the average 65-year-old in the early days of social security. It was acknowledged, however, that a rise in the retirement age might pose hardships for older workers in poor health and for those who became unemployed. The argument for declining replacement rates over time rested on the judgment that society's obligation to successive generations of retirees can be fulfilled by guaranteeing an *absolute* rather than a *relative* standard of living, or at least that it does not require retirement benefits of future generations of retirees to rise *pari passu* with the wages of future generations of workers.

Not surprisingly, it was not easy for Congress to choose between raising taxes and reducing benefits in a program that currently has 36 million beneficiaries and that ultimately will affect virtually the total population. Although there had been several recent studies and reports (Advisory Council on Social Security, 1979; National Commission of Social Security, 1981; President's Commission on Pension Policy, 1981), President Reagan appointed a bipartisan National Commission on Social Security Reform at the end of 1981 in the hope that a political compromise might be effected. The commission's report (1983) identified a $150-200 billion shortfall for the years 1983-1989, and a long-range deficit (1981-2056) equal to 1.80 percent of taxable payroll. A "consensus" package of recommendations supported by 12 of the 15 members was estimated to meet the short-run problem completely and to cover about two-thirds of the long-run problem. For dealing with the remaining one-third of the long-run deficit the 12 members disagreed; 7 advocated raising the retirement age and 5 proposed increasing the payroll tax by about .5 percent beginning in 2010.

The commission's report provided the hoped for basis for compromise, and Congress enacted a financing bill in March 1983. Its principal provisions were as follows: (1) The payroll tax was increased from 6.7 to 7.0 percent in 1984, to be offset by a .3 percent income tax credit in that year; the remaining scheduled increases in the payroll tax remained largely unchanged, with the rate reaching 7.65 in 1990. (2) *Newly hired* federal employees as well as all employees of nonprofit organizations were mandatorily covered beginning in 1984. (3) The retirement age at which full benefits may be received will increase to 66 by the year 2009 and to 67 by 2027. (4) A sliding scale income tax formula was applied to social security benefits such that some tax liability will exist if 50 percent of benefits plus other income exceeds $25,000 for individuals and $32,000 for those filing joint returns. (5) Cost-of-living adjustments, (COLA) which had hitherto gone into effect in July of each year, were to be delayed until the following January; if after 1984 the OASDI trust fund falls below 20 percent of estimated outgo for any year, the COLA will be based on the increase that has occurred in prices *or* wages, whichever is lower. (6) The credit for retiring after the age at which full benefits are payable will increase gradually to an ultimate 8 percent by 2010. (7) The retirement test was liberalized by reducing benefits by $1.00 for every $3.00 (rather than the current $2.00) of earnings over the specified level, effective in 1990.

While these changes were expected to resolve the financial problems of OASDI for at least the next 75 years, a moment's reflection should indicate that it is not possible to be completely confident of this. As has been seen, both in the short run and in the long run a large number of factors that are very difficult to predict have profound effects on income to and payments from the OASDI trust funds. However, realistic acknowledgment of this fact is by no means to suggest that the OASDI system is in continuous peril. On the contrary, the impressive fact is that relatively minor adjustments that in no way compromise the essential character or integrity of the program have been and almost certainly will continue to be adequate to keep the program actuarially sound. In this context, perhaps the most significant aspect of the report of National Commission on Social Security Reform (1983) is the following *unanimous* recommendation:

> The members of the national Commission believe that the Congress, in its deliberations on financing proposals, should not alter the fundamental structure of the Social Security program or undermine

its fundamental principles. The National Commission considered, but rejected, proposals to make the Social Security program a voluntary one, or to transform it into a program under which benefits are a product exclusively of the contributions paid, or to convert it into a fully-funded program, or to change it to a program under which benefits are conditioned on the showing of financial need.

Medicare financing problems. Unlike the combined OASDI trust funds, the HI trust fund in the early 1980s had a comfortable surplus, amounting in 1982 to almost $21 billion, or over 50 percent of estimated annual outgo. Indeed, substantial loans were made by the HI to the OASI fund in order to allow the latter to continue to pay benefits. However, this rosy status of the HI fund is not destined to last. According to intermediate cost estimates, if no changes are made in the current law, the fund is expected to be depleted by 1990 and to have deficits of about $400 billion by 1995. Currently scheduled payroll taxes would cover less than one-third of the projected costs in 2055. The basic reason for the difficulty lies in the high rates of increase in hospital costs, which are projected to continue. Increasing proportions of older persons are also a contributing factor but a less important one than hospital costs.

The National Commission for Social Security Reform made no recommendations for Medicare, because a Social Security Advisory Committee had been appointed to consider that program. It is clear that there must be either substantial increases in revenues or much more heroic measures for controlling hospital costs than have hitherto been tried. So far as revenues are concerned, many observers have noted that because the incidence of medical expenses is unrelated to prior earnings there is less justification for payroll taxes in the case of HI than for OASI. Hence, payment of some or all of the cost from general revenues has been suggested.

NOTES

1. Newly hired federal employees will be covered under amendments adopted in 1983.

2. The reason for ending the process at age 60 is that the benefit calculation is made for the time when the individual is first eligible for retirement benefits (age 62), but there is a two-year lag in the availability of data on average annual earnings of all workers.

3. Of the 43 years between 1940 and 1982 there were only twelve in which real average weekly wages declined: eight of these occurred between 1970 and 1982.

QUESTIONS FOR DISCUSSION

1. To what extent, if any, would income maintenance programs be necessary in the absence of a poverty problem?

2. Differentiate between social insurance and social assistance. Do you regard the distinction to be hard and fast? In your view, is it desirable to have both types of programs?

3. Are social insurance programs really "insurance"? Irrespective of your response, might it have made a difference if the OASI program had been called OASC (Old Age and Survivors' Compensation?).

4. Had the income maintenance system in the United States been mapped out in its entirety in advance, how do you think it would differ from what we now have?

5. What do you see as the major principles underlying OASDHI? Discuss the significance and the relative importance of each.

6. Is OASDHI a "good deal" for someone entering the labor market today? Do you regard this to be a relevant and sensible question? How confident should a 20-year-old be of receiving an old age benefit upon retirement?

7. How do you react to the 1983 amendments to the Social Security Act? Given the nature of the financial problems faced by the OASDI trust funds, are there alternative solutions you would have preferred?

12

Unemployment Compensation and Workers' Compensation

Unemployment and work-connected injury and illness are pervasive sources of economic insecurity. During the decade of the 1970s in the United States, the proportion of individuals with work experience during a year who experienced some unemployment ranged between 14 and 20 percent; in recent years the incidence of occupational injury and illness has been in the neighborhood of 9 per 100 full-time workers, with 3 or 4 involving at least some loss of time from work.

Unemployment Compensation (UC) and Workers' Compensation (WC) are social insurance programs designed to provide a degree of protection against these risks. Both provide partial compensation for income loss; WC, in addition, covers the medical costs attributable to work-connected illness and injury. Although the federal government plays an important role in the case of UC, both UC and WC are essentially state programs and thus vary considerably among states. In this chapter we describe the essential features of each program and examine some of the important policy issues relating to each.

UNEMPLOYMENT COMPENSATION

While the principal and most obvious purpose of unemployment compensation is to protect workers against some of the income loss resulting from unemployment, the program serves at least two additional social purposes. First, it serves as an economic stabilizer by pumping purchasing power into the hands of consumers when unemployment begins to swell during a recession, thus preventing the economic decline from being as deep as it otherwise would be. Moreover, as we will see, the firm's UC tax rate is inversely related to the amount of unemployment it has "caused," which at least theoretically provides employers with an economic incentive to stabilize employment. Second, UC serves as a subsidy to job search, removing some of the pressure on an unemployed individual to take the first job that comes along. Aside from the obvious advantage that this creates for the individual, it at least potentially results in a more nearly optimal allocation of human resources.

The evolution of unemployment compensation. Great Britain adopted the first national system of unemployment insurance in 1911, and nine other nations had developed compulsory programs by the time the Social Security Act was passed in the United States in 1935. Although there were legislative attempts as early as 1916, it remained for the economic collapse of the early 1930s to produce a real explosion of interest in unemployment insurance in the United States; in 1933 there were a total of 83 bills under consideration in state legislatures.

Despite this flurry of legislative activity, only one state—Wisconsin—had enacted an unemployment insurance law by 1935. The chief impediment to the adoption of legislation was each state's fear that the enactment of a law would place employers at a competitive disadvantage relative to employers in other states. This log jam was broken in an ingenious way by the Social Security Act. While the act did not create a national system of UC, it imposed a 3 percent payroll tax on employers with the stipulation that employers who paid taxes into an approved state UC system would be permitted to deduct their maximum state tax liability[1] from the amount of the federal tax up to 90 percent of the federal tax. What this meant was that if a state failed to enact a UC law, the employers in that state would pay a 3 percent payroll tax to the federal government and workers would have none of the advantages of UC; if, on the other hand, the state enacted an approved UC law with a maximum tax rate of 2.7 percent, employers would pay 0.3 percent to the federal government and a rate not exceeding 2.7 percent to the state. Little wonder that within two years all of the states had enacted legislation.

The conditions that state laws had to meet in order to qualify employers for the tax offset were very few and related more to procedure than to substance. Indeed, the only substantive requirement was that a state could not disqualify a worker from benefits for refusing to accept a job that (1) was vacant because of labor dispute, (2) would require membership in a company-dominated union or prohibit membership in a bona fide union, or (3) had substandard wages, hours, or working conditions. Thus, states were almost completely free to develop whatever eligibility requirements and benefit rights they chose, and the laws are characterized by considerable diversity.

Eligibility. All of the state laws require a stipulated amount of recent work experience in employment subject to the UC tax as a condition for receiving unemployment benefits. We turn first, then, to the question of what employments are covered by the laws. When the Social Secuirty Act was first passed, the federal payroll tax for UC was applicable to employers of eight or more persons, with a number of excluded categories of employment. Because the tax offset provisions of the law applied only to covered employment, the state laws almost without exception had the same coverage limitations so that only about 60 percent of all wage and salary jobs were initially covered. Over the years the size-of-firm limitation was first reduced and then eliminated, and most of the originally excluded types of employment were subjected to the payroll tax. As a consequence, coverage currently extends to over 95 percent of all wage and salary workers, the only significant exclusions being agricultural workers on small farms and most domestic servants.[2]

There are several different methods for defining the recent employment experience required for eligibility. All state laws specify either a minimum amount of wages or a minimum number of weeks of employment, or both, that the worker must have accumulated within a recent 12-month period known as the *base period*—most commonly the first four of the last five calendar quarters prior to filing a claim for benefits. The requirements are designed to assure that benefits go only to persons with reasonably firm attachment to the labor force. Although they are not stringent—20 weeks of employment and/or $600-$700 of earnings would allow an individual to qualify in most states—they do preclude the payment of benefits to new entrants to the labor market, to reentrants who have been absent from the market for more than a year, and to individuals whose recent labor market experience has been only casual.

In addition to these qualifying requirements, all states require as a condition of eligibility that the unemployed individual be able to work and available for work. In this context, the laws almost universally require the claimant to register for work at a public employment office; refusal to accept a referral to a suitable job is a basis for disqualification. In addition, most of the laws require the climant to make an independent search for work. Despite the ability-to-work requirement, several states have provided that a temporary spell of illness during an uninterrupted period of unemployment will not preclude the receipt of benefits.

All but about a dozen states require a one-week waiting period before benefits can be paid; that is, the first week of unemployment in any year is noncompensable. However, a number of states with a waiting period requirement provide for the retroactive compensation of the waiting week if the spell of unemployment exceeds a specified duration.

Even when all of the foregoing eligibility requirements are met, an individual may be disqualified from the receipt of benefits for a variety of reasons that are spelled out in the laws. The most important causes of disqualification—which appear in all of the laws—are (1) voluntarily quitting a job without just cause; (2) discharge for misconduct; (3) refusal of suitable work; and (4) unemployment resulting from a labor dispute. Each of these is obviously far from unambiguous, and it is not surprising that the administrative agencies and the courts in the states have had to hear a large number of cases involving them. Moreoover, the wording of the provisions is not uniform from state to state. For these reasons it is not possible to review in detail the interpretations that have been placed upon the disqualification provisions; however, some broad generalizations can be made.

What constitutes good or sufficient cause for a voluntary quit (i.e., so that it will not be disqualifying) varies among the states, but generally is confined to causes *related to the job* or *attributable to the employer.* Thus, a person who leaves a job because a disabled relative needs the individual's attention at home would almost invariably be disqualified from the receipt of benefits upon reentering the labor market. Disqualification for misconduct likewise relates to misconduct on the job. In some states discharges for certain types of misconduct (e.g., stealing) invoke more severe disqualifications than discharges for less serious offenses.

Most of the state laws contain criteria for deciding what constitutes "suitable work." These typically include the degree of risk to the individual's health, safety, and morals; the claimant's physical fitness and prior training, experience, and earnings; the distance of the job from the claimant's residence; and the duration of unemployment in relation to the claimant's prospects of finding local work in a customary occupation. The last criterion suggests that the claimant is expected to adjust job requirements downward to some extent as the job search continues to be unsuccessful. Some states make this expectation more explicit by formally providing for the redefinition of suitable work as the spell of unemployment is prolonged. To illustrate, Maine's law provides that after 12 weeks of unemployment an individual's prior wage is no longer to be considered in determining whether a job is suitable; the Wyoming law provides that after 4 weeks of unemployment a "suitable wage" is one that is as much as 75 percent of the claimant's prior earnings.

The labor dispute disqualification has a different motivation than those that have been described above. The latter are designed to restrict the payment of benefits to claimants who are in some sense responsible for their unemployment; the purpose of the labor dispute disqualification, on the other hand, is to preserve the "neutrality" of the unemployment compensation system in labor-management disputes. From this point of view the denial of benefits during work stoppages (which prevents UC from providing "strike benefits") is regarded to be the analogue of the provision that prohibits disqualification for refusing a job vacant because of a labor dispute (which prevents UC from operating as a "strike-breaking" agency).

Even if one accepts this point of view, there are obvious difficulties in deciding what kinds of disputes should be disqualifying and which categories of individuals becoming unemployed by virtue of a work stoppage should have unemployment benefits denied. With respect to the first of these issues, very few state laws contain a definition of a labor dispute, but about one-third of the laws exclude lockouts from the disqualification and several exclude disputes resulting from an employer's failure to comply with a labor law and/or the provisions of a collective bargaining agreement. With respect to the second, most of the laws confine the disqualification to workers employed by the establishment in which the work stoppage occurs, exclude individuals from the disqualification provision if neither they nor any workers of the same grade or class of workers are "participating in," "financing," and/or "directly interested in" the dispute.

Although there is considerable uniformity among the states in the *causes* for disqualification, there is substantial variation in its *duration*. The greatest uniformity in this regard prevails in the labor dispute disqualification, which in all but two states is for the duration of the work stoppage. The two exceptions are New York and Rhode Island, where benefits are payable after the strike has lasted seven and six weeks, respectively. In the other causes for disqualification there are two major patterns. Most of the state laws disqualify the worker for the duration of the spell of unemployment that is attributable to the disqualifying act—such as voluntarily quitting a job—and require the individual to become reemployed and to earn a specified amount of wages before regaining eligibility for benefits. A minority of states have a less punitive arrangement under which the disqualification is for a specified number of weeks after which benefits can be paid if the individual remains unemployed. The laws with this type of provision appear to take the view that even if the initial unemployment was the worker's fault, once it continues for, say, five or six weeks it is attributable to the state of the labor market rather than the worker's original act.

Benefits. For unemployed workers meeting all the eligibility requirements, what amount of benefits will be payable? When UC was first developed in the United States, the notion was that the program should make up about one-half of the lost earnings of the unemployed worker. The overwhelming majority of states adhere to this standard, although it is implemented in a variety of ways. The most common arrangement is to compute the weekly benefit amount (WBA) as a fraction—generally from 1/22 to 1/26—of the claimant's highest quarterly earnings during the base year. A fraction of 1/26 would be equivalent to 50 percent of the average weekly wage during the quarter for a regularly employed full-time worker.

There is a maximum weekly benefit in every state, which means that high-wage workers will not achieve the 50 percent wage replacement described above. The maxima were originally specified in absolute dollar amounts, which required repeated legislative action if wage replacement ratios were not to be eroded by rising prices and wages. To meet this problem, most states today specify the maximum WBA as a percentage (50-70) of the statewide average weekly wage in covered employment. As of mid-1983, the maximum WBA for a worker without dependents ranged from $84 in Indiana to $223 in West Virginia, with most states falling within the range of $125-$175. When dependents' allowances are included (in the dozen states that provide for them), the highest maximum benefit was $258 (in Massachusetts).

In addition to benefits for total unemployment, all of the states provide compensation for partial unemployment, which is defined as a situation in which a worker's earnings, as a result of involuntary loss of work, are less than what the WBA for total unemployment would be. Most states calculate the benefit for partial unemployment by substracting the part-time earnings, less a specified amount that is disregarded, from the WBA for total unemployment. The provision for disregarding a portion of earnings is designed to make part-time employment more attractive than total unemployment, but the amount of the "disregard" is frequently too small to accomplish this result.

All of the state laws limit the number of weeks of benefits during any benefit year (i.e., the 12-month period following the filing of a claim). In all but a few states the maximum is 26 weeks, but it is as low as 20 in one state and ranges between 30 and 34 in four. In addition, several states provide for longer durations when state unemployment rates exceed specified levels. In some states all eligible individuals are entitled to the maximum number of weeks of benefits if their unemployment lasts that long; in most states, however, the duration of benefits depends upon the extent of the individual's employment and/or earnings during the base year.

Since 1970 there has been a program of extended benefits that is jointly financed by the federal and state governments and that is "triggered" when unemployment exceeds prescribed levels. Originally the "triggers" were defined in terms of either state *or* national unemployment levels, but legislation adopted in 1981 at the behest of the Reagan administration eliminated the national trigger and imposed more restrictive requirements for the state trigger. When extended benefits are triggered in a state, they allow benefits for an additional period equal to one-half of the regular benefit duration (but no longer than an additional 13 weeks).

How to protect large numbers of workers who exhaust their rights to UC benefits during recession has perennially plagued the UC system. The earliest response to this issue occurred in the recession year of 1958, when Congress passed the Temporary Unemployment Compensation Act allowing the payment of up to 13 additional weeks of benefits. On one other occasion (1961) prior to the adoption of the permanent extended benefit program and on several occasions since, temporary legislation has extended the maximum duration of benefits. The most recent illustration is the Federal Supplemental Compensation Act of 1982, which authorized a temporary program of additional benefits—within more stringent eligibility requirements—ranging between 6 and 10 weeks depending upon unemployment conditions in the state. Experience with these provisions raises the question of whether ad hoc changes in benefit duration under UC are the most effective way of dealing with the problem of large-scale, long-term unemployment. Some careful students of UC have concluded that they are not (Hamermesh, 1977: 107-108).

As the result of an early ruling of the Internal Revenue Service, UC benefits were exempt from federal income taxation until 1979 when some portion of benefits became taxable for individuals whose income exceeded specified threshold levels. As of 1983 these thresholds were $12,000 for single taxpayers and $18,00 for married individuals filing joint returns.

Financing. As has been seen, there is a Federal Unemployment Tax levied on the payrolls of covered employers against which state taxes may be offset up to a prescribed maximum of 2.7 percent. As of 1983, the gross federal tax rate (before the offset) was 3.5 percent levied on the first $7,000 of annual wages paid to each employee (the so-called *tax base*). Thus, the *net* federal tax was 0.8 percent. Revenues from the federal tax are used for three purposes: (1) to make grants to the states covering the administrative costs of both UC and the public employment service; (2) to pay the federal share of the cost of extended benefits; and (3) to make loans to states whose UC funds are threatened or depleted.

Except for three states in which a tax is imposed also on the wages of employees, state UC programs are financed exclusively by payroll taxes on employers. The tax base in most states is the same as for the federal tax, but more than 20 states use a higher base. All states use a system of *experience rating*, which relates the employer's tax rate to the unemployment experience of the firm. There are several methods of accomplishing this, the most common of which (used in 32 states) is the reserve ratio system. In this system every employer has an account that is credited with the taxes that the firm has paid (and a proportionate share of interest earnings on the state's fund) and debited with the benefit payments made to the firm's employees. The balance in the account at any moment of time is referred to as the employer's reserve and is expressed as a percentage of the average payroll of the firm. The higher this *reserve ratio*, the lower the employer's tax rate, within limits prescribed by a schedule contained in the law. Actually, the law contains several schedules with different levels of rates. The schedule in use in a given year depends on the size of the state's fund relative to total covered payrolls. As of mid-1983 minimum tax rates ranged between 0 and 3.7 percent; the range for the maximum rates was from 2.9 to 10 percent.

It is important to note that the firm's tax rate depends upon the amount of benefits that have been *paid* to workers. Employers thus have an incentive to contest the payment of benefits and to lobby for more restrictive disqualification provisions. This is one of the factors that accounts for the fact that the disqualification provisions of state laws have become increasingly restrictive over the years.

Administration. Each state has an employment security agency responsible for the administration of UC, and the Bureau of Employment Security in the United States Department of Labor is charged with the federal responsibilities under the program. As one of the conditions for receiving administrative grants, states are required by the Social Security Act to provide an opportunity for appeals to claimants whose benefits have been denied. Accordingly, all states have a system in which *either the claimant or the employer* can have the decision of the administrative agency reviewed by a quasi-judicial hearing officer, and about half of the states provide for another level of appeal to a review tribunal. The parties then have recourse to the state courts.

Operating statistics. Table 12.1 shows the very substantial variation in the number of unemployment compensation claims and in the amount of benefit disbursements as economic conditions change. In 1973, when the overall unemployment rate (CPS) was 4.9 percent, about 5.3 million workers collected $4.0 billion in benefits; two years later, when the unemployment rate had climbed to 8.5 percent, the number of claimants exceeded 11 million and benefits reached almost $12 billion. In the earlier year about 1.5 workers exhausted their benefit rights, 28 percent of the total number of claimants; in 1975 there were 4.2 million exhaustees, 38 percent of the total.

Average weekly benefits have risen considerably over the past three decades in real terms, and have even risen slightly more than average weekly earnings. Between 1950 and 1980 the average weekly UC benefit for total unemployment rose from $20.76 to $98.92, an increase of 376 percent. Over the same 30-year period

TABLE 12.1   Unemployment Compensation Operating Statistics, 1973-1982

Item	1973	1975	1980	1982
Number of recipients (in thousands)	5,328	11,160	10,001	11,617
Average weekly number of insured unemployed (in thousands)	1,632	3,986	3,350	4,054
Exhaustees	1,495	4,195	3,076	4,164
Total benefits (billions of dollars)	4.0	11.7	14.4	21.5

SOURCE: *Social Security Bulletin*, August (1983: 54).

average weekly earnings of production and nonsupervisory workers in the private sector of the economy rose from $53.13 to $235.10, a rise of 342 percent.

Some economic issues in UC. In the early days of UC, experience rating was a hotly debated issue, but this method of financing has by now become so firmly entrenched that the issue is largely academic. In their original UC laws, a number of states simply imposed a flat 2.7 percent tax on all employers. In light of the 90 percent tax offset provision of the Social Security Act, this was the rate that would allow the largest portion of the federal tax to redound to the advantage of the state. Experience indicated, however, that the UC program did not require that high a tax rate. Given the provisions of the Social Security Act, the only way in which a state could reduce its tax on employers without requiring them to pay correspondingly higher federal taxes was through experience rating. It was therefore not long before all of the states had adopted it.

The principal argument for experience rating is that it gives employers an economic incentive to stabilize their employment. Additionally, because it give employers an economic stake in the decisions made by the administrative agency, it is argued that employers will help to police the system against fraudulent receipt of benefits. Finally, some observers contend that economic justice and efficiency are served by requiring every industry and firm to pay for its own unemployment.

On the other side, it has been noted that unemployment is largely beyond the control of individual employers and that there is ample economic incentive to stabilize employment even in the absence of experience rating to the extent that employers are able to accomplish this. Opponents acknowledge that employers are motivated by experience rating to police the administration of the system but argue that many employers have been unduly assiduous in contesting claims and in lobbying for more restrictive disqualification provisions in the state laws with the result that UC programs have been subverted from their purpose of providing adequate protection.

Daniel Hamermesh's review of the evidence on the economic effects of UC has led him to conclude that experience rating has probably had some "slight stabilizing effect" as compared with a UC system financed by a uniform tax (Hamermesh, 1977: 72). He argues, however, that employers already paying the maximum tax rate are encouraged to increase the seasonality of their operations, and therefore advocates complete experience rating, with a minimum tax rate of 0 percent and no maximum.

Hamermesh (1977, 1981) has come to a number of other significant conclusions about the economic effects of UC that may be summarized briefly. However, it is only fair to point out (as Hamermesh acknowledges) that the evidence on which some of the conclusions rest is both incomplete and conflicting.

(1) The average (median) recipient of UC gets about one-half of after-tax earnings. For low-wage workers the corresponding fraction exceeds three-fourths.

(2) The ratio of average weekly UC benefits to average weekly earnings in covered employment has ranged between 32 and 37 percent since 1947, but varies substantially across states (e.g., 31 percent in Oregon and 43 percent in Colorado in 1977).

(3) Higher benefit levels induce longer spells of unemployment. A 20 percent increase in UC benefits may be expected to result in an increase of one-half to one week in average duration of unemployment.

(4) A longer potential duration of benefits induces lengthier spells of unemployment, but the effect is smaller during recessions than at other times.

(5) UC benefits under the regular state programs have offset only about 10 percent of the decline in purchasing power in recessions.

(6) Taking into account all of its effects, UC probably increases measured unemployment from what it would be in the absence of the program. The magnitude of the effect is about 0.7 percentage point when unemployment is low (e.g., 4 percent) and about .45 percentage point when unemployment is high (e.g., 7 percent).

Recommendations of the National Commission on Unemployment Compensation

The most comprehensive recent review and evaluation of the UC program in the United States is that made by the National Commission on Unemployment Compensation, a tripartite commission representing workers, employers, and the public that was appointed under a congressional mandate enacted in 1976. In July 1980 the commission made its report containing a large number of recommendations. Only the most important of these will be summarized here.

With respect to benefits, additional federal standards were recommended, including the requirement that the maximum UC benefit in each state be at least 55 percent of the average weekly wage starting in 1982 and rising ultimately to 66.67 percent in 1986. Below the maximum, the weekly benefit was to be at least 50 percent of the claimant's average weekly wage. To the states the commission advocated a goal of a 60 percent benefit level and urged liberalization of disqualification provisions. Greater protection for older workers and for all workers during periods of heavy unemployment were recommended to Congress. Extended durations up to a maximum of 52 or 65 weeks, depending upon the level of unemployment, were recommended. For workers 60-64 years of age meeting specified OASDHI coverage requirements, the suggestion was for a "lifetime reserve" of a maximum of 52 weeks of benefits to be used when other UC benefits had been exhausted. The exclusion of UC benefits from taxable income was also among the commission's recommendations.

The commission recommended expansion of UC coverage among farm and domestic workers and made several recommendations designed to put the UC program "on a sound financial footing." The most important of these was developing a flexible tax base for the federal unemployment tax by relating it to the level of covered wages. The base was to be 50 percent of average covered wages in 1983 and was to increase in stages to 65 percent in 1989. The commission estimated that the taxable base under this proposal would become $8,000 in 1983 and rise to $16,100 in 1989.

The commission's chairman was Professor Wilbur J. Cohen, a long-time student and administrator of social security programs in the United States. In his introductory statement to the commission's report in which he pleaded for favorable consideration of the recommendations, he said the following:

Members of the Commission and the staff have worked diligently and creatively to develop recommendations that are responsible and practical. I believe that the proposals are responsible and practical. I believe they are conservative because they will help to preserve the Federal-State system. I believe they are feasible. I believe they are within our ability to pay, and I believe they are completely consistent with the underlying philosophy of the Federal-State system.

One may agree with Professor Cohen, but the political climate in the early 1980s was not conducive to the liberalization of social insurance programs.

WORKERS' COMPENSATION

Historically, the legal status of the risk of industrial injuries differed substantially from the risk of unemployment, which helps to account for some of the differences in the development and the current characteristics of workers' compensation and unemployment compensation. In the case of unemployment, employers historically had no responsibility—and certainly no legal liability— for periods of unemployment that befell their employees. Even if a long-service worker was terminated permanently and without warning simply because this suited the purposes of the employer, the latter had no obligation to compensate the worker for his or her loss. In the case of industrial injuries on the other hand, a long tradition under the English common law recognized the liability of the employer, at least to the extent that the employer's negligence was responsible for the injury. From this point of view, workers' compensation is an institution that insures the *employer* against liability as well as insuring the worker against the risks of work-connected injury and disease.

Historical development. Actually, the employer's liability under the common law was less complete than the foregoing statement might suggest. Even if negligent, the employer might escape liability by successfully invoking any of three common law defenses—contributory negligence, the fellow servant rule, and voluntary assumption of risk. In the case of the first of these, if it could be shown that negligence on the part of the injured worker— even in small part—contributed to the injury, the employer was exonerated. The same was true if the injury resulted in part from the negligence of a fellow worker, for the law took the position that a worker stood in a different relationship to the employing establishment than an outsider and thus could not—as the latter could—hold the employer liable for the negligent acts of agents of the employer (i.e., fellow workers of the injured employee). Finally, the voluntary assumption of risk doctrine held that the commonly recognized hazards that attached to certain occupations should be presumed to be known to the incumbents so that serving in the occupation signified that the worker had voluntarily assumed its inherent risks.

It takes relatively little imagination to realize that this kind of legal framework provided woefully inadequate protection to workers. Lawsuits were expensive and rarely successful, and while an occasional fortunate litigant might win a large reward, many injured workers were not compensated (Millis and Montgomery, 1938). The first type of reform was employer liability legislation, which restricted the employer's common law defense and introduced other changes that stacked the deck less markedly against the worker. Still, even under these laws there was the necessity for expensive and uncertain lawsuits.

It was in this context that interest developed early in this century in what was then called "workmen's compensation," the central idea of which was that compensation in industrial injury cases should be paid "without regard to fault." Such a program had been instituted in Germany as early as 1884. In 1908 Congress passed a statute of this kind covering federal civil servants in hazardous employments, and several states adopted analogous laws for workers in the private sector in 1911. Between 1911 and 1920 all but six states had enacted statutes of this kind, although it was not until 1948 that the last state (Mississippi) followed suit. In order to meet the tests of constitutionality that courts were then imposing, many of the early laws applied only to specified hazardous industries and even here made coverage elective. In the words of the National Commission on State Workmen's Compensation Laws (NCSWCL) these early constitutional doctrines, although no longer applicable, have left an "unmistakable imprint" on the current workers' compensation system (NCSWCL, 1972: 34).

In 1969, the Federal Coal Mine Health and Safety Act established a federal program of disability and survivors' benefits applicable to coal miners suffering from black lung disease (pneumoconiosis), which had been excluded from coverage under the state programs. In the following year Congress passed the Occupational Safety and Health Act (see Chapter 14), one of whose provisions created the NCSWCL to evaluate the existing WC system and to make recommendations for improvement. The commission's report (1972) made almost 100 recommendations for change, 19 of which were designated as being "essential." Most of these will be referred to in the ensuing description of the characteristics of the existing WC system in the United States.

Coverage: categories of workers. About 79 million workers—88 percent of total wage and salary employment—were covered by WC programs as of 1980. Although there had been a substantial increase in the extent of coverage over the preceding decade— from about 80 percent of the wage and salary work force in 1970, the NCSWCL recommendation for universal compulsory coverage had not yet been achieved. Departures from complete coverage result primarily from the total or partial exclusion of certain types of employment and from size-of-firm restrictions and, to a lesser extent, from the existence of elective laws in a few states.

Domestic servants, farm workers, and state and local government workers are among the groups for whom coverage is most typically restricted. Over a dozen states exclude most farm workers and almost two dozen fail to cover all state and local government employees. About a dozen states exclude from coverage workers in firms with fewer than a specified number of employees (two to six). The number of states with laws providing for elective coverage has declined substantially in recent years—from 19 in 1972 to fewer than 5 in 1980. Employers in such states generally elect coverage anyway because those who do not cannot take advantage of the common law defenses against liability in the event of a lawsuit. Finally, railroad workers and seamen are excluded from state laws because they are covered under federal employers' liability laws, which preserve their right to sue for damages.

Unlike the situation in unemployment compensation, there are no service or work experience qualifications for benefits in the case of workers' compensation. An individual achieves instant eligibility upon starting to work in a covered job. The difference between UC and WC in this respect obviously stems from the difference in the nature of the risk against which the programs are designed to provide protection.

Coverage: types of risk. There are three requirements for benefits under WC laws: There must be (1) an *impairment*, caused by (2) an *injury or disease* that is (3) *work connected* (NCSWCL, 1972: 49). An impairment is a medical condition—"any anatomic or functional abnormality"—which may or may not create a disability. If it does there will be cash benefits; even if it does not there will at least be medical benefits. So far as the definition of "injury" is concerned, the traditional criterion for compensability was the occurrence of an "accident" (i.e., a sudden, traumatic event). By this criterion, for example, a hernia that developed as the result of continuous heaving lifting would not be compensable but one produced by slipping while carrying a heavy load would be. This narrow interpretation of "accident" has largely disappeared, and the NCSWCL recommended its complete elimination.

Because of the traditional requirement of an accidental occurrence for compensability, occupational diseases were not ordinarily covered under the early WC legislation. This deficiency was first met by listing in the laws specific occupational diseases (e.g., lead poisoning) that were compensable. As time went on more and more states shifted to complete coverage of occupational diseases—that is, those that are produced by chronic exposure to specific occupational environments or activities. By 1972 there were 41 jurisdictions that had such laws, and the NCSWCL recommended in that year that it become universal. By 1978 all states had full coverage of work-connected diseases.

The criteria for deciding whether an injury or illness is work related have been the thorniest legal issue in workers' compensation. All of the state laws require that the impairment have arisen "out of and in the course of employment," but there is no uniformity of interpretation among or, indeed, even within states. The questions that have to be resolved relate to where and when an injury occurs (e.g., falling in the firm's parking lot at the end of the day) and to the nature of the activity of the individual at the time of the injury (e.g., playing table tennis in the company recreation room during lunch hour). Even more difficult are some of the issues relating to the compensability of occupational diseases—for example, how does one ascertain whether a heart disease has arisen "out of and in the course of employment"? Despite the obvious difficulties involved, the NCSWCL recommended the retention of the criterion.

Benefits. Three categories of benefits are provided by WC programs—cash, medical, and rehabilitation. Cash benefits are payable when the work-related impairment results in a disability, which may be either temporary total, permanent total, or permanent partial. Benefits are also paid to the survivors of workers who die from causes related to their work. A large majority of all claims for cash benefits under WC laws are for temporary total disability—the period of recuperation before the victim of an industrial injury returns to work. There is typically a waiting period of 3 or 7 days before benefits become payable, although retroactive payment is generally made if the disability exceeds a specified duration (ranging from 5 to 42 days). Fewer than one-half of the states have a maximum waiting period as short as 3 days or provide for retroactive compensation after as few as 14 days—one of the "nonessential" recommendations of the NCSWCL.

All of the WC laws specify the proportion of the worker's average weekly wage that is to be replaced up to a specified maximum. In both of these respects there have been significant improvement in recent years. In 1969 almost one-half of the states specified a replacement rate of under two-thirds; by 1977 all but 3 states had achieved that level. Maximum weekly benefits were also raised substantially, almost doubling between 1973 and 1977. In the latter year 42 states had flexible maximums, typically specified at 100 percent of the statewide average weekly wage. Nevertheless, 13 states still had maximum benefits that were under two-thirds of the statewide average weekly wage. Dependents' allowances, in addition to the basic cash benefit, are provided by 11 states.

The actual wage-replacement rate that prevails in a particular claim depends upon the worker's wage, the state maximum benefit, the required waiting period, and the duration of the worker's disability. For a three-week disability—approximately the average duration—the actual replacement rate in 1977 ranged between about 30 percent in Texas to about 70 percent in Iowa or (if dependents' allowances are included) 100 percent in Massachusetts. In most states the rate was 66.7 percent; the weighted national average rate was 58 percent for a worker with no dependents, up from 44 percent in 1969 (Price, 1979: 15).

Despite dramatic improvements over the past decade, prevailing benefit levels are below those recommended by the NCSWCL. It proposed a weekly benefit equal to 80 percent of *spendable earnings* (i.e., after taxes), and the elimination of dependents' allowances. It illustrated how this would work for a person earning the national average (1972) wage of $150. The weekly benefit would be $105.53 in the case of a family of four, or $97.49 for a single individual. By way of comparison, the conventional formula (two-thirds of gross weekly earnings) would yield a benefit of $100. The commission's recommendation for the maximum benefit was 200 percent of the statewide average weekly wage, to be achieved by 1981.

Permanent total disability and death claims account for under 1 percent of all compensable claims but for close to 15 percent of cash benefit payments. For such claims the gross weekly replacement rate and the maximum weekly benefit are generally the same as for temporary total disability, but a number of states impose limits on the duration of benefits. The NCSWCL recommended the elimination of all such restrictions.

Permanent partial disability benefits are payable to individuals who suffer a permanent impairment as the result of a work-connected injury or disease, without being completely disabled. There are two major types of permanent partial benefits. One is paid for "scheduled" losses—a list of specific impairments (e.g., loss of an index finger; loss of one arm at the elbow) for each of which a specified number of weeks of compensation is provided. The second type of permanent partial benefit is based on the extent of disability as measured by loss of wage-earning capacity.

Permanent partial disability is the most expensive aspect of workers' compensation, accounting for over 60 percent of cash benefits and over one-half of combined cash and medical benefits. In the words of the NCSWCL, it is also "the most controversial and complex aspect," with "more variations among the states" and "more divergence between statutes and practices" than any other category of benefits. The commission found the existing system for compensating permanent partial impairments to be quite unsatisfactory but refrained from making substantive recommendations, calling instead for a separate study and report on the issues involved.

Medical benefits account for one-third of all benefit payments under workers' compensation laws; less than one-fourth of all workers who suffer work-connected impairments remain disabled long enough to qualify for cash benefits. A large majority of the state alws provide full medical benefits for industrial injuries and occupational diseases, although restrictions are somewhat more common in the case of the latter than the former. The NCSWCL recommended the elimination of all statutory limits on the duration or dollar amounts paid for medical or physical rehabilitation services.

The NCSWCL found that WC provides satisfactory medical care during the acute and healing stages of the worker's impairment, but frequently leaves something to be desired with respect to physical rehabilitation and is even less satisfactory when it comes to providing adequate vocational rehabilitation services. It recommended strengthening the programs in both these respects.

Finally, it found that job placement services for rehabilitated workers generally need improvement, although it acknowledged that the second-injury funds that exist in all but a handful of states are helpful in this respect. These are funds from which compensation is paid to handicapped workers who suffer a subsequent injury. Their purpose is to assure full compensation to such an employee while charging the employer only for the benefits attributable to the second injury. To illustrate, in the absence of such an arrangement an employer might be reluctant to hire an employee who had previously lost an eye because a similar injury to the other eye would result in permanent total disability. With a second injury fund, however, the employer would be charged only for the permanent partial benefits payable for the loss of one eye.

Administration and financing. Like unemployment compensation in most states, workers' compensation is financed by charges paid by employers. Unlike unemployment compensation, however, workers' compensation in most states does not involve a state fund. There are actually three ways in which employers finance the payment of the statutory WC benefits to their employees: through the purchase of insurance from a private insurance carrier, from a state fund, or through self-insurance. Most of the states provide only for private insurance or, for employers who can demonstrate financial responsibility, self-insurance, However, 18 states have a state insurance fund; in 12 of these the state fund operates in competition with private carriers, and in the other 6 it is the exclusive insurance carrier for workers' compensation. Private insurance accounted for a little more than one-half of all WC cash and medical benefit payments in 1980; state and federal fund disbursements accounted for about one-third of the total; and self-insurance accounted for the remaining one-sixth.

A perennial source of controversy in WC has been the relative merits of state funds versus private insurance. The ratio of benefits to premiums is higher for the former than the latter, but there are a number of reasons why this does not provide a reliable answer to the question, including difficult-to-measure differences in the quality of claim service and accident prevention activities. The NCSWCL concluded that "the most serious problems [of WC] . . . can be solved without restructuring basic insurance arrangements" (NCSWCL, 1972: 113).

Analogous to experience rating in unemployment compensation, a system of merit rating in WC—which was the inspiration for the idea in UC—relates an employer's insurance premium to accident experience. There is first a series of rates for industry categories, and large employers within each of these have further differentiated rates based upon their individual experience. Although there is no good evidence that this sytsem has its intended effect of promoting industrial safety (Chelius and Smith, 1983) and although it stimulates employers to contest even legitimate claims, the NCSWCL advocated its retention and the extension of merit rating to smaller employers within industrial categories (NCSWCL, 1972: 97-98).

There is variation in the structure and functions of the agencies that administer WC. In about half the states the chief administrator of the WC system has administrative functions only and generally reports to the governor, to a cabinet officer (e.g., Secretary of Labor), or to members of a commission that operates as an appeals board. In most of the other states the adjudicating and administrative functions are combined; either the entire appeals tribunal has administrative responsibilities or one of its members is designated as the chief administrative officer. In five states there is no special tribunal for handling contested claims; they are heard by the regular state courts.

Operating statistics. WC benefits in the United States in 1980 (including black lung benefits) totaled $13.4 billion, of which 61 percent represented cash disability benefits, 10 percent went for cash survivors' benefits, and 29 percent paid the costs of medical care. Total premium costs amounted to $22 billion, or 1.94 percent of covered payroll. The ratio of benefits to covered payroll was 43 percent higher in 1980 than it had been in 1972 when the report of the NCSWCL was issued.

The National Commission's evaluation of WC. On the basis of its intensive analysis of the state WC programs, the NCSWCL (1972: 25) concluded that state WC laws

> are in general neither adequate nor equitable. While several States have good programs, and while medical care and some other aspects of workmen's compensation are commendable, strong points too often are matched by weak.

The commission considered several alternatives to a state system of WC but concluded that for the foreseeable future the best approach lies in strengthening the existing system along the lines of its recommendations. While it rejected the substituion of a federal system, it emphasized the important role the federal government could play and recommended that the president appoint a commission to provide encouragement and technical assistance to the states.

Finally, it recommended that if the states had not adopted its "essential" recommendations by 1975, there should be congressional action to guarantee compliance. As has been seen, substantial improvements have been made in the state programs in the decade since the appearance of the commission's report, but the WC system is still a long way from meeting the benefit and the coverage recommendations that the NCSWCL regarded to be essential, and no federal standards have been imposed. The concluding sentence of an analysis of the WC developments of the 1970s (Price, 1979: 24) appears to be still appropriate: "It is not yet clear . . . whether and how how the remaining problems will be solved within the current system."

NOTES

1. Employers were pemitted to deduct not only the amount of tax they *actually* paid, but also—if the state had variable tax rates depending on the employer's unemployment experience—the difference between that amount and the "normal" rate under the state law.

2. Railroad workers are also excluded, but this is because they are covered under a separate federal statute—the Railroad Unemployment Insurance Act.

QUESTIONS FOR DISCUSSION

1. To what extent are the differences between unemployment compensation and workers' compensation in the United States attributable to differences in the risk against which they provide protection? Which of the two do you regard to be more nearly an "insurance" program?

2. What are the several purposes that an unemployment compensation program serves? Do you see any potential conflicts or tradeoffs among these? Does the pursuit of one impede the achievement of another?

3. What is your reaction to the disqualification provisions of unemployment compensation laws? Which arrangement do you think is better social policy: duration disqualification, or disqualification for a specified number of weeks?

4. With respect to duration, for how much of the unemployment problem ought unemployment compensation be expected to

provide protection? Assuming that unemployment compensation protection is less than total, what supplementary arrangements do you recommend?

5. What is your appraisal of the recommendations of the National Commission on Unemployment Compensation? Are there any additional changes you would suggest?

6. How do you react to the experience (merit) rating provisions in (a) unemployment compensation; (b) workers' compensation?

7. Leaving aside the question of political feasibility, do you think we would be better served by a national system of (a) unemployment compensation; (b) workers' compensation?

8. How do you react to the recommendations of the National Commission on State Workmen's Compensation Laws?

13

Public Assistance

As we have seen, social insurance programs provide only partial protection against income loss—not necessarily enough to sustain all individuals who are eligible for payment, especially if they have no other resources and/or if the deprivation of earnings is protracted. Moreover, for persons without the required work experience social insurance provides no protection at all. Thus if society is to assure individuals of some minimum level of sustenance, there is need for what Robert Lampman (1981: 9) has called a "second line of defense." This is the role of public assistance, which makes benefits available on the basis of demonstrated need.

HISTORICAL DEVELOPMENT

Cash programs. Except for programs aiding veterans—which appeared as early as 1766—there were no examples of federal public assistance until the 1930s. Indeed, until about the end of the nineteenth century the responsibility for assuring adequate levels of support to individuals fell on their families, on private charities, and, as an occasional last resort, on the local community. At about the turn of the century, however, there were examples of state aid—for the blind in Ohio and for needy mothers and children in Illinois and Missouri. By 1935, 30 states had programs of assistance to the elderly, 27 had programs for the blind, and nearly all had plans for orphans (Lynn, 1977: 58).

To alleviate the widespread misery created by the collapse of the economy, the New Deal administration of Franklin Roosevelt introduced a variety of public assistance and work relief programs administered by the Federal Emergency Relief Administration (FERA) and the WPA. The passage of the Social Security Act in 1935 created three federal-state categorical programs—Old Age Assistance (OAA), Aid to the Blind (AB), and Aid to Dependent Children (ADC). Each of these was administered by the states but financed jointly by the state and national governments.

Several major changes were subsequently made in this basic structure. In 1950 a new category of cash benefits was introduced—Aid to the Permanently and Totally Disabled (APTD). In 1962 ADC became Aid to Families with Dependent Children, and states were for the first time authorized to make payments under certain circumstances to intact families in which the father was unemployed, thus partially removing the incentive for the father to move out of the house in order to allow his family to be provided for. About one-half of the states have introduced this AFDC-UF program.

Two important modifications in the AFCD program were made in 1967 in an effort to induce greater work effort on the part of AFDC recipients. The "carrot" was a change in the rules regarding earned income. Instead of the dollar-for-dollar reduction in AFDC benefits, which had amounted to an implicit tax rate of 100 percent, a "thirty plus one-third" rule was introduced under which the first $30 per month of earnings was disregarded and the remainder was "taxed" at the rate of 66.67 percent. The "stick" was the Work Incentive Program (WIN) under which benefits were to be denied to adult AFDC recipients who could profit from work-training programs but refused to register for them. Under a 1971 amendment, mothers of preschool children were exempt from the requirement but were required to register as soon as their children reached school age.

The "adult" categorical programs—OAA, AB, and APTD—have always been less controversial than AFDC. For one thing, they are less expensive. But what is even more important, the issue of "work versus welfare" does not arouse popular excitement with respect to these programs, because almost nobody is inclined to argue that their beneficiaries should be expected to work. Consequently, it was easier to generate support for eliminating the inequities in these programs that resulted from interstate variation in eligibility rules and benefit levels than for doing the same for the equivalent inequities in the AFDC program.

Accordingly, amendments to the Social Security Act were adopted in 1972 that nationalized the "adult" categorical programs, effective in 1974. The new program was called Supplemental Security Income (SSI) and provided for nationally uniform eligibility rules and benefit levels for the needy aged, blind, and disabled that were to be automatically adjusted upward each year in response to increases in the CPI. In order to assure that those then on the benefit rolls would not be worse off as the result of the change, states that had been paying higher benefits were *required* to supplement the federal payment to such persons, and were *permitted* to continue supplemental benefits for newly enrolled beneficiaries.

In-kind assistance. Programs that make available specific types of goods or services to the needy have become an important part of the public assistance program in the United States, accounting currently for over one-fourth of total expenditures. The motives for providing these in-kind rather than cash benefits are several. They may, for example, reflect a desire to serve some constituency other than the direct beneficiaries (e.g., farmers, in the case of food distribution). They may be designed to meet some other objective of social policy—the elimination of hunger or the improvement of health. Finally, they may reflect a basic distrust of the recipients' ability to spend cash benefits wisely in their own self interest—or an unwillingness to bear the costs of cash benefits if they are going to be spent on beer rather than bread.

The earliest major food transfer program was the direct distribution to the needy of surplus agricultural commodities by the FERA in 1933. This was replaced later in the decade by a food stamp program; a total of 1,741 counties and 88 cities had food stamp plans at one time or another between 1939 and 1943 (Lynn, 1977: 62). The origin of the current food stamp plan, however, dates from pilot programs in eight areas that were established by President Kennedy in 1961. Three years later Congress passed a law authorizing the establishment in local communities of *either* food stamp or commodity distribution plans; but it was not until 1973 that the food stamp program became mandatory and universal.

Housing assistance to the needy dates from the New Deal. As early as 1933 the National Industrial Recovery Act authorized the construction of low cost public housing, and in 1937 the National Housing Act provided for grants to local housing authorities for the construction of housing for low income families. A variety of additional plans developed in the 1960s, and in 1973 the Nixon administration embarked on a new plan under which the Department of Housing and Urban Development subsidizes the owner of housing that is rented to eligible families. The subsidy equals the difference between a "fair market rent" and what the family is expected to pay (15-25 percent of its income).

Medical benefits first became available to the recipients of OAA, AB, APTD, and AFDC in 1950, when an amendment to the Social Security Act provided for federal cost-sharing for such benefits. In 1960 this program was extended to the "medically indigent" aged—namely, those who were judged to be unable to pay medical bills, even if not qualifying for OAA. The Medical Assistance (Medicaid) program enacted in 1965 in effect extended this arrangement to the populations served by AB, APTD, and AFDC, although later legislation restricted the income limits for determining eligibility.

The National Defense Education Act of 1958 provided the first higher education benefits to needy families in the form of low interest loans. In 1965 the Higher Education Act provided for federal scholarships (Educational Opportunity Grants) to needy college students as well as for federally insured student loans for families with incomes under $15,000. A program of Basic Educational Opportunity Grants (BEOG) was authorized by legislation in 1972.

Energy assistance constitutes yet another form on in-kind assistance to the needy. This program was introduced in 1979 in the form of block grants to states in order to help low income families meet the sharp increases that had occurred in the price of fuel.

The development of a "nonsystem." Even this very cursory review of the development of the current public assistance programs in the United States indicates a very substantial expansion of aid to the needy over the past two decades. It also indicates, however, that the existing arrangements constitute a crazy-quilt of individual pieces, with very little in the way of integration and rationalization. All observers of "welfare" in the United States are struck with this characteristic. Lynn (1977: 84) cites the Joint Economic Committee of Congress:

> it is no longer possible—if, indeed, it ever was—to provide a convincing rationale for the programs as they exist in terms of who is

covered and who is excluded, benefit amounts, and eligibility conditions. . . . Additionally, the programs are extraordinarily complex, and the eligibility conditions and entitlement provision lack uniformity even among programs with similar objectives and structures.

Again, the President's Commission for a National Agenda for the Eighties (1980: 73) states,

One might consider the case of a recently widowed mother with children, one of whom is disabled. Under present conditions, this mother must apply to at least seven different programs to recieve the aid to which she is entitled. In a typical jurisdiction, she needs to travel to at least four different offices and fill out at least five different forms, answering 300 separate questions. The programs may treat this information differently. . . . Because each welfare program follows its own traditions, it may take 1,400 pieces of information just to determine accurately the woman's income.

MAJOR COMPONENTS OF PUBLIC ASSISTANCE

AFDC. AFDC is the largest of the cash public assistance programs. In 1980 it involved money payments of about $12.5 billion to an average of more than 3.5 million families with close to 7.5 million children. As has been mentioned, AFDC was designed for children who have been deprived of parental support. However, the composition of the beneficiaries has changed considerably since the program originated. In 1949 about two-fifths of the mothers in supported families were widows; by the mid-1960s this proportion had dropped to 6 percent. Thus, support goes overwhelmingly to homes in which the parents have either been divorced or separated or have never been married. Since the change in federal law in 1961 allowed payment to homes in which there is an able-bodied male if he is unemployed, 27 states have availed themselves of this UF (unemployed father) option under AFDC. The eligibility requirements, however, are both complex and restrictive. The man must have had 6 calendar quarters of work out of the 13 prior to his application, he must currently be working less than 100 hours per month, and he must be ineligible for unemployment compensation and be registered with the public employment service. Only about 5 percent of total AFDC benefits are paid under the UF program.

The federal share of the cost of AFDC varies depending on the per capita income of the state, but averages slightly under 60 percent. Administration of the program, however, rests exclusively with the states, in about half of which local government units also play a role. Each state establishes its own eligibility requirements and level of benefits, and there is wide variation in respect to each. For example the definition of "need" for a family of four ranged in 1978 from $187 to $566 per month (with a median of $334); but only 22 states actually paid the full level of need. Benefits per person in that year ranged from $26 per month in Mississippi to $120 in Wisconsin. In no state was the level of benefits sufficiently high to keep a family out of poverty if there was no other income or in-kind assistance. In early 1981 the national average monthly benefit was about $288 per family, or about $100 per person. Over the preceding decade the average benefits for a family of four had fallen almost 30 percent in real terms.

Recent longitudinal evidence from the University of Michigan Survey Research Center indicates that there is considerable turnover among AFDC recipients. Over the ten-year period 1969 to 1979 about one-fourth of the population received cash benefits or food stamps for at least some period of time; of this number, one-third received such aid in only one year and about one-fourth in six or more years. Less than 20 percent were in families in which public assistance accounted for the major portion of family income in eight or more years. Thus, contrary to a widespread popular belief, AFDC is more typically a means of dealing with temporary adversity than a means of making welfare a "way of life."

Nonetheless, the program remains the most controversial element in the public assistance program, largely because of the large increase that has occurred in benefit rolls and because of the character of its clientele. In 1980 the number of recipients of AFDC was about ten times as great as in 1940. Moreover, as Lynn (1977: 74) has observed,

> the program was becoming increasingly urban and black, and more and more involved fathers who had deserted their wives or who were not married to the children's mothers. No aspect of our national ideology was consistent with a continuation of this situation.

He then goes on to comment that the most remarkable aspect of the history of public assistance in the recent past is that "the problems of the AFDC program . . . are still largely unresolved."

SSI. At the beginning of 1983 about 3.9 million persons were receiving SSI payments—1.6 million aged, 2.2 million permanently and totally disabled, and 78 thousand blind. Total payments in 1981 amounted to $8.5 billion. As of July 1983, the nationally uniform basic benefit payable in the absence of other income became $304.30 for an individual and $456.40 for a couple. These amounts—which rise each year with increases in the CPI— represented about 75 and 90 percent of the respective poverty levels for one- and two-person families.

Many states supplement federal benefits to all or some categories of beneficiaries, and payments under state supplements in early 1983 amounted to about 20 percent of total benefits or 25 percent of the federal payments. The national average monthly payment per individual was $196—$146 for the aged, $242 for the blind, and $230 for the disabled. There was, however, considerable variation in these averages among the states. For instance, the average monthly benefit for the needy aged ranged between $83.79 in Maine and $211.60 in California.

These variations in the average level of benefits in part reflect the effects of state supplements and in part reflect interstate differences in the economic circumstances of the recipients. Federal law provides for a "disregard" of stipulated amounts of income in establishing eligibility and determining benefits and for a reduction in benefits equal to 50 percent of income over those limits. The limits are adjusted upward each year by the percentage increase in the CPI. In 1980 they stood at $65 per month for earned income and $20 per month for social security and other income. There are asset as well as income restrictions on eligibility for SSI. Assets (excluding the value of a home, automobile, property for self support, and life insurance policies under $1,500) may not exceed $1,500 for an individual or $2,250 for a couple.

General assistance. In addition to the categorical assistance programs that have been described, general assistance is available in most states for needy individuals who fall outside the categories provided for under the Social Security Act. There is wide variation in coverage and benefits, with some states providing only medical and burial expenses. As of the end of 1980 there were close to 800 thousand cases, involving almost 1 million individual beneficiaries. Illinois, New York and Pennsylvania accounted for two-thirds of the total case load and the same proportion of the total annual outlay of $1.4 billion in 1980. The monthly outlay per recipient averaged $130 for the nation, ranging between $13 in Mississippi and $160 in New Jersey.

Food stamps. The emergence and growth of the food stamp program is without question one of the most significant developments in public assistance during the past two decades. The reason for the importance of this program lies not only in the large number of persons that it serves, but more fundamentally in the facts that (1) it involves uniform national eligibility and benefit levels, and (2) it is noncategorical. The former characteristic helps to make interstate variation in *total* benefits accruing the AFDC and SSI recipients less unequal; the latter means that aid is available to the working poor irrespective of family structure.

The program is one in which eligible individuals are given coupons that can be used for the purchase of food in regular retail outlets. The federal government pays the cost of the stamps and part of the administrative costs; administration resides in the states. Families at or below the official poverty line are eligible for the stamps in amounts that depend primarily upon family size and the level and sources of family income. The maximum allotment is adjusted semiannually to reflect changes in the CPI; in 1980 it stood at $209 per month for a family of four.

In calculating the food stamp benefit, the first $75 of earned income is ignored and further allowances for work-related expenses and taxes are permitted up to 20 percent of earned income. The maximum allotment is reduced by 30 percent of income over and above the allowable deductions. To illustrate, in 1980 a family of four with a monthly income of $500 and allowable work-related expenses equal to the full 20 percent would have been eligible to receive $111.50 in food stamps, calculated as follows:

Income	$500
Basic disregard	−75
Allowable deductions	−100
Net earnings	325
Maximum allotment	209
Implicit tax (30% of 325)	−97.50
Food stamps	111.50

The number of recipients of food stamps grew from 6 million in 1972 to 20 million in 1980; expenditures rose from $1.9 billion to $8.7 billion. Among the reasons for this growth were the wider availability of benefits (universal availability was achieved by 1975); liberalization of benefits; higher rates of unemployment; and more widespread information about the program.

Medicaid. All of the states except Arizona provide medical benefits to individuals who receive federally supported public assistance, and more than 30 states extend benefits also to the "medically indigent." The costs of the program are shared by the federal and state governments, with the federal share being at least 50 percent or more, depending on the state's per capita income. The benefits provided by states vary, depending on which, if any, of a list of optional benefits listed in the federal law the particular state wishes to provide. To illustrate, payments per recipient exceed $1,000 per year in some states (e.g., Minnesota and New York) but are under $400 in others (e.g., Mississippi and Pennsylvania). Total federal expenditures on the program equalled $14.2 billion in 1980. There were 23 million recipients in that year, two-thirds of whom were below the poverty line.

THE ISSUE OF WELFARE REFORM

Welfare reform has been a perennial issue in the United States during most of the years after World War II. At the risk of some oversimplification, the following assertions appear to be warranted: (1) Very few students of public assistance find existing arrangements satisfactory; (2) there is a substantial consensus on the criteria for a good public assistance system; (3) most, but not all, observers agree that these criteria are for the most part not met by existing programs; (4) there is no consensus about what kind of reform is most desirable and most likely to succeed. In this section we examine briefly the criteria of a good needs-tested income maintenance system; point up the discrepanices between existing arrangements and those criteria; describe proposals for change that were made by the Nixon and the Carter administrations; and consider the relative merits of incremental change versus a fundamental overhaul.

Criteria for a good system. Barth, Carcagno, and Palmer (1974) have specified nine goals for an income-tested welfare system. Among the most important are the payment of adequate benefits, target efficiency, horizontal and vertical equity, and the preservation of work incentives. The meaning of benefit adequacy is, of course, clear although even persons who agree with the goal in principle may well disagree on the standard of living that society ought to be expected to underwrite. Target efficiency requires the program to be rather sharply focused on those who (by whatever definition) are in need, without "wasting" resources on those who are not. Horizontal equity requires individuals in similar economic circumstances to be treated equally—regardless of geographic location, of whether or not there are children in the family, and of whether need results from the absence of work or from low earnings. Vertical equity means that the amount of benefits should be systematically related to the degree of need and that families with higher earnings should receive more *total* income than those earning less. This is related to the work incentive goal, which means that the program ought to operate so that benefit recipients who are able to work will find it in their economic interest to do so.

In addition to these characteristics, a good program should contain incentives for family stability, or at least not induce family dissolution. It should also encourage self-reliance and independence among recipients and allow them to maintain their dignity. Finally the system should be coherent and administratively efficient. That is, considered as a whole it should be internally consistent and intelligible; it should be designed to achieve its objectives at the lowest possible cost and to be as simple as possible both for administrators and beneficiaries.

One of the major dilemmas of a public assistance program is that some of these goals are mutually incompatible. Consider the objectives of adequacy, target efficiency, and preservation of work incentives. Every income-conditioned assistance program involves three crucial variables: (1) the basic guarantee—the benefit that goes to an individual or family with no other income; (2) the implicit tax rate—the amount of benefits that must be given up for each dollar of earned income; and (3) the "break-even" point—the level of earned income at which no benefits are received. The adequacy criterion argues for a high guarantee; the work incentive criterion argues for a low tax rate; and the target efficiency criterion argues for a low break-even point. The problem lies in the fact that the three variables are arithmetically related to one another in the following manner:

$$\text{Break-even point} = \text{guarantee/tax rate.}$$

Thus, if the basic guarantee is $400 a month for a family of four and the tax rate is 50 percent, any level of earnings up to $800 a month or $9,600 per year will entitle the family to some benefits. On the other hand, with the same basic guarantee and a tax rate of 25 percent, families with earned incomes up to $19,200 a year will qualify. In other words, with any given level of adequacy, increasing incentives to work can be accomplished only by sacrificing some target efficiency. Albrecht (1982: 20) points out that this dilemma can be in part overcome by having a two-track system—one with a high guarantee and a high tax rate for groups that are unemployable or whose nonemployment society is willing to subsidize; the other with a lower guarantee and a lower tax rate for those whom society believes ought to be at work. But an arrangement of this kind appears to violate the principle of horizontal equity.

The ideal criteria versus existing programs. Virtually all of the criteria of a good welfare system are violated by the arrangements that currently prevail in the United States. To begin with, it is clear that no one can claim coherence or administrative simplicity for the nonsystem that has developed. Second, there are blatant horizontal inequities between the working and nonworking poor, and even more especially in the wide interstate variation that exists *within* particular programs—especially AFDC and Medicaid. Third, there are serious work disincentives resulting not only from high implicit tax rates (especially in AFDC) but also because of the "notch" phenomenon—a situation in which a small increase in earnings can result in an actual decrease in total income. For example, in the AFDC-UF program any work over the 100 hours per month maximum allowable for eligibility leads to the complete loss of benefits. As a more important example, Medicaid is an all or nothing proposition. As soon as earned income exceeds the break-even point, *all* Medicaid benefits are lost. Finally, the AFDC program, particularly in those states that do not have the UF component, encourages family breakups, for the presence of an able bodied male in the home precludes eligibility of the family for benefits.

The Nixon and the Carter proposals. In response to some of these problems the Nixon administration proposed a dramatic change in public assistance that would have gone far in reducing inequities among residents of different states and between the working and nonworking poor. The proposed Family Assistance Plan (FAP) would have abolished AFDC and have replaced it with a program of uniform national benefits for needy families with children.

The basic guarantee would have been $500 per year for each of the first two family members and $300 for each additional member, thus amounting to $1,600 for a family of four—about 40 percent of the poverty threshold as of 1970. Eligibility was to be limited to families whose resources (excluding home, household furnishings, and personal effects) did not exceed $1,500. Recipients were to be permitted to keep 50 percent of nonearned income (including social security benefits) and the first $720 of earned income per year without reduction in benefits. Beyond these limits (plus certain other exceptions, including the value of food stamps) benefits were to be reduced by $1.00 for every $2.00 of income (i.e., a 50 percent implicit tax rate). Bills containing two different versions of FAP were passed by the House of Representatives, one in 1970 and the other in 1971. Each was rejected by the Senate, however, largely because it was regarded by liberals to be too niggardly and by conservatives to be too costly.

The next major welfare reform proposal to receive serious congressional attention was President Carter's 1977 Program for Better Jobs and Income (PBJI), which would have replaced SSI, AFDC, and food stamps with a plan providing cash, tax credits, and jobs to low income persons. Unlike FAP, PBJI would have been available irrespective of the presence of children.

The amount of the basic guarantee would have varied for different categories of recipients (e.g., for aged, blind, and disabled, $3,750 per couple; for able-bodied adults under 65 without children, $2,200 per couple, for single-parent families, amounts ranging up to $6,000 depending on number of children). For those with total incomes high enough to be taxable, additional benefits equal to 20 percent of such taxable income would be paid. In order to prevent any current public assistance beneficiaries from being damaged by the proposed changes, state supplementation would be encouraged in such cases by federal cost-sharing.

In addition to the incentives to work that were incorporated in the proposal, job opportunities were to be created in the form of a "job-search assistance" program and the creation of 1.4 million additional public service jobs at the minimum wage. Those categories of PBJI applicants who were expected to work would have to make themselves available for such opportunities in order to be eligible for any cash benefits. PBJI was estimated to involve a net additional cost of $17.4 billion to the federal government and a reduction in costs to the states of $3.4 billion (Myers, 1981: 620).

When the initial bill for PBJI was unsuccessful in 1978, a somewhat scaled-down version was introduced in the following year but again was unsuccessful. As in the case of FAP the proposal was too much for those who objected to increased government spending and too little for those who believed that not enough public sector jobs were being provided or that the minimum wage that was contemplated for such jobs would damage regular public sector employees (Albrecht, 1982: 16).

Incrementalism versus overhaul. Even among those who believe that public assistance programs in the United States do not adequately discharge society's obligations to its needy members, there is disagreement about the best strategy for reform. The most basic issue is whether continued piecemeal improvements or a fundamental revamping of the system is the better alternative. One of the most frequently discussed means of achieving the latter is by means of a negative income tax (NIT), which would replace most if not all of the existing programs. While specific proposals vary considerably, the basic idea calls for an income guarantee that would vary only according to family size, and for benefit reductions (i.e., an implicit tax rate) on income beyond a specified "disregard." The NIT, in other words, would be similar to Nixon's FAP except that it would not be restricted to familes with children.

The relative merits of incrementalism versus fundamental change have been admirably summarized by Lynn (1977: 113-115). The basic arguments in favor of the incremental approach are its "proven record of success in reducing poverty" and the greater likelilhood that piecemeal changes will be accepted. Indeed, incrementalism

> is not *an* approach, it is *the* approach to policymaking given existing institutions. To put the point differently, the only practical way to achieve the elimination of poverty and income redistribution in this country is to do it gradually, incrementally, and, to avoid a middle class revolt, inefficiently.

In addition, fundamental change may involve unperceived flaws or unanticipated side effects; "incrementalism is the most practical way to learn how to solve social problems and how not to solve them."

On the other side, it is difficult to see how incremental change can overcome the horizontal inequities, the perverse incentives, and the inefficiencies that pervade the current system. Moreover, some of the obstacles to political acceptability of fundamental reform have been weakened. For instance, recent research evidence has shown that a negative income tax would have less serious adverse effects on work incentives than many had earlier believed (Moffitt, 1982: 213) and that there is greater turnover among welfare recipients than had been generally realized.

Another factor in this regard is the precedent of universal eligibility established by the food stamp plan, which means that an NIT would not have the effect of making entire new categories of individuals eligible for public benefits. Thus Lynn believes that "the sum total of experience with the existing system and the results of research on poverty have irrevocably altered the content of the welfare reform debate in a manner that should be favorable" to fundamental reform.

The President's Commission for a National Agenda for the Eighties (1980: 75), after reviewing various proposals for change, recommended just such a basic reform—"a minimum security income for all Americans" ranging between two-thirds and three-fourths of the poverty level, with a 50 percent implicit tax rate on earnings. The proposal would replace AFDC and food stamps, but would leave SSI in force because the higher income guarantee of that program is appropriate for groups that are not expected to work.

The inauguration of President Reagan not long after the commission rendered its report of course made this recommendation academic, for the new president was committed to reduce rather than expand federal programs and expenditures. Moreover, at least one student of public assistance in the United States argues that all substantial welfare reform in the United States—whether incremental or comprehensive—is dead. William Albrecht (1982) argues that despite its shortcomings, the existing system is pretty good and has been successful in almost eliminating poverty; movement toward a more uniform federal system would not necessarily be an improvement "since for any benefit generated by the reforms there would be a cost . . . [and] it is not entirely obvious that the net benefits would be positive" (p. 27). In any case reform is politically impossible because "too many people have a stake in the existing system to permit changes that are significant enough to be labeled reform" (p. 26). Thus, Albrecht concludes, demands for welfare reform are both unwarranted and futile. The latter characterization would seem to be less controversial than the former!

The Reagan administration's agenda for public assistance. In pursuit of his objective of reducing the power and expenditures of the federal government with respect to functions other than national defense, President Reagan proposed a number of changes in public assistance programs aimed at making them more restrictive, as well as a redivision of responsibilities between federal and state governments for AFDC, food stamps, and Medicaid.

Expressed in terms of dollars of constant (1981) purchasing power, Reagan's budget for fiscal year 1983 called for a reduction from 1981 levels of $5.7 billion (−32 percent) for food stamps and other nutrition programs (a 20 percent decline for food stamps alone), $2.6 billion (−14 percent) for Medicaid, $2.2 billion (−27 percent) for AFDC, and $0.2 billion (−3 percent) for SSI. In current dollars federal expenditures for these programs amounted to $33.7 billion in 1981; the proposed expenditure level for 1983 was $26.8 billion, a decrease of 21 percent, or a drop of from 1.18 percent to 0.78 percent of GNP (Aaron et al., 1982: 108, 115).

The Reagan proposals also called for turning over to the states beginning in fiscal yᴄᴙr 1984 sole responsibility for the financing as well as the administration of both AFDC and food stamps. In return, the federal government would assume full responsibility for Medicaid. If implemented, these changes would almost certainly result in even greater interstate variation in benefits than now exists as well as a lower average level of assistance. Medicaid benefits, on the other hand would become more uniform, but probably at a lower level than currently prevails in the states with more liberal benefits.

Congress was less inclined to honor the administration's requested budget cuts for public assistance in 1983 than it had been in the previous year. For AFDC, Medicaid, and food stamps combined, the administration had asked for cuts over a three-year period totaling $18.4 billion; the actual cuts approved by Congress totaled $3 billion. Nor had the proposed realignment of federal and state responsibilities been enacted by the end of fiscal year 1983. Indeed, as late as September 1982 eight former Secretaries of Health, Education and Welfare who served under all the presidents from Eisenhower through Carter proposed a move in the opposite direction, calling for a uniform national minimum benefit for AFDC.

In which direction policy will move remains to be seen. However, as of the end of fiscal year 1983 the prospects for improving—or indeed even maintaining—the pre-Reagan contours of public assistance in the United States appear to be dim.

QUESTIONS FOR DISCUSSION

1. Describe the major contours of social assistance in the United States. In your opinion, are there valid reasons for having both cash and in-kind programs?

2. How does the popular stereotype of welfare recipients correspond with whatever evidence is available? How do you account for whatever differences you perceive? Why does the SSI program evoke less opposition than AFDC? How would you formulate the work-versus-welfare issue? What is your personal view on this issue?

3. What several meanings attach to the phrase "welfare reform?" In your view, is substantial modification of the public assistance program (a) desirable? (b) feasible?

4. If you believe that some change is desirable, how do you stand on the issue of incrementalism versus fundamental overhaul? Under each of these headings, what types of changes appear to you to be most desirable?

5. If there were to be a universal negative income tax with a guarantee sufficiently high to eliminate poverty, would you advocate the elimination of all other income support programs? If not, which should remain, and why?

14

Aspects of
Human Resource Utilization

In Chapter 1 we defined human resource utilization as relating to the terms and conditions under which employment is offered by individual firms. Human resource utilization, in other words, is largely a matter of the personnel (human resource) practices and policies of particular employing establishments. However, there are a number of respects in which these policies and practices are regulated or controlled by government, and such controls are manifestations of *public policy* on human resource utilization. In this chapter we examine three largely unrelated examples of government regulation in this realm—minimum wage legislation, health and safety legislations, and fair employment practices (antidiscrimination) legislation. In each of these the federal government plays a major (although not exclusive) role; each is characterized by a number of highly controversial issues.

MINIMUM WAGE LEGISLATION

The Fair Labor Standards Act. The major minimum wage statute in the United States is the Fair Labor Standards Act (FLSA), enacted in 1938 after previous efforts at both the state and federal levels. Following precedents established in Australia in 1896 and in Great Britain in 1909, Massachusetts enacted the first minimum wage law in the United States in 1912, applicable to women and children. In the next year several other states followed suit, and by 1923 there were laws on the books of 16 states, the District of Columbia, and Puerto Rico. In that year the movement came to a halt with the Supreme Court's Adkins v. Children's Hospital decision, which invalidated the District of Columbia's statute as an unconstitutional infringement on freedom of contract.

With the advent of the New Deal administration of Franklin Roosevelt, minimum wages were included in the codes of fair competition of the National Industrial Recovery Act of 1933. However this statute also failed to pass the scrutiny of the Surpeme Court, as did New York State's minimum wage law, which had been couched in language that its framers had hoped would overcome the constitutional objections that the Supreme Court had enunciated in the Adkins case. By 1937, however, the Court had changed its mind on this as well as several other issues, and it upheld the minimum wage statute of the state of Washington. In the following year the FLSA not only successfully introduced a federal minimum wage for workers in interstate commerce but also required premium (time-and-a-half) pay for hours in excess of a standard work week and sharply curtailed child labor.

At the time of its passage, the FLSA imposed a minimum wage of $.25 per hour and a standard work week of 44 hours, which were to change by 1945 to $.40 per hour for a week of 40 hours. The law has been amended six times, increasing the minimum and extending the coverage of the act. Under the 1977 amendments, the minimum wage became $3.35 in 1981, with no further increases scheduled. Despite the large nominal increase in the minimum wage over the years, its relation to average wages in the economy has remained fairly stable or even declined. The $.75 minimum that became effective in 1950 represented 56 percent of the average hourly earnings of production and nonsupervisory workers in the private nonagricultural sector of the economy—a level that was not again achieved until the $1.60 minimum became effective in 1968. During the decade of the 1970s and the early 1980s the ratio fluctuated within the narrow range of 43 to 47 percent.

The coverage of the statute, on the other hand, has been very substantially extended—from about one-third of nonsupervisory private sector employment when the FLSA was first passed to about 90 percent after the 1977 amendments. As of 1980 well over one-half of all excluded private employment consisted of executive, administrative, and professional workers (13.1 million) and outside sales workers (2.4 million), whose exemption makes little or no difference from the standpoint of the minimum wage but is significant from the viewpoint of the hours provisions of the law. Of the remaining 7.5 million excluded workers, 4.2 million were in retail trade or service establishments with annual gross receipts below the level required for coverage, and 0.8 million were in small agricultural establishments. These three industrial sectors account for about three-fourths of all workers employed at or below the minimum wage (Minimum Wage Study Commission, 1981: 109-111). In the public sector federal employees are covered and state and local employees were for a time, until the Supreme Court in 1976 found this to be a violation of rights guaranteed by the Constitution to the states.

State laws. About three-fourths of the states have statutes establishing minimum wages, and almost all of those that do not are in the South. There is a great deal of variation, however, in their characteristics and their effectiveness. Some apply only to minors; some cover only particular industries; some have statutory minimum rates while others provide for industry committees or "wage boards" to establish minimum rates, generally after holding public hearings. In regard to level, about a dozen states match the minimum established by the FLSA, and some of these provide for automatic increases when the federal minimum is raised. Alaska and Connecticut require wage rates higher than the federal minimum. At the other extreme, however, a half dozen states have minimum wage rates under $2.00 per hour.

Controversy over minimum wage legislation. Minimum wage legislation has been an article of faith among "liberals" and social reformers for as long a time as such laws have been held to be pernicious by orthodox economists. To the former, minimum wage laws are a weapon for combating poverty, a method of preventing unfair competition in the labor market, and/or a means of promoting economic stability by bolstering the purchasing power of low income groups. To the latter, they result in the misallocation of resources and the distortion of the wage structure (see Chapter 5); what is worse, they impose special hardships on their intended beneficiaries by reducing employment opportunities for individuals whose marginal productivities are below the legislated minimum.

A large number of empirical studies have attempted to assess the economic consequences of minimum wage legislation. By far the most comprehensive of these is the work that has been done by the Minimum Wage Study Commission (MWSC), established pursuant to provisions of the 1977 amendments to the FLSA. Consisting of eight members—two each appointed by the Secretaries of Agriculture; Commerce; Labor; and Health, Education, and Welfare—the committee was charged with studying the "social, political, and economic ramifications" of the FLSA. It was to address itself particularly to 12 specific issues, including the demographic characteristics of minimum wage workers; the effects of the minimum wage on employment and unemployment, poverty, inflation, and wages above the minimum; the desirability of indexing the minimum wage to wages or prices; and the desirability of a subminimum for youth.

Over a three-year period the commission's staff reviewed previous research, conducted their own studies, and contracted with outside experts for additional research. The results were published in seven volumes in 1981, the first of which summarized all of the findings and contained the commission's recommendations (MWSC, 1981). The fact that the commission members were appointed by cabinet members in a Democratic administration created some suspicion about the impartiality of the research findings, but comparison of the results with those produced under the auspices of the conservative American Enterprise Institute reveals substantial comparability with no grounds for believing that either is biased (Eccles and Freeman, 1982: 227). The major findings of the MWSC on the issues listed above will be briefly reviewed.

Who are the minimum wage workers? In 1980. when the minimum wage under FLSA was $3.10 per hour, data from the CPS indicated that 10.6 million workers, or 12.4 percent of all wage and salary employees, were earning no more that that amount. Of these "minimum wage workers" (MMWs) about four-fifths were in establishments covered by the FLSA. As might be expected, the ratio of MWWs to total employment in nonsubject firms was much higher than in subject firms—30 percent versus 10 percent. A majority of MWWs are concentrated in two occupational and two industrial categories; almost three-fifths are in clerical (16 percent) or service (42 percent) occupations; and two-thirds are in retail trade (36 percent) or service (30 percent) industries.

The likelihood of being an MWW varies considerably by age, sex, and race. The proportions are as high as 44 percent among 16-to-

19-year-olds and 38 percent among persons 65 and older. About one-half of all MWWs are below the age of 25. Women are twice as likely as men to be MWWs (17.7 versus 8.2 percent); the rate is 18 percent among blacks and 11 percent among whites.

From the standpoint of the relationship of minimum wage legislation to the poverty problem perhaps the most informative data concern the distribution of MWWs among families with varying numbers of workers and at different income levels. Over one-half (54 percent) of all MWWs are in married-couple families with multiple earners. An additional 15 percent are in families headed by women, and 13 percent are either living alone or outside of family households. With regard to family income, about one-fourth of MWWs were in units with 1978 incomes under $6,000, but almost two-fifths (38.2 percent) were in families with incomes of $15,000 or more.

A full-time worker earning exactly the minimum wage in 1980 would have had an annual income of $6,200 ($3.10 × 2,000). The poverty threshold in that year was $4,256 for a single individual and $8,400 for a family of four. Only 11 percent of all MWWs were in units whose income put them below the poverty line; three-fourths were in families with incomes at least 1.5 times the poverty threshold.

The foregoing data help to explain why the minimum wage is not an efficient tool for combating poverty however desirable it may be for other reasons. All of the studies reviewed by the MWSC that have attempted to assess the impact of the minimum wage on income distribution point to the conclusion that "the minimum wage does little to ameliorate poverty," and that transfer payment mechanisms "would be more effective in providing income support" (MWSC, 1981: 88, 103).

Employment and unemployment effects. Scores of studies over the years, varying widely in sophistication, have attempted to assess the effects of minimum wages on employment and unemployment. Employment is probably a more appropriate dependent variable than unemployment for measuring whatever "harm" minimum wages inflict. For one thing, it is the variable the conventional theory links to wage level. Moreover, even if a minimum wage does in fact result in decreased employment, unemployment may not rise if workers leave the labor force in discouragement. Conversely, it is possible for unemployment to rise even without a decrease in employment opportunities if persons are lured into the labor force by the higher wage established by the minimum wage law (Brown et al., 1982).

Most recent studies using reasonably sophisticated econometric methods have focused on the effects of the minimum wage on the employment of teenagers, as they constitute such a large proportion of MWWs. The typical study has been based upon time-series data and has used as the explanatory variable a measure that captures increases in either the level of the minimum or the extent of coverage under the FLSA; also generally included in the multivariate framework are variables that control for business conditions, seasonal and secular trends, and the relative size of the youth population.

The evidence produced by about two dozen studies, although by no means uniform, suggests that the minimum wage does have an adverse effect upon the employment of teenage youth but that the effect is not very large; a 10 percent increase in the minimum wage reduces the employment of teenagers by between 1 and 3 percent. At 1981 levels of teenage employment, this represents between 77,000 and 231,000 jobs. There is no consistent evidence of a differential impact by either race or sex. The impact of the minimum on the employment of young adults (20-24) appears to be much smaller. Finally, although the character of the evidence is less satisfactory, it seems fair to conclude that minimum wage legislation has curtailed employment to some extent in low-wage industries, particularly in the manufacturing sector (MWSC, 1981: 35-45; Brown et al., 1982).

A subminimum for youth? Concern about high rates of unemployment among teenagers and about the probable role of the minimum wage in contributing to that problem has prompted periodic proposals for a lower minimum wage ("subminimum") for youth. The proposal has taken a variety of forms, ranging from a simple differential in which the minimum for teenagers would be 75 or 85 percent of the regular minimum to the 1983 Reagan administration's proposal under which a $2.50 youth minimum would apply only during the summer months (May through September). A special differential under the FLSA already exists for full-time students employed in retail and service establishments and in higher education. Under this Student Certification Program, students may be paid a wage no lower than 85 percent of the basic minimum for no more than 20 hours per week when school is in session and 40 hours at other times.

The principal argument against the youth subminimum is that it would substitute adult for youth unemployment, and organized labor has vigorously fought all such proposals. This danger is recognized by proponents of the change; most of the proposed bills have contained provisions prohibiting employers from substituting youth for adults, but these would be difficult if not impossible to enforce in view of the complex and subtle ways in which such substitution could occur. After examining the arguments pro and con and the limited evidence relating to the likely effects of a subminimum the MWSC concluded that "the record does not justify the establishment of a youth differential." In addition to the threat that it would pose to employment opportunities for adults, the commission emphasized its limited contribution to lowering teenage unemployment rates and the inequitable departure it would entail from the principal of equal pay for equal work. Moreover, the commission pointed out that the problem of teenage unemployment will probably be ameliorated as the baby boom generation passes into adulthood (MWSC, 1981: 57-58).

Inflationary effects of minimum wages. Estimating the effects of increases in the minimum wage on the rate of increase in prices is by no means a straightforward exercise. In addition to calculating the increases in wages paid to workers who were previously being paid less than the (new) minimum, one must estimate the indirect effects on the wages of workers who were previously above the minimum (the "ripple" effect), the effects of these changes in wages on the mix of various grades of labor and capital used in the productive process, and the impact of all these changes on productivity, unit labor costs, and prices.

According to one econometric simulation executed by the staff of the MWSC, if the minimum wage had been 10 percent higher than it was in each year between 1974 and 1979, total wages would have been higher by 0.8 percent and consumer prices higher by somewhat less than 0.3 percent. The *actual* increases that were legislated by the 1974 and 1977 amendments to the FLSA caused the minimum to rise from $2.00 to $2.90 between 1974 and 1979. This increase was estimated to have produced a 0.6 percent increase in the total wage bill and a 0.2 percent increase in consumer prices over the period. In view of the fact that the actual average annual rate of increase in the CPI over the 1974-1979 period was 9.3 percent, the contribution of the minimum wage to inflation was clearly quite small (MWSC, 1981: 69-70).

Indexation of the minimum wage. One problem faced by any legislated minimum wage is that its impact in *real* terms is quickly eroded during periods in which prices and wages are changing rapidly. As prices rise, the floor of real income provided by the minimum wage sinks; as the average level of wages in the economy increases, the *relative* protection provided by the minimum declines. The way in which the FLSA has handled this problem has been to provide for a schedule of rates over a specified period of time each time the law has been amended. However, as rates of inflation and of wage increase cannot be foreseen with any accuracy, this procedure by no means guarantees a stable relationship between the minimum and either prices or wages. To illustrate, the 1977 amendments to the FLSA provided for minima in each of the following four years that represented annual increases of 15.2, 9.4, 6.9, and 8.1 percent, respectively. The first of these was double the 7.6 percent rise in the CPI between 1977 and 1978, but each of the other three fell short of the inflation rate. However, because wage increases also lagged behind the inflation rate, the ratio of the minimum to average hourly earnings remained stable between 1978 and 1980 at about 47 percent and dropped to 46 percent in 1981. By 1982 the unchanged minimum wage ($3.35) had fallen to 43.6 percent of average hourly earnings.

On the basis of its evaluation of several methods of indexing the minimum wage, the MWSC recommended that it be tied to average hourly earnings in the private economy, with an automatic adjustment each year based on the previous year's change in earnings. The commission asserted that such "regular and predictable increases in the minimum wage would be noninflationary and would be easier for business to adjust to than the irregular increases of the present system (1981: 84).

Noncompliance with FLSA. A 1979 survey of a randomly selected sample of 15,000 establishments conducted at the request of the MWSC by the Department of Labor's Wage and Hour Division provides the basis for estimates of the extent of noncompliance with the wage and overtime provision of the FLSA. Violations of the wage provisions were found in 5 percent of the 2.6 million establishments subject to the act; among firms that had scheduled overtime work, 21 percent were found to be in violation of the overtime provisions of the law. In all, 13 percent of the establishments had violated one or both of the provisions. Two-thirds of a million workers were found to have been paid less than the minimum wage—a number that represents slightly over 1 percent of the 56 million workers subject to the act, but almost 12 percent of the subject employees whose earnings are at or below the minimum wage. About 90 percent of the violations occurred in retail trade and in the service industry. The MWSC found this level of noncompliance unacceptable and made several recommendations for tightening up the enforcement of the act.

Coverage recommendations of the MWSC. The MWSC evaluated the coverage provisions of the FLSA and made a number of recommendations for change. The most important of these was to bring within the protection of the law employees of low-volume retail trade and service establishments. As of 1978 there were about 1 million such establishments employing over 4 million nonsupervisory employees, about 1 million of whom were being paid less than the minimum wage. These low-wage workers were concentrated in one-half of the exempt firms. The commission pointed out that the elimination of this exemption would bring under the umbrella of the law the largest single group of nonsupervisory workers who are currently excluded.

THE OCCUPATIONAL SAFETY AND HEALTH ACT OF 1970

Efforts to protect the safety of workers through government action are over 100 years old in the United States, although it was not until the passage of the Occupational Safety and Health Act (OSHA) in 1970 that a comprehensive system of regulation was instituted. Massachusetts had enacted the first law regulating safety hazards in the workplace in 1877, and by 1970 almost all of the other states had passed safety legislation of one kind or another; however, with a few notable exceptions—New York and California—they were largely ineffective. The federal government had played a very limited role in this area, the most general example of which was the Walsh-Healey Public Contracts Act of 1936. In addition to providing that prevailing wages be paid by establishments holding government contracts in excess of $10,000, this statute authorized the Secretary of Labor to establish safety standards applicable to work under such contracts.

Ashford (1976) attributes the passage of OSHA and of the Coal Mine Health and Safety Act that had been enacted in the preceding year to a combination of factors, chief among which was the reversal of the long-run downward trend in injury rates during the 1960s. Between 1961 and 1970 injury rates increased by 29 percent; and while part of this shift was subsequently shown to be attributable to the high level of economic activity that prevailed during most of the period and to the influx into the labor force of large numbers of young, inexperienced workers, part of it remains unexplained (Chelius, 1983; Smith, 1976). A second factor was the increasing awareness of and sensitivity to certain forms of occupational disease, such as pneumoconiosis (black lung), beryllium disease, and the cancers produced by asbestos and vinyl chloride. The development of the environmental movement, which sensitized the population generally to environmental health hazards both off and on the job, was yet a third factor. Finally, the higher average level of educational attainment of the labor force operated to enhance the potency of each of these other factors.

Provisions. OSHA covers all employees in business affecting interstate commerce except those covered by other more specialized federal statutes (e.g, the Coal Mine Health and Safety Act). About 65 million workers in about 5 million workplaces fall under the protection of the law. Federal employees are also covered, with each agency being required to develop a safety and health program consistent with the OSHA standards applicable to private employers. State and local government workers are excluded from coverge, except that states that operate approved private sector programs (described below) must assure comparable protection for state and local government employees.

The "general duty" clause of the statute imposes on every covered employer the obligation to "furnish a place of employment . . . free from recognized hazards that cause or are likely to cause death or serious physical harm to employees." In addition, employers must comply with the specific safety and health standards that are promulgated under the act, and firms with 11 or more workers must keep records of all occupational injuries and diseases.

The chief enforcement agency is the Occupational Safety and Health Administration (OSHA) in the Department of Labor, which is empowered to set standards, conduct inspections, issue citations, and assess penalties. The development of standards, of which there are over 4,000 (at least half of which apply to the construction and maritime industries), may be initiated by OSHA itself or at the request of any interested party. In any case, all standards that OSHA intends to implement must first be published in the *Federal Register* with an opportunity for a public hearing if one is requested.

The inspection function of OSHA has been subject to considerable controversy and has been substantially modified in recent years. The law authorizes inspectors to enter establishments without delay and without advance notice. As the result of a Supreme Court decision, however, a search warrant is required if an employer demands one. With only a little over 1,000 compliance officers to inspect about 3 million workplaces, it is clear that inspections must be infrequent, perfunctory, or both. Under the Reagan administration, the agency has followed the policy of "targeting" inspections on higher-risk industries. Moreover, if a firm's records indicate that its injury rate is below the national average, no inspection of the premises is made. These policies, together with the elimination of "nit-picking" standards that had begun even under the Carter administration, have somewhat mollified industry while the AFL-CIO and certain public interest groups (e.g., Ralph Nader's Center for the Study of Responsive Law) have charged that the law is being emasculated.

The act assigns responsibilities to three agencies in addition to OSHA. The Occupational Safety and Health Review Commission is an independent quasi-judicial board of three members appointed by the president for three-year terms. Any ruling of OSHA challenged by an employer is heard by a commission-appointed officer whose report may be reviewed by the commission. An order by the commission may be appealed to the courts by the employer or by OSHA. The National Institute for Occupational Safety and Health (NIOSH) is a research organization within the Department of Health and Human Services that develops and recommends health and safety standards. Finally, the National Advisory Committee on Occupational Safety and Health, consisting of representatives of labor, management, occupational safety and health professionals, and the public, advises the Secretaries of Labor and of Health and Human Services on matters relating to administering the act.

Role of state safety and health programs. Under the federal law, states are permitted to develop and operate their own safety and health programs if they are at least as effective as the federal program. The federal government provides 90 percent of the developmental costs and 50 percent of the administrative costs when a state plan has been approved. Once final approval of a state plan is granted by OSHA, compliance is exclusively in the hands of state officers although the federal government continues to monitor the program. At the end of fiscal year 1982, 24 states were operating their own programs.

Implementation problems. There are a number of fundamental problems that make the setting of standards in a program like OSHA inherently difficult. For one thing, the diversity, complexity, and rapidity of change of productive processes make almost impossible the task of identifying all potential hazards and developing safeguards against their occurrence. For another, especially in the case of health hazards there is the question of whether the use of a substance or a process should be prohibited until proven safe, or permitted until proven unsafe. Third, there is the factual question of how unsafe a process actually is—that is, what level or degree of exposure to a potentially harmful substance constitutes what degree of risk? And finally, even if the degree of risk to health and safety can be precisely quantified, what costs ought society be willing to incur to reduce or eliminate it?

The Supreme Court has provided some guidance with respect to at least two of these questions. In a 1980 case the Court invalidated a benzene standard that had been promulgated by OSHA on the ground that a "significant risk" had not been demonstrated. In a 1981 cotton dust case, however, the Court held that so long as there is a significant risk and so long as a standard that will reduce or eliminate it is feasible, OSHA can legally impose the standard without showing that the benefits justify the costs. The Court, in other words, interpreted literally the act's requirement that health standards be established that assure "to the extent feasible . . . that no employee will suffer material impairment of health." The decision went on to suggest, however, that it is appropriate for OSHA to consider the "least costly alternative" in developing a standard.

On the basis of these guidelines, OSHA has developed a set of policies and procedures that it has dubbed the "Regulatory Management System." As described by the U.S. Department of Labor's Chief of Staff (Cowan, 1982), it consists of (1) ascertaining that a hazard constitutes a significant risk to workers; (2) verifying that the proposed standard would substantially reduce the risk; (3) setting the most protective exposure limit that is both technologically and economically feasible (with economic feasibility meaning that the standard must not eliminate the entire industry); and (4) utilizing the most cost-effective methods for achieving the result. It has been suggested that these criteria allow a considerable amount of desirable discretion to OSHA in its regulation of occupational health (Chelius, 1983).

Nevertheless, there appears to be no way of escaping a considerable amount of uncertainty in standard setting, as is illustrated by the experience with the vinyl chloride standard (Lave, 1980: 146-148). After almost incontrovertible evidence that exposure to vinyl chloride in plastic manufacture subjected workers to the risk of a rare form of liver cancer, OSHA proposed an exposure standard of 1 part per million, the feasibility of attaining which was disputed by the industry. The Firestone Tire and Rubber Company estimated a cost ranging from $450 million to $1 billion, but did not believe that even these expenditures would allow the standard to be met. When OSHA actually imposed the standard, industry-initiated research discovered a technology for meeting the standard at "virtually no cost," as it resulted in the recovery of much of the chemical that had previously been wasted.

Impact of OSHA. It is very difficult to assess empirically the impact of OSHA on injury rates in the United States because the character of the relevant data base changed with the introduction of the law. Nevertheless, the consensus of a number of indirect studies is that the law has had little or no effect on injury rates (Chelius, 1983). Smith (1976) has pointed out that most injuries result from some behavioral problem or transitory hazard. Only one-fourth of the total are estimated to result from a more-or-less permanent condition that is susceptible to regulation. Moreover, Smith observes that even in these cases there are virtually no incentives for compliance with the law prior to inspections. First, as has been seen, the probability of being inspected is small. Second, even when inspections occur, inspectors rarely discover or cite all violations. Third, penalties are trivial, averaging $170, or $25 per violation. Only a miniscule proportion of the violations for which penalties are assessed (1.2 percent) are what the act describes as "serious," with average fines of $648. The remainder draw fines that average $16. Smith's analysis antedated the changes in

OSHA policy initiated by the Reagan administration. The general relaxation of enforcement procedures (including reductions in the level of fines) that have occurred make Smith's generalizations even more pertinent in the early 1980s than when they were originally written.

Chelius (1983: 126) has concluded that the potential of OSHA in the realm of occupational health is considerably greater than in occupational safety. In the latter case, unlike the former,

> both workers and employers are felt to have sufficient information and motivation as to safety hazards and preventive techniques, and certainly more insight than government agencies into the specific problems of individual worksites.

Despite this judgment, which many students of the subject share, OSHA had devoted more of its resources to safety than to health. Only 11 health standards had been promulgated by the agency as late as 1983 and very few citations under them had been made. Finally, Chelius cites a number of studies that suggest that OSHA's health regulation has been inefficient in the sense of paying inadequate attention to achieving the greatest protection of lives and health that available resources permit. As we "simply cannot eliminate all risks, . . . it is sensible to regulate in a manner which generates the greatest results from our efforts" (Chelius, 1983: 172).

ANTIDISCRIMINATION REGULATION

The earliest government action aimed explicitly at combating labor market discrimination in the United States began to appear in the 1940s in the form of limited presidential executive orders and state statutes of varying degrees of effectiveness. However, not until the 1960s did the major elements of federal policy in this area emerge. The principal instruments were (1) the Equal Pay Act of 1963 (EPA), which prohibits sex differentials in pay for "equal work on jobs the performance of which requires equal skill, effort, and responsibility, and which are performed under similar working conditions;" (2) Title VII of the Civil Rights Act of 1964, which outlaws employment discrimination of any kind based on race, sex, religion, or national origin; (3) Executive Order 11246 of 1965, which makes discrimination illegal in establishments holding federal contracts; and the Age Discrimination in Employment Act of 1967 (ADEA), which prohibits discrimination against persons between 40 and 70 years of age.

The first fair employment practice (FEP) law was enacted by the state of New York in 1945. By the time the federal legislation of the 1960s took effect, about one-half of the states had such legislation. By the early 1980s FEP laws were on the statute books of all of the states except six (Alabama, Arkansas, Louisiana, Mississippi, Texas, and Virginia) plus the District of Columbia and Puerto Rico. Programs exist in some communities as well, so that the Federal Equal Employment Opportunity Commission (EEOC), which has the responsibility for enforcing Title VII, the EPA, and the ADEA, cooperates through work-sharing agreements with 69 state and local agencies in processing discrimination charges. The state laws vary considerably in the vigor with which they are enforced, and some are almost completely ineffective.

Title VII of the Civil Rights Act. The most comprehensive proscription of labor market discrimination is contained in Title VII of the Civil Rights Act, which applies to employers of 15 or more workers and, since 1972, to federal, state, and local government agencies. It forbids discrimination against an individual in hiring or discharge or "with respect to . . . compensation, terms, conditions, or privileges of employment because of such individual's race, color, religion, sex, or national origin." Unions and employment agencies are likewise prohibited from engaging in such discrimination.

Enforcement was vested by the act in the five-member EEOC, which subsequently (1979) also acquired responsibility for enforcing the EPA and the ADEA (hitherto the responsibilities of the Department of Labor). Through its 49 field officers and staff of about 3,500 employees, the EEOC has the authority to investigate charges of discrimination and attempt to resolve them through conciliation. If unsuccessful, it may seek enforcement through the Department of Justice or, since 1972, through suits initiated by itself. Aggrieved individuals may also bring suit if the EEOC chooses not to do so. It is important to note that the EEOC is not a quasi-judicial agency; it has no authority to issue compliance orders or to impose fines but must seek redress through the courts.

Executive Order 11246. Issued by President Johnson in 1965, E.O. 11246 (as subsequently amended by E.O. 11375 and E.O. 12080) prohibits employment discrimination based on race, sex, color, religion, or national origin by federal contractors and, further, requires such contractors to take "affirmative action" to assure equal employment opportunity. Enforcement is in the hands of the Office of Federal Contract Compliance Programs (OFCCP—formerly OFCC). OFCCP also administers the affirmative action provision of the Rehabilitation Act of 1973 applying to handicapped individuals.

Despite its more restrictive coverage, there are at least two respects in which the OFCCP can wage a more vigorous fight against discrimination than can the EEOC under Title VII. First, whereas the EEOC must await charges of discrimination, the OFCCP may on its own initiative seek to identify and eliminate it. Second, Title VII contains an explicit prohibition against quota hiring although such arrangements are permissible as a means of redressing violations of the law. E.O. 11246, on the other hand, actually *requires* contractors to take affirmative action including the setting of numerical "targets" to ensure that employment opportunities are extended to qualified women and minority group members. This issue will be discussed further below.

Although the OFCCP may impose sanctions, including the cancellation of a firm's eligibility for government contracts, such sanctions are rarely used; there was an average of only two "debarments" per year between 1971 and 1977. The agency "has preferred to adopt a positive, nonconfrontational approach emphasizing conciliation to achieve compliance and technical assistance to aid employers in meeting their contractual obligations" (U.S. Department of Labor, 1982b: 49). During fiscal year 1982 there were 3,081 compliance reviews of contractors employing 2.4 million workers. Complaints alleging discriminatory treatment led to 2,589 investigations. The agency executed 259 agreements in which contractors committed $7.3 million to redress violations, including back pay awards of $2.1 million to 1,133 individuals.

The Age Discrimination in Employment Act (ADEA). Although efforts were made to include age as one of the forms of discrimination prohibited by the Civil Rights Act of 1964, it was excluded "ostensibly because not enough was known about the nature and extent of the problem" (McConnell, 1983: 163). Instead, the Department of Labor was instructed to carry out a study of age discrimination. Its subsequent report to Congress noted that 50 percent of all job openings were closed to applicants 55 and older and that 25 percent were off limits to persons 45 and over. These and other findings led to the passage of the ADEA in 1967. The act prohibits employers (including government units after 1974), employment agencies, or labor organizations from discriminating on the basis of age in such matters as hiring, job retention, compensation, and other terms or conditions of employment.

As originally passed, the law covered workers between 40 and 65 years of age, and one of its effects, therefore, was to prohibit mandatory retirement at any age below 65. As amended in 1978, the upper age limit was raised to 70 and for most federal government employees mandatory retirement was outlawed at any age. Excluded from the higher mandatory retirement age in the private sector were executives entitled to an annual pension of at least $27,000. These individuals may be mandatorily retired on their sixty-fifth birthday.

Charges of age discrimination have grown dramatically in recent years, from about 5,400 in 1979 to almost 9,500 in 1981. The reason for the increase is not entirely clear, but may be the greater awareness of the act generated by the extensive discussion of the mandatory retirement issue during the debate on the 1978 amendments. Men accounted for almost two-thirds of all charges filed in 1981, and among both men and women almost one-half of the charges were brought by individuals in their fifties. Of the 15,000 alleged violations of the act, one-half involved discharge, layoff, or involuntary retirement, and 12 percent related to hiring; only 7 percent alleged discrimination in wages or benefits (McConnell, 1983).

What constitutes "discrimination"? It is one thing to outlaw labor market discrimination; it is quite another to decide precisely what constitutes discriminatory conduct. As the result of administrative guidelines and court decisions, a vast body of fair employment practice law has developed, only some basic elements of which can be hinted at here.

The prohibition of discrimination allows as exceptions preferential hiring based on bona fide occupational qualifications (BFOQ). To illustrate, the exclusion of women from "contact" positions in an all-male maximum security prison has been held to be permissible; a 35-year-old maximum hiring age for Greyhound bus drivers and a 40-year maximum for American Airline pilots have been held to be legal BFOQs on grounds of public safety. On the other hand, a circuit court has rejected the argument of an oil company that because its South American clients would refuse to deal with a woman the position of Director of International Relations required a male incumbent.

With respect to recruitment and selection, any procedure that has the effect of denying opportunities to qualified members of protected groups is illegal. For instance, recruitment by word of mouth through a firms's all-white work force would be a violation of the law. A requirement that applicants have a high school diploma in the absence of a showing that the requirement is related to job performance would likewise be illegal. A minimum height requirement that cannot be justified by the requirements of the job and that has the effect of excluding a higher proportion of women and Hispanic-Americans than of non-Hispanic males constitutes illegal discrimination. Motive or intent in these instances is irrelevant. If the *effect* of any requirement or test is to weed out a disproportionate number of minority members or of women and if the requirement cannot be shown to be related to job performance, its use is a violation of the law.

A number of rulings have exclusive relevance to sex discrimination. Protective state labor legislation that applies only to women has been held to violate the law. The Pregnancy Discrimination Act of 1978 requires pregnancy to be treated as any other physical condition in determining eligibility for employment or benefits. Sexual harassment is a prohibited form of sex discrimination and includes any conduct that has "the purpose or effect of substantially interfering with an individual's work performance or creating an intimidating, hostile, or offensive working environment." The employer is liable for the illegal behavior of supervisory personnel under all circumstances, but for the behavior of other employees only if the employer or its agents are in a position to know about it.

Two of the most recent sex discrimination issues relate to pensions and to the circumstances under which equal wages for men and women can be construed to constitute illegal discrimination. The latter issue—"comparable worth"—will be discussed below. With regard to pensions, the courts have held that the greater average longevity of women as compared to men does not justify differential treatment in pension benefits. In a 1978 case (Los Angeles v. Manhart) the Supreme Court ruled that it is illegal sex discrimination to require larger contributions to a retirement plan from women than from men. In 1983 (Arizona v. Norris) the Court held that the payment of lower monthly retirement benefits to women was also a violation of the law.

Has antidiscrimination policy been effective? The sensory perceptions of almost everyone over 35 years of age would suggest that antidiscrimination policies have had some effect. Black and female television anchorpersons, male telephone operators, and female bus drivers and coal miners were virtually unheard of thirty years ago. Nevertheless, economists have spent a considerable amount of research effort attempting to ascertain whether Title VII of the Civil Rights Act and E.O. 11246 have had their intended effects, and the findings have been mixed (Brown, 1981). Some of the studies, particularly those based upon comparisons of firms with and without government contracts, have shown no positive impact of E.O. 11246 on the relative position of blacks. Moreover, studies of the administrative processes of the EEOC and the OFCCP have raised doubts about their probable effectiveness. Lack of sufficient resources has been a persistent problem. In fiscal year 1973, EEOC had a professional staff of under 1,300 to deal with about 50,000 discrimination cases. A backlog fo 130,000 cases had developed by 1977. In the case of OFCCP, fewer than one-fifth of all contractors were subject to compliance reviews in the three-year period 1970-1972. EEOC has also been criticized for an unwise allocation of resources, devoting relatively too little effort to attacking "systemic" discrimination as opposed to cases involving single individuals.

In recent years some of these problems have been mitigated. An improved procedure for dealing with complaints has been developed by EEOC and greater emphasis has been placed on instances of systemic discrimination. The backlog of cases has fallen considerably, from 99,000 in December 1977 to 20,000 at the end of fiscal year 1981. On the other hand, a retrogression appears to be in progress under the Reagan administration. The number of federal contractors required to file affirmative action plans has been sharply reduced, as has the frequency of compliance reviews. Moreover, the administration has taken the position, contrary to court interpretations, that numerical goals for hiring and promotion are inappropriate even for organizations that have been pursuing discriminatory policies.

In any case, Brown's comprehensive review (1981) of the evidence produced by evaluative studies leads him to conclude that "the labor market position of minorities improved more rapidly in the past 15 years than might have been expected on the basis of prior trends, general business conditions, or the relative educational attainment of minorities." Female earnings, on the other hand have not increased appreciably relative to those of males, possibly as the result of the rapid rise in female labor force participation (Brown, 1981: 48). A more recent unpublished study of the U.S. Department of Labor has concluded that affirmative action has been effective in promoting the employment of blacks, women, and Hispanics. Between 1974 and 1980 total employment in firms holding government contracts grew more slowly than in firms not doing business with the government (+3 percent versus +8 percent). Nevertheless, minority employment rose by 20 percent in the former and 12 percent in the latter firms; the corresponding gains in female employment were 15 percent and 2 percent (Pear, 1983).

The issue of "reverse discrimination." By far the most controversial issue in antidiscrimination policy—and one which the courts have not yet fully resolved—relates to the use of quotas to rectify racial or sex imbalances in employment. As has been mentioned, the Civil Rights Act has been interpreted to permit this approach as a means of rectifying violation of the law but explicitly prohibits granting preference to protected groups purely as a means of compensating for prior discrimination in society at large. In implementing the affirmative action requirements of E.O. 11246, on the other hand, the OFCCP has required subject employers to establish "targets" for the employment of minorities and women.

The Supreme Court has expressed itself at least on the periphery of the issue in two important cases, the earlier of which (Bakke, 1978) did not involve alleged discrimination in employment but in admission to a University of California Medical School. In filling its 100 openings, the school had developed a special admissions program for economically or educationally disadvantaged minorities under which 16 students were to be admitted. Allan Bakke, an unsuccessful applicant under the regular program, claimed that the university's quota system was responsible for his failure to be admitted and thus had deprived him of his rights under the Fourteenth Amendment and violated Title VI of the Civil Rights Act, which prohibits discrimination under any program receiving federal financial assistance.

In a complex decision involving six separate opinions set forth in about 200 pages, a bare majority of the Supreme Court held that the University of California's quota system was unlawful but acknowledged that a university might take race into account in its admissions program either to counterbalance the effects of past discrimination in its admissions or to achieve racial or ethnic diversity among its study body.

In the 1979 Weber case, the Court considered the claim by Brian Weber, a white, that he had been unlawfully discriminated against by an agreement between the United Steelworkers and Kaiser Aluminum and Chemical Company providing for admissions to a training program based on seniority but equally divided between black and white employees. Weber, whose seniority on the white list was not sufficient to gain him admission, was able to show that several blacks were admitted who had less seniority than he. The Court denied Weber's claim, holding that Title VII does not prohibit voluntary affirmative action plans "designed to eliminate conspicuous racial imbalance in traditionally segregated job categories."

Quite aside from the law, the question of "reverse discrimination" poses difficult economic and moral dilemmas. On the one hand it is clear that reverse discrimination creates the same threat to economic efficiency as the discrimination for which it attempts to "atone"; that it is inequitable to those harmed by the preferential treatment (e.g., white males) who have not themselves been responsible for prior discrimination; and that it is demeaning to the preferred group itself whose successful members can never be sure that they "made it" on their own.

On the other hand it is also clear that preferential treatment for minorities and/or women would not intrude into a world in which other personnel decisions are made strictly according to merit or, indeed, in which merit can be precisely measured. Moreover, in view of the influence exerted by tradition and stereotypes even among those intellectually committed to nondiscrimination (e.g., Are you fully at ease with a male telephone operator? How would you feel as a passenger in an aircraft piloted by a 55-year-old woman?), it may perhaps be necessary to bend over backward to some extent in order to be assured of standing up straight. Considerations of these kinds make the appropriate public policy in this regard far from clear (at least to me). What is clear is that in the context of racial discrimination there is no completely satisfactory way of undoing the damage created by two centuries of criminal insanity.

The issue of "comparable worth." The doctrine of "comparable worth" has loomed large in recent discussions of sex discrimination in wages. While the phrase apparently means different things to different people, it has been defined by Alice Cook (1983: 495) as a

> concept calling for measuring the relative values . . . of disparate jobs, specifically of those done primarily by men and those done primarily by women, through the application of job evaluation and other systems that . . . attach . . . objective weights . . . to . . . gradations of skill, effort, responsibility, and working conditions.

According to the proponents of the comparable worth doctrine, the elimination of sex discrimination in wages requires more than equal pay for equal work (the criterion established by the Equal Pay Act of 1963). As they see it, the problem is that the vast majority of women workers are concentrated into a relatively few occupational categories that are paid lower wages than traditionally male jobs of no greater worth or value to the employer. The issue, therefore, is whether "employers should be required to go beyond paying equal wages for equal work to paying equal wages for different, but comparable jobs" (Koziara et al., 1983: 504). A related question is whether Title VII of the Civil Rights Act may require anything more than the EPA with respect to the relationship between male and female wages. This question has already been answered affirmatively by the Supreme Court in the Gunther case (1981) in which female jail matrons in Washington County, Oregon, had claimed that their substantially lower wages than those received by male guards represented sex discrimination. Although Gunther has frequently been referred to as the "comparable worth" case, this is in reality a misnomer as the Court merely ruled that suits under Title VII for sex discrimination in compensation are not limited to cases alleging unequal pay for similar work. In the Gunther case, there was evidence that the county had set the pay scale for female matrons relative to male guards at a lower level than "that warranted by its own survey of outside markets and the worth of the jobs."

The real problem in implementing the comparable worth doctrine, of course, is in developing a means of measuring "worth." As early as 1977 the EEOC commissioned the National Academy of Sciences to study the comparable worth issue. A committee report, issued in 1981, concluded that "women are systematically underpaid" and that, as promoting occupational desegregation will correct this situation only slowly, the concept of comparable worth "merits consideration as an alternative policy of intervention in the pay setting process." Nevertheless, the committee acknowledged that there is no universal standard of job worth and made no recommendations for specific changes in job evaluation plans or for other approaches to deal with the problem (Bureau of National Affairs, 1981).

There has been a great deal of recent activity on the comparable worth issue at the state level. Alice Cook reports that of the 39 states with equal pay statutes in 1982, 16 require equal pay for "comparable work" or "work of comparable character" (Cook, 1983: 497); however, the only judicial interpretations that have been made were in Pennsylvania where the courts have given the language the same interpretation as the EPA. Another type of legislation that has been adopted in more than a half dozen states directs personnel departments to reevaluate job and wage classification systems and to make whatever changes are required to make rates of pay reflect the value of the job irrespective of whether the work is similar.

Where all of this will lead is not as yet clear, but it seems entirely likely that Eleanor Holmes Norton, former Chairperson of EEOC, made a valid prediction in 1979 when she declared that "comparable worth will be the major issue for women in the 1980s."

QUESTIONS FOR DISCUSSION

1. How do you react to the selection of the topics covered in this chapter? Do you agree that each is an aspect of human resource utilization policy? Is there another topic that you would have been inclined to substitute for one of these?

2. In your view, are there legitimate purposes to be served by minimum wage legislation? On what grounds is it easiest for you to justify such legislation?

3. Evaluate the evidence adduced and the recommendations made by the Minimum Wage Study Commission.

4. Outline the principal policy issues relating to the Occupational Safety and Health Act, and present your position on each.

5. What sense does it make to you to argue that health and safety standards ought to be imposed without regard to whether the benefits are commensurate with the costs?

6. What does the term "affirmative action" mean? In your view, does it necessarily imply preferential treatment for the groups toward whom it is directed? Irrespective of your response to the foregoing, are there any circumstances under which you can justify preferential treatment in order to increase the employment opportunities of specified groups?

7. How do you interpret the "comparable worth" issue? What is your position on it?

8. To what degree, if at all, has the antidiscrimination effort in the United States been successful?

9. What do you think would help most in reducing labor market discrimination: additional legislation, better enforcement of existing legislation, or social and cultural changes that occur naturally over time? Do you regard these to be alternatives or complements?

15

Conclusion

Human Resource Policy Issues, 1985-2000

There is need for a summing up. We have defined the domain of human resource policy and have explored a number of major aspects of human resource policy in the United States as of the early 1980s. There is much that has been omitted. We have not dealt at all with the realm of labor-management relations (collective bargaining), which would require another volume at least as long as this one. The Public Employment (Job) Service—the principal public institution in the human resource allocative process—has barely been mentioned, with no hint of the difficulties that have hampered the performance of its role. Although the Davis-Bacon Act is mentioned in the introductory chapter, there is no description of its administration and of the controversy concerning its contribution to inflation.

Nevertheless, we have set forth what I think is a useful way of looking at human beings in their productive roles; have become familiar with the types of data and kinds of analysis that contribute to an understanding of human resouce issues; and have taken a fairly careful look at the processes of human resource development, allocation, and conservation in the United States, with particular attention to the role of public policy. We have recognized that policy choices—even by an informed citizenry—are difficult not only because of a diversity of competing social goals but also because the current state of knowledge does not unambiguously identify routes to particular goals. We have attempted repeatedly to illustrate this basic theme in pointing up the specific policy issues that pervade the various topics that have been examined.

It is a fitting conclusion to stand back somewhat from the detail of previous chapters and attempt to identify the several major human resource policy questions that confront the American people and that will likely elicit efforts at solution between now and the end of the century. While it is appropriate to end the book in this way, it is also a difficult and humbling task for at least three reasons. Perhaps the greatest problem is in knowing where to draw boundaries—that is, in being able to separate human resource problems from others that face us as a nation. To take the most extreme example, unless we, together with the rest of the international community, are successful in avoiding nuclear destruction, nothing else matters. *How* we manage this most important end is also exceedingly relevant, for so long as national defense absorbs over one-fourth of the federal budget (as in fiscal year 1984) human resource needs as well as other important social needs are bound to be short changed.

Less far afield than international policy is general economic policy. Learning how to operate an economy at reasonably satisfactory levels without intolerable inflation is not basically a human resource problem, but this problem needs to be solved before some of the most elemental human resource problems can satisfactorily be met. Recent experience does not permit unbridled optimism on this score.

A second difficulty—especially in trying to foresee the issues of the next decade and a half—lies in not having a crystal ball. Already there are differences of opinion among respected experts about the character and extent of technological change that can be expected and about its likely impact upon employment and unemployment. Moreover, almost no future state of affairs is inevitable. To a considerable degree the kinds of human resource problems that will confront American society in the year 2000 depend upon what actions are taken between now and then, and these in turn depend on political events. It is hard to believe that the character of human resource issues in the 1990s will have been unaffected by the results of the 1984 and 1988 presidential elections.

The final problem stems from the fact that issues of any kind are to a large extent in the eye of the beholder. Not only is the position one takes on policy issues affected by one's values; the issues that one elects to talk about are no less a reflection of value orientation. I acknowledge, in other words, that the remainder of this brief concluding chapter should be interpreted as indicating simply what human resource problems are of primary concern to *me,* plus my judgment about the likelihood of their continued relevance over the next decade and a half.

FULL EMPLOYMENT

The point has been made repeatedly in earlier chapters that a full employment economy is a sine qua non of any meaningful human resource policy. While it is admittedly difficult to say precisely what full employment is, there can be no disagreement that it is *not* the 10 percent unemployment rate that prevailed in 1982 and 1983 nor the 9 percent level below which the administration was predicting that unemployment would not fall for at least three years. Thus, it is highly likely that unemployment will continue to be a major human resource issue at least through most of the 1980s.

Part of the problem lies in learning how to do a better job in macroeconomic policy—achieving higher levels of economic activity without generating unacceptable levels of inflation. Another part, however, is dealing more effectively with structural unemployment problems—both those created by the failure of individuals to have acquired useful labor market skills and those created by technological change and shifts in demand that render obsolete skills that once gained access to desirable jobs. For both aspects of the problem, training and retraining will doubtless continue to be useful remedies—eliminating human resource bottlenecks so as to improve the trade-off between unemployment and inflation and at the same time allowing the unemployed to acquire useful skills.

In the same context, public service employment (PSE) constitutes a means of battling both types of unemployment. If properly targeted, public service jobs have the potential of absorbing larger numbers of unemployed with less inflationary pressure than general stimulative policies alone. For the most disadvantaged unemployed, PSE is virtually the *only* sure method of providing employment. Finally, if it is carefully designed PSE can contribute to the satisfaction of a multitude of unmet social needs at the same time that it provides jobs to those who want them. Collapsing bridges and the growing numbers of desolate older persons needing companionship and nonprofessional care illustrate the range of possibilities in this regard. For all these reasons and despite the problems with PSE that have been highlighted by the experience of the 1970s, it will be surprising if such programs do not reappear (with better administrative safeguards, it is hoped).

HUMAN RESOURCE DEVELOPMENT

As the preceding discussion suggests, problems of unemployment need to be attacked on both the supply and demand sides of the labor market. Human resource development policies, therefore, are themselves relevant to the pursuit of full employment and will continue to be in the future. There is ample evidence that many young people are being inadequately prepared for the world of work, and this problem is not likely to disappear, at least during the time span under consideration. The fault lies not only—or perhaps not even primarily—with the educational system, although schools must surely bear part of the blame. Debate on educational policy is therefore likely to be as intense over the next decade or so as it has been in the recent past.

The low levels of fertility since the mid-1960s mean that smaller youth cohorts will be entering the labor market in the 1980s and 1990s, which will help to ease somewhat the problems of transition from school to work. However, human resource development is not a process exclusively relevant to youth. Especially if the rate of technological change accelerates, greater opportunities for career change will be required and the concept of life-long learning opportunities can be expected to continue to attract attention.

INCOME MAINTENANCE

As we have seen in Chapters 11-13, there are enough problems in social insurance and public assistance programs in the United States to guarantee that they will continue to stimulate policy debate. The crazy quilt that constitutes the public assistance program is in particular need of rationalization. While the financial problems of OASDI appear to have been satisfactorily resolved, the multitudes of uncertain factors that affect income and outgo of the funds precludes complete confidence that further difficulties will not emerge. In any case, the problems of Medicare are even more difficult than those that had plagued OASDI. There is no question that considerable attention will have to be paid over the next decade or so not only to that program but to the entire question of how best to provide medical care and to contain rapidly rising medical costs.

Our public assistance programs have become more niggardly during the years of the Reagan administration at the same time that recession has very considerably increased the need for such support. The Congressional Budget Office (1983) has estimated the decrease in outlays between 1982 and 1985 that will have resulted from legislation enacted between January 1981 and July 1983 for selected human resource programs. In total these reductions amounted to 7 percent, but they were 13 percent for AFDC and food stamps, 28 percent for child nutrition programs (e.g., school lunches), 5 percent for Medicare, and 4 percent for housing assistance. In absolute terms, the reductions for these several programs amount to $18.8 billion. Considering all reductions in benefit payments, the impact is largest for low income families. In 1984, for example, the loss in benefits for households with incomes under $10,000 was estimated to amount to $430 as compared with an average loss of $250 over all income categories. Whether this trend is to be maintained, intensified, or reversed is one of the most immediate problems of social policy as of the mid-1980s.

ANTIDISCRIMINATION POLICY

Despite the dramatic innovations over the past two decades in federal policy directed at labor market discrimination, and although there is evidence that the programs have had positive effects, there is a long way yet to go in eliminating manifestations of discrimination. The gains that have been made have on the one hand whetted appetites for more, and on the other have produced a feeling in some quarters that we have gone too far—particuarly in affirmative action programs. That the issue will continue to provoke controversy is virtually certain.

The phenomenal growth in women's labor force participation over the past three or four decades is surely one of the most revolutionary changes in human resource patterns—and, indeed, in the total fabric of American life—that has occurred. While it is easy to be impatient at the road that remains to be travelled in establishing an equitable position for women in the labor market, it is impossible not to be impressed at the remarkable changes that have occurred. Yet, the stubborn persistence of the three-fifths ratio between women's and men's full-time earnings has invited new approaches to the problem of occupational segregation in the form of the comparable worth doctrine, and we will surely see continued advances in this direction. The prospects for the complete elimination of women's disadvantage in the labor market appear to be dim, however, unless society is successful in making further changes in the socialization process and in the culture generally—and particularly in the home.

We know less about the effects of legislation on age discrimination than on discrimination based on race and sex. From one point of view the problem of age discrimination may be exacerbated during the remainder of the century by the increasing numbers of individuals in the 45-to-64-year age range. On the other hand, the decline in the number of young workers (age 18-35) by the year 2000 may actually increase job opportunities for middle-aged and older workers. Much depends, however, on what happens to the total level of demand for labor.

It seems likely that the permissible age for mandatory retirement will be raised further or perhaps eliminated entirely. However, this is unlikely to be of substantial quantitative importance because there is abundant evidence that only a very small proportion of individuals are unwillingly forced out of the labor market by mandatory retirement rules (Parnes and Nestel, 1981). Nevertheless, elimination of mandatory retirement would have the desirable effect of increasing freedom of choice.

A SET OF GOALS

What we are able to achieve through human resource policy will depend in good part upon how we specify our goals and how firmly we are committed to them. The basic principles to which I personally subscribe, shorn of detail and elaboration, can be expressed rather simply in four propositions:

(1) Everyone who wants to work should be guaranteed the opportunity to hold a job for which she or he is qualified. Government should become the employer of last resort.

(2) Individuals should have lifelong opportunities, beginning with the public school system, to prepare themselves adequately for specific occupational roles, including opportunities to change such roles as adults.

(3) Steps should be taken to assure the widest possible freedom of choice in the labor market. As a minimum, this means that all jobs should be equally available to all individuals who qualify for them. It also means, however, that through one's entire lifetime—but especially during youth when educational and occupational decisions are being made—there should be adequate information about alternatives to allow *real choices* to be made.

(4) Public income maintenance programs, in addition to compensating for income loss resulting from retirement, disability, or temporary unemployment, should provide a floor no lower than what is currently defined as the poverty threshold—below which no family's income should be permitted to fall. The guaranteed level should be more generous for those unable to work.

I realize, of course, that a large number of difficult problems are ignored in this brief formulation. Nevertheless, if viewed as guiding principles rather than as a blueprint, I believe they are defensible. What is more, they are attainable if a national consensus on their merit were to be achieved, and if society were willing to bear the costs of their implementation—including, incidentally, not only public expenditures, but the loss of relative advantages that the more fortunate of us enjoy under existing arrangements. I see no possibility of such a consensus emerging—not, at least, by the year 2000.

QUESTION FOR DISCUSSION

1. On the basis of your own analysis and values, summarize your set of goals for human resource policy in the United States.

REFERENCES

Aaron, Henry J. (1982) *Economic Effects of Social Security*. Washington, DC: The Brookings Institution.

———and associates. (1982) Nondefense programs. In Joseph A. Pechman (Ed.), *Setting National Priorities: The 1983 Budget*. Washington, DC: The Brookings Institution.

Adler, Paul S. (1982) The productivity puzzle: numbers alone won't solve it. *Monthly Labor Review* 105, 10: 15-21.

Advisory Council on Social Security (1979) *Report of the Advisory Council on Social Security*. Washington, DC: Social Security Administration. (processed)

Albrecht, William P. (1982) Welfare reform: an idea whose time has come and gone. In Paul M. Sommers (Ed.), *Welfare Reform in America: Perspectives and Prospects*. Boston: Kluwer-Nijhoff Publishing.

Ashford, Nicholas A. (1976) *Crisis in the Workplace*. Cambridge: MIT Press.

Bailey, Martin Neil (1982) Labor market performance, competition, and inflation. In Martin Neil Bailey (Ed.), *Workers, Jobs, and Inflation*. Washington, DC: The Brookings Institution.

Barkley, Paul W. (1977) *Economics: The Way We Choose*. New York: Harcourt Brace Jovanovitch.

Barth, Michael C., George J. Carcagno, and John L. Palmer (1974) *Toward an Effective Income Support System: Problems, Prospects and Choices*, with an *Overview Paper* by Irwin Garfinkel. Madison, WI: Institute for Research on Poverty.

Barton, Paul (1982) *Worklife Transitions: The Adult Learning Connection*. New York: McGraw-Hill.

Becker, Gary S. (1971) *The Economics of Discrimination*. 2nd Edition. Chicago: University of Chicago Press.

Borus, Michael E. (1979) *Measuring the Impact of Employment-Related Social Programs: A Primer on the Evaluation of Employment and Training, Vocational Education, Vocational Rehabilitation, and Other Job Oriented Programs*. Kalamazoo, MI: W. E. Upjohn Institute for Employment Research.

———(1980) Assessing the impact of training programs. In Eli Ginzberg (Ed.), *Employing the Unemployed*. New York: Basic Books.

Boulding, Kenneth E. (1975) The pursuit of equality. In James D. Smith (Ed.), *The Personal Distribution of Income and Wealth*. New York: National Bureau of Economic Research.

Bowen, William and T. Aldrich Finegan (1969) *The Economics of Labor Force Participation*. Princeton: Princeton University Press.

Brittain, John A. (1972) *The Payroll Tax for Security Security.* Washington, DC: Brookings Institution.

Bronfenbrenner, Martin (1973) Equality and equity. *Annals of the American Academy of Political and Social Science* (September): 9-23.

Brown, Charles (1981) The federal attack on labor market discrimination: the mouse that roared? *NBER Working Paper Series,* 669. Cambridge, MA: National Bureau of Economic Research. (processed)

———, Curtis Gilroy, and Andrew Kohen (1982) The effect of the minimum wage on employment and unemployment. *Journal of Economic Literature* 20 487-528.

Bureau of National Affairs (1981) *Employment and Training Reporter,* 13: 32-33.

Burns, Evaline (1954) *Social Security and Public Policy.* New York: McGraw-Hill.

Cain, Glen G. (1976) The challenge of segmented labor market theories to orthodox theories: a survey. *Journal of Economic Literature* 14: 1215-1257.

Carnegie Foundation for the Advancement of Teaching (1983) *High School: A Report on Secondary Education in America.* New York: The Carnegie Foundation.

Chelius, James (1983) The American experience with occupational safety and health regulation. *New Zealand Journal of Industrial Relations* 8: 123-132.

Chelius, James R. and Robert S. Smith (1983) Experience rating and injury prevention. In John D. Worrall (Ed.) *Safety and the Work Place: Incentives and Disincentives in Workers' Compensation.* Ithaca, NY: Cornell Industrial and Labor Relations Press.

Clark, Robert L. [Ed.] (1980) *Retirement Policy in an Aging Society.* Durham, NC: Duke University Press.

Cobb, S. and S. V. Kasl (1977) *Termination: The Consequences of Job Loss.* NIOSH Research Report. U.S. Department of Health, Education and Welfare. Washington, DC: U.S. Government Printing Office.

Congressional Budget Office (1983) Major legislative changes in human resource programs since January 1981. Staff memorandum. (processed)

Cook, Alice H. (1983) Comparable worth: recent developments in selected states. *Proceedings of the 1983 Spring Meeting,* Industrial Relations Research Association: 494-504.

Conant, Eaton H. (1963) Worker efficiency and wage differentials in a clerical labor market. *Industrial and Labor Relations Review* (April): 428-433.

Cowan, Mark D. (1982) Regulatory reform: an OSHA case study. *Labor Law Journal* 33: 763-770.

Cross, Patricia (1978) *The Adult Learner.* Washington, DC: American Association for Higher Education.

Danziger, Sheldon and Robert Plotnick (1982) The war on income poverty: achievements and failures. In Paul A. Sommers (Ed.), *Welfare Reform in America.* Boston: Kluwer-Nijhoff Publishing.

Daymont, Thomas N. (1981a) Changes in black-white labor market opportunities. In Herbert S. Parnes et al. (Eds.), *Work and Retirement: A Longitudinal Study of Men.* Cambridge: MIT Press.

———(1981b) Changes in black-white opportunities among young men: earnings and unemployment. Presented at meetings of the American Statistical Association, Houston, 1981.

————and Paul J. Andrisani (1983) *The Research Uses of the National Longi-tudinal Surveys: An Update.* Report submitted to the Social Science Research Council. (processed)

Donovan, Raymond S. (1981) *Final Report of the Secretary of Labor on the Recommendations of the National Commission on Employment and Unem-ployment Statistics.* Washington, DC: U.S. Government Printing Office.

Douty, H. M. (1980) *The Wage Bargain and the Labor Market.* Baltimore: Johns Hopkins University Press.

Duncan, Greg J. et al. (1983) *Years of Poverty, Years of Plenty.* Ann Arbor, MI: Institute for Social Research.

Eccles, Mary and Richard B. Freeman (1982) What! another minimum wage study? *The American Economic Review. Papers and Proceedings of the Ninety-fourth Annual Meeting* 72, 2: 226-232.

Freeman, Richard (1976) *The Overeducated American.* New York: Academic Press.

Fuerbringer, Jonathan (1982) Washington watch: cutting funds for statistics. *New York Times,* August 2: D2.

General Accounting Office (1982) *CETA Programs For Disadvantaged Adults—What Do We Know About Their Enrollees, Services, and Effectiveness?* Washington: General Accounting Office.

————(1983) *Federal Job Training: A Comparison of Public and Private Sector Performance.* Washington: General Accounting Office.

Goodlad, John I. (1983) *A Place Called School: Prospects for the Future.* New York: McGraw-Hill.

Gordon, David M. (1972) *Theories of Poverty and Underemployment: Orthodox, Radical, and Dual Labor Market Perspectives.* Lexington, MA: Lexington Books.

Grasso, John T. and John R. Shea (1979) *Vocational Education and Training: Impact on Youth.* New York: Carnegie Council on Policy Studies in Higher Education.

Gueron, Judy (1980) The supported work experiment. In Eli Ginzberg (Ed.), *Employing the Unemployed.* New York: Basic Books.

Guttman, Robert (1983) Job Training Partnership Act: New help for the unem-ployed. *Monthly Labor Review* (March): 3-10.

Hamermesh, Daniel S. (1977) *Jobless Pay and the Economy.* Baltimore: Johns Hopkins University Press.

————(1982) The interaction between research and policy: the case of unemploy-ment insurance. *The American Economic Review. Papers and Proceedings of the Ninety-fourth Annual Meeting* 72, 2: 237-241.

Harbison, Frederick H. and Charles A. Myers (1964) *Education, Manpower, and Economic Growth: Strategies of Human Resource Development.* New York: McGraw-Hill.

Haveman, Robert H. (1980) Direct job creation. In Eli Ginzberg (Ed.), *Employing the Unemployed.* New York: Basic Books.

————and Barbara L. Wolfe (1983) Education and economic well-being: the role of non-market effects. Institute for Research on Poverty Discussion Paper 716-782.

Hoagland, G. William (1982) The effectiveness of current transfer programs in reducing poverty. In Paul A. Sommers (Ed.), *Welfare Reform in America.* Boston: Kluwer-Nijhoff Publishing.

Institute for Research on Poverty (1982) Poverty in the United States: where do we stand? *Focus* 5, 2: 1-11.

Jaffe, A. J. and Charles D. Stewart (1951) *Manpower Resources and Utilization.* New York: John Wiley.

Johnston, Janet W. (1980) An overview of federal employment and training programs. In National Commission for Employment Policy *Sixth Annual Report.* Washington, DC: National Commission for Employment Policy.

———(1981) The national employment and training "system." In National Commission for Employment Policy, *Seventh Annual Report: The Federal Interest in Employment and Training.* Washington, DC: National Commission for Employment Policy.

Kendrick, John W. (1977) *Understanding Productivity: An Introduction to the Dynamics of Productivity Change.* Baltimore: Johns Hopkins University Press.

Kerr, Clark (1954) The Balkanization of labor markets. In E. Wight Bakke (Ed.), *Labor Mobility and Economic Opportunity.* New York: John Wiley.

Koziara, Karen S., David A. Pierson, and Russell E. Johannesson (1983) The comparable worth issue: current status and new directions. *Proceedings of the 1983 Spring Meetings,* Industrial Relations Research Association: 504-509.

Lampman, Robert J. (1973) Measured inequality of income: what does it mean and what can it tell us? *The Annals of the American Academy of Political and Social Science* (September): 81-91.

———(1982) Goals and purposes of social welfare expenditures. In Paul M. Sommers (Ed.), *Welfare Reform in America: Perspectives and Prospects.* Boston: Kluwer-Nijhoff Publishing.

Lansing, John B. and Eva Mueller (1967) *The Geographic Mobility of Labor.* Ann Arbor: University of Michigan Institute for Social Research.

Lave, Lester B. (1980) Health, safety, and environmental regulations. In Joseph A. Pechman (Ed.), *Setting National Priorities: Agenda for the 1980s.* Washington, DC: Brookings Institution.

Lebergott, Stanley (1964) *Manpower in Economic Growth: The American Record Since 1800.* New York: McGraw-Hill.

Levitan, Sar A. and Clifford M. Johnson (1982) *Second Thoughts On Work.* Kalamazoo, MI: The W.E. Upjohn Institute for Employment Research.

Lippman, Steven A. and John J. McCall (1976) The economics of job search: a survey. *Economic Inquiry* 14: 155-189.

Lipsey, Richard B. (1965) Structural and deficient-demand unemployment reconsidered. In Arthur M. Ross (Ed.) *Employment Policy and the Labor Market.* Berkeley: University of California Press.

Lynn, Laurence E., Jr. (1977) A decade of policy developments in the income-maintenance system. In Robert H. Haveman (Ed.), *A Decade of Federal Antipoverty Programs: Achievements, Failures, and Lessons.* New York: Academic Press.

Mangum, Garth (1981) 20 years of employment and training programs: whatever happened to the consensus? *Industrial Relations Research Association Proceedings of the 1981 Spring Meeting,* 508-513.

Mare, Robert (1979) Sources of educational growth in America. In Institute for Research on Poverty, *Focus* 3, 2: 5-6, 12.

Marshall, Ray (1974) The economics of racial discrimination: a survey. *Journal of Economic Literature* 12: 849-871.

Masters, Stanley H. (1975) *Black-White Income Differentials: Empirical Studies and Policy Implications.* New York: Academic Press.

McConnell, Stephen R. (1983) Age discrimination in employment. In Herbert S. Parnes (Ed.), *Policy Issues in Work and Retirement.* Kalamazoo, MI: The W.E. Upjohn Institute for Employment Research.

Millis, Harry A. and Royal E. Montgomery (1938) *Labor's Risks and Social Insurance.* New York: McGraw-Hill.

Mincer, Jacob (1962) On-the-job training: costs, returns, and some implications. *Journal of Political Economy,* Supplement. *Investment in Human Beings* (October): 50-79.

Minimum Wage Study Commission (1981) *Report of the Minimum Wage Study Commission.* Washington, DC: U.S. Government Printing Office.

Moffitt, Robert A. (1982) The effect of a negative income tax on work effort: a summary of the experimental results. In Paul M. Sommers (Ed.), *Welfare Reform in America: Perspectives and Prospects.* Boston: Kluwer-Nijhoff Publishing.

Morgan, James N.(1975) Using survey data from the University of Michigan's Survey Research Center. *American Economic Review: Papers and Proceedings* (May): 250-256.

Munnell, Alicia (1983) Financing options for Social Security. In Herbert S. Parnes (Ed.), *Policy Issues in Work and Retirement.* Kalamazoo, MI: The W.E. Upjohn Institute for Employment Research.

Myers, Robert J. (1981) *Social Security.* Homewood, IL: Richard D. Irwin.

Nathan, Richard P. (1980) Public service employment. In Eli Ginzberg (Ed.), *Employing the Unemployed.* New York: Basic Books.

National Commission on Employment and Unemployment Statistics (1979) *Counting the Labor Force.* Washington, DC: U.S. Government Printing Office.

National Commission on Excellence in Education (1983) *A Nation at Risk: The Imperative for Educational Reform.* A Report to the Nation and to the Secretary of Education, U.S. Department of Education.

National Commission on Social Security (1981) *Social Security in America's Future—Final Report of the National Commission on Social Security.* Washington, DC: U.S. Government Printing Office.

National Commission on Social Security Reform (1983) *Report of the National Commission on Social Security Reform.* Washington, DC: National Commission on Social Security Reform. (processed)

The National Commission on State Workmen's Compensation Laws (1972) *Report of the National Commission on State Workmen's Compensation Laws.* Washington, DC: U.S. Government Printing Office.

National Commission on Unemployment Compensation (1980) *Unemployment Compensation: Final Report.* Washington, DC: U.S. Government Printing Office.

Okner, Benjamin A. (1975) Individual taxes and the distribution of income. In James D. Smith (Ed.), *The Personal Distribution of Income and Wealth.* New York: National Bureau of Economic Research.

Okun, Arthur M. (1975) *Equality and Efficiency: The Big Tradeoff.* Washington, DC: The Brookings Institution.

Organization for Economic Cooperation and Development (1961) *Policy Conference on Economic Growth and Investment in Education,* Volumes 1-5. Paris: Author.

———(1965) *Wages and Labour Mobility.* Paris: Author.

Parnes, Herbert S. (1954) *Research on Labor Mobility: An Appraisal of Research Findings in the United States.* New York: Social Science Research Council.

———(1960) The labor force and labor markets. In Herbert G. Heneman, Jr., et al. (Eds.), *Employment Relations Research: A Summary and Appraisal.* New York: Harper and Brothers.

———(1970) Labor force participation and labor mobility. In *A Review of Industrial Relations Research,* Volume 1. Madison, WI: Industrial Relations Research Association.

———(1975) The National Longitudinal Surveys: New vistas for labor market research. *American Economic Review. Papers and Proceedings* (May): 244-249.

———(1981) The retirement experience. In Herbert S. Parnes et al. (Eds.), *Work and Retirement: A Longitudinal Study of Men.* Cambridge: MIT Press.

———(1982) *Unemployment Experience of Individuals Over a Decade: Variations by Sex, Race, and Age.* Kalamazoo, MI: The W.E. Upjohn Institute for Employment Research.

———(1983) Introduction and overview. In Herbert S. Parnes (Ed.), *Policy Issues in Work and Retirement.* Kalamazoo, MI: The W.E. Upjohn Institute for Employment Research.

———and Gilbert Nestel (1975) Early retirement. In Herbert S. Parnes et al. *The Pre-Retirement Years: A Longitudinal Study of the Labor Market Experience of Men.* Volume 4. U.S. Department of Labor Manpower R and D Monograph 15. Washington, DC: U.S. Government Printing Office.

Pear, Robert (1983) Study says affirmative rule expands hiring of minorities. *New York Times,* June 19: 16.

Pechman, Joseph A. and Benjamin A. Okner (1974) *Who Bears the Tax Burden?* Washington, DC: Brookings Institution.

Perry, Charles R. et al. (1975) *The Impact of Government Manpower Programs.* Philadelphia: University of Pennsylvania Industrial Research Unit.

Phillips, A. W. (1958) The relation between unemployment and the rate of change in money wage rates in the United Kingdom, 1861-1957. *Economica* 25: 283-299.

President's Commission for a National Agenda for the Eighties (1980) *A National Agenda for the Eighties.* Washington, DC: U.S. Government Printing Office.

President's Commission on Pension Policy (1981) *Coming of Age: Toward a National Retirement Income Policy.* Washington, DC: U.S. Government Printing Office.

The President's Committee to Appraise Employment and Unemployment Statistics (1962) *Measuring Employment and Unemployment.* Washington, DC: U.S. Government Printing Office.

Price, Daniel N. (1979) Workers' compensation program in the 1970's. *Social Security Bulletin* 42,5: 3-24.

———(1983) Workers' compensation: coverage, benefits, and costs, 1980. *Social Security Bulletin* 46,5: 14-19.

Radner, Daniel B. (1981) Adjusted estimates of the age distribution of family income for 1972. U.S. Department of Health and Human Services. Social Security Administration. Office of Research and Statistics Working Paper Series, 24. (processed)

Reynolds, Lloyd G. (1951) *The Structure of Labor Markets.* New York: Harper and Brothers.

Rottenberg, Simon (1956) On choice in labor markets. *Industrial and Labor Relations Review* 9: 183-199.

Saks, Daniel H. and Steven H. Sandell (1980) The economic environment, fiscal policy and employment in the 1980's. In National Commission for Employment Policy, *Sixth Annual Report*. Washington, DC: U.S. Government Printing Office.

Samuelson, Paul A. (1980) *Economics*. 11th edition. New York: McGraw-Hill.

Sawhill, Isabel V. and Lauri J. Bassi (1980) The challenge of full employment. In Eli Ginzberg (Ed.), *Employing the Unemployed*. New York: Basic Books.

Schlesinger, Arthur M., Jr. (1957) *The Age of Roosevelt: The Crisis of the Old Order, 1919-1933*. Boston: Houghton Mifflin.

———(1983) The "hundred days" of FDR. *New York Times*, April 10, Section 3: 8.

Schultz, Theodore W. (1961) Investment in human capital. *American Economic Review* 51: 1-17.

Schulz, James (1980) *The Economics of Aging*. 2nd Edition. Belmont, CA: Wadsworth.

Smith, Robert Stewart (1976) *Occupational Safety and Health Act: Its Goals and Its Achievements*. Washington, DC: American Enterprise Institute for Public Policy Research.

Solow, Robert M. (1980) Employment policy in inflationary times. In Eli Ginzberg (Ed.), *Employing the Unemployed*. New York: Basic Books.

Stigler, George J. (1962) Information in the labor market. *Journal of Political Economy, Supplement, Investment in Human Capital* (October): 94-105.

Thurow, Lester C. (1970) *Investment in Human Capital*. Belmont, CA: Wadsworth.

U.S. Department of Labor (1982a) Bureau of Labor Statistics, Bulletin 2121. *Economic Projections to 1990*. Washington, DC: U.S. Government Printing Office.

———(1982b) *Seventieth Annual Report, Fiscal Year 1982*. Washington, DC: U.S. Department of Labor.

U.S. President (1981) *Economic Report of the President*. Washington, DC: U.S. Government Printing Office.

———(1982a) *Economic Report of the President*. Washington, DC: U.S. Government Printing Office.

———(1982b) *Employment and Training Report of the President*. Washington, DC: U.S. Government Printing Office.

———(1983) *Economic Report of the President*. Washington, DC: U.S. Government Printing Office.

Watts, Harold W. (1980) Panel suggests changes in BLS family budget program. *Monthly Labor Review* (December): 3-10.

Webster's New World Dictionary of the American Language (1974) Second College Edition. Cleveland: New World.

Wolfbein, Seymour (1964) *Employment and Unemployment in the United States: A Study of the American Labor Force*. Science Research Associates, Inc.

INDEX

ABOUT THE AUTHOR

Herbert S. Parnes, Professor Emeritus of Economics at Ohio State University, began his career of teaching and research in labor economics in 1947. *Peoplepower* represents his perception of an appropriate introduction to the field at either the undergraduate or graduate level.

He has authored or coauthored numerous articles and almost twenty books and monographs, among the most influential of which have been *Research on Labor Mobility* (1954), *Forecasting Educational Needs for Economic and Social Development* (1962), and *Work and Retirement* (1981). The last of these, named by Princeton University's Industrial Relations Section as one of the ten outstanding books in industrial relations in 1981, is based on the data from the National Longitudinal Surveys—the "Parnes data"—that he directed from the mid-1960s to the late 1970s.

Parnes' professional activities as well as his writings have reflected his interest in issues of public policy. He has served as Chairman of the Ohio Advisory Council on Employment Security, member of the Columbus-Franklin County Manpower Advisory Council, and consultant to a number of federal agencies and international organizations, including the Organization for Economic Cooperation and Development (OECD). For the OECD he spent a year in Europe in the early 1960s developing the methodology for a major exercise in educational planning by six Mediterranean countries.